OGILVY ON ADVER-TISING
IN THE DIGITAL AGE

Bloomsbury USA
An imprint of Bloomsbury Publishing Plc

1385 Broadway   50 Bedford Square
New York   London
NY 10018   WC1B 3DP
USA   UK

www.bloomsbury.com

First published in Great Britain by Goodman 2017
First U.S. edition published by Bloomsbury 2018

ISBN: HB: 978-1-63557-146-2
          ePub: 978-1-63557-147-9

Library of Congress Cataloging-in-Publication Data is available.

2 4 6 8 10 9 7 5 3 1

Printed in China

To find out more about our authors and books visit www.bloomsbury.com.
Here you will find extracts, author interviews, details of forthcoming events,
and the option to sign up for our newsletters.

Bloomsbury books may be purchased for business or promotional use. For
information on bulk purchases please contact Macmillan Corporate and
Premium Sales Department at specialmarkets@macmillan.com.

OGILVY ON ADVER-TISING
IN THE DIGITAL AGE

MILES YOUNG
NON-EXECUTIVE CHAIRMAN OF OGILVY & MATHER

B L O O M S B U R Y
NEW YORK · LONDON · OXFORD · NEW DELHI · SYDNEY

CONTENTS

6   **INTRODUCTION**
VIEW FROM TOUFFOU

8   **1 CODETTA**

12   **2 THE DIGITAL REVOLUTION**

20   **3 THE SHORT MARCH**

30   **4 THE DIGITAL ECOSYSTEM**

46   **5 TO BE OR NOT TO BE A MILLENNIAL**

54   **6 THE POST-MODERN BRAND**

72   **7 CONTENT IS KING; BUT WHAT DOES IT MEAN?**

98   **8 CREATIVITY IN THE DIGITAL AGE**

98   **"GIVE ME GOLD"**

101   **ART OR SCIENCE?**

107   **PERVASIVE CREATIVITY**

120   **9 DATA: THE CURRENCY OF THE DIGITAL AGE**

132   **10 "ONLY CONNECT"**

150   **11 CREATIVE TECHNOLOGY: THE SWEET SPOT**

164   **12 THE THREE BATTLEGROUNDS**

164   PUTTING THE SOCIAL BACK INTO SOCIAL MEDIA

174   THE JOY OF MOBILITY

180   CONTINUOUS COMMERCE

192   **13 DIGITAL TRANSFORMATIONS**

192   DIGITAL POLITICS

197   DIGITAL GOVERNMENT

200   DIGITAL TOURISM

204   DIGITAL SOCIAL RESPONSIBILITY

210   **14 FIVE GIANTS OF ADVERTISING IN THE DIGITAL AGE**

210   BOB GREENBERG

216   AKIRA KAGAMI

220   MARTIN NISENHOLTZ

224   MATIAS PALM-JENSEN

228   CHUCK PORTER

236   **15 MY BRAIN HURTS**

248   **16 THE NEW SHAPE OF THE WORLD**

266   **17 CULTURE, COURAGE, CLIENTS AND CASTANETS**

272   **18 EPILOGUE**

274   ENDNOTES

278   INDEX

286   ACKNOWLEDGEMENTS

288   PICTURE CREDITS

INTRODUCTION
VIEW FROM TOUFFOU

Unlike authors who have to worry about why they are writing at all, my purpose is very narrow. The point of this book is to persuade people to read or re-read *Ogilvy on Advertising* by David Ogilvy. It is still pure, pure gold. Yes, the cast has changed, the scenery is different, the plumbing is new, but the tragic and comic plots, sub-plots and counter-plots of this business remain persistently and defiantly unchanged. Of course, this irritates some people who really would rather all had changed completely.

I am writing these words in Touffou, the home David retired to in South West France, in the room he used as his study. The desk on which *Ogilvy on Advertising* was partly written is still here, although in a different room. The shelves in the study contain a range of books, which testify to his belief that the most productive people read the most widely. There's history, biography, architecture, travel – spines with titles that sum up a man's life. And, of course, there are the advertising books.

Below Touffou evolved over several centuries, but the original keep, built for defence, dates from the twelfth century.

The house nestles between some low wooded elevations and the banks of the River Vienne as it winds lazily through the countryside of Poitou. David settled here in 1973 with his third wife, Herta. The couple spent the next decades restoring Touffou, turning the grounds into a magnificent garden and creating a grand but friendly home.

David died here in 1999, and his ashes are scattered in the garden. Herta remains Ogilvy & Mather's materfamilias; and we continue to hold Board meetings, Executive Committee meetings, client meetings and workshops here.

In 2013, I called our Digital Council to Touffou. This was a group of young enthusiasts from around the world and from around the eco-system – mobile, customer relationship management (CRM), social, creative, technology. Our previous meetings had taken place in Palo Alto, CA, but there did not seem anything incongruous in talking about the future of communication in a medieval setting. In fact, it gave us something that we simply could not so easily get in California: perspective. Well into Ogilvy & Mather's own digital transformation, I wanted a discussion of a more fundamental kind. What is digital? Is it an evolution or a revolution? Is it so novel and specialized that we should treat it apart? Or it is something that needs to be baked into the heart of the business, an integrator in itself? We had guidance, in part, from a videotaped last testament that David left. He called it "View from Touffou". We still play it in training sessions. It makes a point about press advertising, but one that helped us answer the questions.

His argument provided a flash of illumination, bringing into high relief the primacy of content over form. The meeting continued along a path divergent from the one being followed by so many others. It led us to see "digital" not as a "discipline" but rather as just a channel, a dramatic enhancer of "traditional" business, but not a parallel universe.

Above *David and Herta in San Francisco, 1984.*

Below *David's 'View from Touffou' video provides a posthumous take on digital. He would have viewed digital as a channel not as a discipline, one that cries out for rich content, and always in the service of selling.*

1 CODETTA

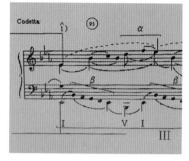

Above *A codetta, or "little tail" in its native Italian, is a brief conclusion in music. It leads back into an exposition or recapitulation of the work before, or occasionally, to a section that develops the piece further. My codetta does the latter – building on David's book by adding some fresh notes on the nuances of the Digital Age.*

A codetta is what ends a musical sequence.

Ogilvy on Advertising begins with a chapter called Overture. It is classic David Ogilvy. Plainspoken, forthright and resonant with his concise prose, it includes his famous line: "I *hate* rules."

The book is a simple yet demonstrative expression of David's breadth of knowledge, containing illustrative references to, among other things, eighteenth-century obstetrics and Horace. And it sparkles with his wit and good humour, ending with this note: "If you think it is a lousy book, you should have seen it before my partner Joel Raphaelson did his best to delouse it. *Bless you, Joel.*"

My codetta rounds off what David began, though it will not be the last word.

Ogilvy on Advertising was written in the 1980s. Joel, David's literary amanuensis, recalls the speed with which it was produced: David posted a chapter to Joel every week. Joel was on sabbatical in Colorado, but his job was to edit it and make suggestions. Written partly in Touffou, at David's desk in his study, and partly in a chalet in Switzerland, it is a polemic.

David did not think it was his best book, and he was right. *Confessions of an Advertising Man* (1963) deserves that appellation. It is more literary: while many copywriters have found it difficult to extend short form into book form, David had a natural gift for book writing.

But *Ogilvy on Advertising* was something else: a most elegant rant against what he believed to be a legion of misconceptions about our business; a primer for anyone interested in advertising; an expression of some very dogmatic views, skillfully excused as brevity; and a showcase for the work he admired most (including a sizeable chunk of his own oeuvre).

Within months of publication, *Ogilvy on Advertising* was a storming success. It has become an advertising classic, remaining in print for over three decades, translated into multiple languages, and featured in legions of syllabi around the world. More than that, many people I meet, whether they're in the industry or not, tell me that the book is the first or only point of contact they have had with the agency he founded.

I first met David in 1982, as a young Account Director in our London advertising agency. I was working in my small office there in the early evening. He happened to walk past, saw there was someone new inside, retraced his steps, came in and flopped in a chair. "Who are you?" Then,

CHÂTEAU DE TOUFFOU
86300 BONNES

March 19, 1982

Dear Joel:

Your telex today has given me a <u>huge</u> lift.

Fancy the Harvard Business Review buying our piece.* I did not think they would. It is a first for Ogilvy & Mather--in thirty-three years. Let us hope that Tony Houghton never sees it.

How <u>wonderful</u> that you had a good meeting with Bill Phillips on the house campaign. And what a relief that I don't have to get into the act.

*   *   *

While I write this letter on Touffou paper, I am actually holed up in a chalet in Switzer-land, working on my book. It has to be 80,000 words--twice as long as Confessions, and pro-fusely illustrated.

I wonder if you could be persuaded to edit the draft when it is ready, sometime around August 15. It would take you longer than it took me to edit your much shorter book--although I did both versions of yours. What I shall need to be told is stuff like this:

    Repetitious
    Incomprehensible
    Clumsy sentence
    Bad taste
    Inconsistent
    Just plain nonsense
    Wrong order

*How come you heard this when I haven't? Have you a relation at the HBR?

    Dangerously tactless
    Boring
    Egotistical
    Senile
    Flogging a dead horse

If you cannot face it, say so. I shall probably be in a hurry, because the thing has to be de-livered to the publisher on October 1.

Yours,

David

Right *David produced the original manuscript for* Ogilvy on Advertising *with characteristic efficiency, sharing a chapter every week with his friend and literary confidante, Joel Raphaelson.*

Above *This is the cover of David's original book, first published in 1983 – from which I've drawn inspiration for this version, and wisdom throughout my entire career.*

Above right *David's appearance on* Late Night with David Letterman *in 1983 for the launch of* Ogilvy on Advertising.

"What are you doing?" I was full of our recent win of the Guinness business, what wonderful work we were doing. He just looked at me and asked: "But are they *gentlemen*?" Some months later, their CEO, Ernest Saunders, "fell like Lucifer". David had a prescience that was often uncanny.

He did not, however, predict the Digital Revolution, which has transformed what we think and do in so many ways, creating new concepts, new languages and new techniques. Nor, I sense (judging by his reaction to then the current phrase "creative revolution"), would he have liked the description very much.

But it would be childish to criticize him for that, especially since he had spent much time since his retirement working on his "first and last love", direct marketing. When I started working in our Paris office, in 1994, to consolidate the IBM account in Europe, I discovered there were two offices: the "posh" advertising office just off the Avenue George V, and the "down and dirty" direct marketing office in the decidedly un-posh Rue Brunel. This was where my team was based, and also where David in retirement chose to have his office. It was a very deliberate gesture. He was cocking a snook at the self-indulgence, distaste for accountability and snobbishness of what was then seen to be the senior discipline. As a refugee from that discipline myself, I could feel some sympathy with the point.

One of the last working meetings David attended was a summit of our direct marketing leaders in the Château d'Esclimont, a turreted pile outside Paris. David was there as a treasured icon rather than as an active contributor, and played a passive role for most of the meeting, apparently peacefully somnolent at the rear of the room. Then the head of the Austrian office started a presentation of unprecedented complexity. It was a small triumph of process over content. After five minutes, the explosion happened.

"STOP!" David bellowed. "FOR GOD'S SAKE, STOP." And then slightly softer and more pained: "I cannot understand or see the usefulness of what you are saying." And then, with acute pain: "And from the land of *Mozart*!" It was a mortifying and terrifying moment which no one in

Right *A rather analogue picture from my early days in advertising. The last 30 years have witnessed a period of immense digital transformation, yet many of the principles drummed into me early on are as important as they ever were.*

the room will easily forget, least of all that hapless Austrian colleague. He shouldn't feel bad about it if he's reading this now. But this is a clue for me about how David would respond to much of the verbiage, hype, redundancy, over-complication and ungrounded optimism that surrounds the Digital Revolution, observing and undermining the enormous gifts it brings.

In his Overture, David stated that one of his objectives was to separate "the eternal verities from the passing fads".

The refrain of this Codetta, so many years on, is that these verities still exist, as true as ever. Conflict between what is significant and what is not is perennial. The digital world has merely spurred a flurry of new fads, but we are just reaching the time where some perspective is possible.

The time to reassert the verities has arrived.

HALL OF FAME

The Digital Revolution has been punctuated by work that has, from time to time, helped to define it. I have put together six case studies, dotted through the book – a Hall of Fame – of those all-time greats, which have stood the test of time, and which still carry lessons today. Like all selections, it's very personal, and I am happy to be challenged!

2 THE DIGITAL REVOLUTION

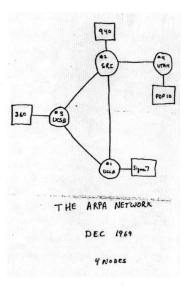

THE ARPA NETWORK

DEC 1969

4 NODES

In 1958 President Eisenhower established the Advanced Research Projects Agency (ARPA). The agency operated largely in the dark, but one of its undertakings, the creation of the ARPANET, was more or less an open secret. Its goal was simple but daunting: to create and ensure the survival of networked communications following the infrastructural disablement of a nuclear strike. The formation of ARPANET ultimately engaged the brightest minds in various fields, including electrical engineering, information architecture, mathematics, computer science, and even psychology, an ad hoc consortium of experts employed by the government (primarily the Department of Defense and NASA), private corporations and leading universities.

The first digital message transmitted over the network, on 29 October 1969, travelled from a Sigma 7 computer at the University of California, Los Angeles (UCLA) to a SDS 940 Host computer at the Stanford Research Institute (SRI), in Menlo Park, California. The system crashed mid-message, but the internet was born that day.

Of course, it was just two nodes on one network. Within a year, that had grown to 14 nodes, then later to 100, and then to thousands. It started off as just one network but soon it linked up many others into a network of networks – an *internet* – talking through a common language still in use today.

And that was the primary motivation of the Digital Revolution: a military research program devised to ensure the survival of networked communications following the infrastructural disablement of a nuclear strike.

Top *On 29 October 1969 the first message was transmitted over the ARPANET from 3420 Boelter Hall at UCLA's School of Engineering to Stanford Research Institute over 350 miles away. It crashed. The system managed a paltry "Lo" before stalling on the "g" of its intended command, "Login". We now send 200 billion emails and 50 billion text messages every day.*

Above *This is the origin of today's internet, scribbled as if on the back of an envelope. In December 1969 four nodes – the connection points between computers – were successfully linked for the first time.*

Digital Comes of Age

There has always been a yearning to designate someone as the inventor of the internet. History in this epoch is not so simple. Before, during and after the work of ARPANET, scores of individuals helped invent it. To each his own fame, but I believe – with the benefit of a reasonable amount of perspective – one can define 15 individuals who share a higher amount of responsibility than others for the Digital Revolution (see chart overleaf).

What these men speak to is both the incremental way in which the internet evolved and that, after its first mission of national defence, the internet has been a technology looking for a commercial model, rather than one of commerce seeking a technological solution.

ANALOGUE VS DIGITAL PROCESS

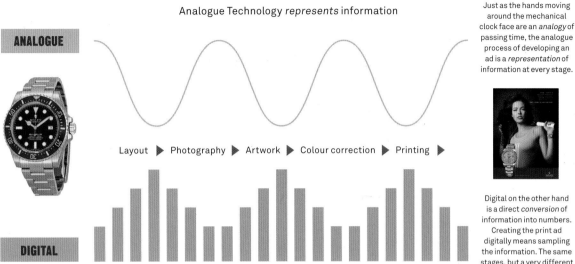

Analogue Technology *represents* information

ANALOGUE

Just as the hands moving around the mechanical clock face are an *analogy* of passing time, the analogue process of developing an ad is a *representation* of information at every stage.

Layout ▶ Photography ▶ Artwork ▶ Colour correction ▶ Printing ▶

DIGITAL

Digital on the other hand is a direct *conversion* of information into numbers. Creating the print ad digitally means sampling the information. The same stages, but a very different process.

Digital technology *converts* information

Above *The digital age hasn't called time on the analogue era, but it has offered an entirely different way of capturing information. Take the production process for developing a print advertisement. Whereas analogue technology represents information – like film negatives in a 35mm camera or the groove in a vinyl record – digital converts it into data, simple 0s and 1s. We may produce a final print ad that looks the same regardless of the method, but one is a representation while the other is a high-fidelity approximation.*

Following pages *From its inception, the internet was a collaborative effort. These are the 15 people whose unique contributions democratized information technology and switched on the digital age.*

The internet's now-ubiquitous force is transforming, among many other worlds, the world of advertising. In this arena, the challenges and opportunities presented by digital media are not unlike those faced by David Ogilvy – and Bill Bernbach, Rosser Reeves, Ted Bates and a whole legion of admen – upon the arrival of the previous great disruptor, television, in the 1950s.

As a transmitter, storer and generator of digital information, this internet with many diverse parts is what enables advertising in the digital age.

Of course, since that first digital message in 1969, digital has not completely replaced analogue technology: a Rolex watch, for instance, where the hands represent passing time as an analogy, can still be more informative than its digital counterpart.

There is something profound in the philosophical as much as the practical impact of digital technology. It's down to the digits.

Analogue work is whole and of a piece, but digital is a binary approximation – albeit one of enormous fidelity – of the analogue world. Perhaps inevitably, a way of working which reduces everything to digits must be less holistic than one which does not. Here lies the real digital divide: the parts versus the whole. Which do you value most?

The answer is neither. The rate of digital advancement is so high that the two are easily confused. Amazing breakthroughs or the total package? You need both: but you need to be very clear what is, in fact, the end point you desire, and which is just a means of getting there.

Perhaps, because of this uncertainty around its essence, the internet that has emerged is riven by conflict. It can best be described as the combination of frustrated idealism and strongly vested interests.

15 FOUNDERS OF THE INTERNET

Robert William "Bob" Taylor

American (1932-). Director of IPTO in years leading to first ARPANET transmission. Recognized need for networked time-sharing computer at Pentagon with those at UC-Berkeley and the System Development Corporation. This was ARPANET. In 1968, co-authored paper with Licklider laying out development of the internet. Headed Xerox PARC, which developed WYSIWYG word processing, the laser printer, and the Alto computer (on which the Mac was based).

Joseph Carl Robnett Licklider

American (1915-1990). Intellectual giant who earned undergraduate degrees in physics, maths, and psychology, and a PhD in psycho-acoustics. Helped establish MIT Lincoln Laboratory in 1951. Two years later, became director of the Information Processing Techniques Office (IPTO). In 1962, wrote memo imagining an electronic commons open to all, "the main and essential medium of informational interaction for governments, institutions, corporations, and individuals". In other words, the internet.

Douglas Engelbart

American (1925-2013). Founder of Augmented Research Center (ARC) at non-profit Stanford Research Institute (SRI) in Menlo Park, CA, in 1966. Led team that created multilayered computer collaboration system NLS (oN-Line System). NLS broke ground by combining disparate computational elements, including hypertext links, graphical-user interface (GUI), mouse, information organized by relevance, screen windowing, and presentation programs (like PowerPoint).

Lawrence Roberts

American (1937-). Neighbour and friend of Bob Taylor. Taylor recruited him to join ARPA's IPTO in 1966. While at ARPA, built system connecting large computers at MIT and UCLA. "Two-node" system paved way for additional connection of computers at the Universities of Utah and Stanford. Influenced by Licklider's writing, Roberts wrote code that enabled packet-switching. First such message transfer took place in October 1969 between computers at UCLA and Stanford.

Donald Davies

British (1924-2000). Co-inventor of packet-switching. Packet-switching methodology developed by ARPA incorporated ideas advanced by Americans Leonard Kleinrock, Paul Baran and Lawrence Roberts. Gordon Welchman coined the term "packet" as a unit of digital data, and co-invented packet-switching. Davies visited MIT in early 1960s, observing choke points in advanced time-sharing computer systems. Back in the UK, devised "packet switching", which divided computer messages into packets of code that could be tagged and sent independently, ultimately converging for reconstitution at a singular IP address. Packet-switching was central to the functioning of ARPANET.

Paul Baran

Polish-born American (1926-). Developed the concept of packets and packet-switching, but used different terminology. In 1960, joined RAND Corporation and led development of distributed array, or network, of packet-switching nodes. Later work expanded distributed communications idea to include OFDM (orthogonal frequency-division multiplexing), the notion that data could be transferred via several closely related channels. OFDM is the basis of digital broadband, DSL internet access, wireless networks and 4G mobile.

Robert Kahn

American (1938-). Electrical engineer who invented TCP/IP protocols with fellow UCLA alumnus Vint Cerf. Worked closely with Cerf after recruiting him to continue development of ARPANET, in 1973. Also with Cerf, served on Internet Engineering Task Force, getting ARPANET up and running. In 1972, Kahn demonstrated ARPANET's packet-switching technology at a public conference, considered a watershed event in development of the internet.

Bernard Marti

French (1943-). Co-inventor of France's Minitel, a predecessor to the World Wide Web (WWW), launched locally in Brittany, France, in 1978, and nationwide in 1982 (ceased operating in 2012). Minitel was an integrated videotext online system that enabled ecommerce and had text chat, video chat and email. Minitel charged users for time spent online and took percentage of online purchases, establishing digital revenue models still in use.

Robert Cailliau

Belgian (1947-). Co-worker of WWW inventor Tim Berners-Lee at CERN, Switzerland. Information engineer and computer scientist switched from working on CERN's Large Hadron to lead organization's Office Computing Systems in Data Handling division. In 1989, Berners-Lee proposed hypertext system to give CERN researchers access to all of CERN's documents, in all forms. Berners-Lee created the system – World Wide Web – in Autumn 1990. Cailliau co-authored the WWW funding proposal, and later co-developed first web browser for the Mac OS, MacWWW.

Tim Berners-Lee

British (1955-). With bachelor's degree in Physics from Oxford, started career as programmer, writing typesetting software for intelligent printers. At CERN in 1989, proposed hypertext project to facilitate sharing and updating of information among researchers. Prototype called ENQUIRE led to creation of World Wide Web. Took hypertext and connected it to the Transmission Control Protocol and domain name system to create the Web.

Vinton "Vint" Cerf

American (1943-). Original digital renaissance man. Co-created TCP/IP protocols with Kahn. Led engineering of MCI Mail, the first internet-connected commercial email service in 1982–86. Worked on systems capable of concurrent transmission of data, information, voice and video over the internet. Now Google's Vice President and Chief Internet Evangelist.

Paul Mockapetris

American (1948-). Co-creator of DNS (Domain Naming System). Researcher at USC (with Postel) was part of the ARPANET team. Postel presented Mockapetris, inventor of SMTP (Simple Mail Transfer Protocol), with five proposals to improve domain service via host.text system. Mockapetris ignored proposals and co-wrote DNS with Postel. DNS distributed domain hosting across wide server network, providing redundancy to keep websites operating if any one server failed. Chief Scientist and Chairman of the Board of IP address infrastructure software provider Nominum since 1999. Has overseen DNS upgrades and security-software development, as well as creation of spam blacklist, which diverts messages from known malicious IP addresses into email spam folder.

John McCarthy

American (1955-2011). Coined the term artificial intelligence in 1955. Implemented CTSS (Compatible Time-Sharing System) to allow use of computer resource (such as a networked machine of application) by many users through multi-programing and multi-tasking at the same time. During speech at MIT's centennial celebration, in 1961, suggested time-sharing could be sold like water, gas and electric utilities – the business model of cloud computing.

Jon Postel

American (1943-1998). Keeper of ARPANET RFCs, key to formation of ICANN (Internet Corporations for Assigned Names and Numbers). Part of UCLA contingent who formed ARPANET. Played key role in creating internet's structure. From 1969 until his death, wrote, edited and catalogued RFCs (Requests for Comment), the papers that shaped the the internet. Central figure in practical operation of internet. With Vint Cerf, in 1972, Postel devised "socket number" tracking system for internet domains. With colleague Paul Mockapetris, created DNS (Domain Name System).

Marc Andreessen

American (1971-). With fellow University of Illinois student Eric Bina, co-developed Mosaic web browser, the first web browser. A year later, introduced the Netscape search engine, which redefined the internet as potentially democratic, empowering, and enabling of digital transactions of every kind.

The frustrated idealism stems from many of the founders, especially those close to the World Wide Web. They really did believe they were ushering in something that was free and equal, a virtual world that would be very much better and nobler than the real one. In many ways, they have been sadly disappointed, but that is another book. Suffice it to say that the internet is not free, and it is not equal. (They also thought it would be democratic: history has already shown that in the wrong hands it can be very undemocratic indeed. Look how it has been used to suborn elections or enable shadowy state actions; or how it can create an unreal bubble of misinformation. The Oxford Dictionaries declared 2016's International Word of the Year to be "post-truth", an idea brought to you by the internet.)

As the internet grew, the idea that it might just be better if it had a funding model – in other words, if the user paid – was ideologically unacceptable. When traditional media moved towards digital, they compounded the issue by giving their premium analogue content away for free. Only slowly have users' subscriptions been seen to be a necessary part of the model – and even now there are holdouts and deniers a-plenty.

For the advertising industry, these are very important points, as it has had to step in and fund much of the internet. No Google search you perform is really "free": it is paid for by advertising. How strange it is that it still seems free to so many people. In fact, Google makes an average $3.25 profit each year from every person on Earth. If you count only those of us who are connected, that figure jumps to $7.25. Google isn't free.

The idealism of the commercial internet is a persistent gene, though, however misleading it may be. It has found full expression in the so-called Sharing Economy, a name that implies something essentially altruistic. I entirely fall on the side of those who recognize this as a piece of seductive re-framing that does not stand up to scrutiny. The transactions offered by Uber and Airbnb – enormously useful – are not about sharing: they are a rental agreement, that's all. And there are discounts to the real rental costs, which are absorbed by the unlevel playing fields in which they operate and which the user does not see. These platforms disintermediate, but they are not truly disruptive. If you really want to share a house/room, I suggest couchsurfing.com.

As the internet has had to become more commercial, it has evolved into a set of highly vested media interests. It is these, much more than governments, which have given shape to the chaos. They have engaged in an orgy of wall building, and the gardens behind the walls have become chargeable properties. Entirely understandably, they have created a rhetoric of digital advertising that supports their agenda. It has a number of themes, including:

- It's all or nothing: either you are with us or against us. Old media are irretrievably dead: as of *now*.
- This is the world of new. Only new matters. This new is unlike any other previous new in every way possible.

"...the internet that has emerged is riven by conflict. It can best be described as the combination of frustrated idealism and strongly vested interests."

Opposite Airbnb is an almost entirely digital presence, but it still defaults to analogue communications in some areas, with billboards and print ads. Renting advertising space in areas with a large availability of rooms, or in the publications that sit within them, just goes to show that to "belong anywhere" means being everywhere.

Above Sometimes dismissive of traditional advertising, Google nonetheless has embraced non-internet channels to drive product interest, such as using television commercials in India and Pakistan to demonstrate the potential of search to bring people together.

It is the rhetoric of digital exclusivity and of digital exceptionalism. It is not so much philosophically driven as rooted in the hard need to attract advertising dollars; but it has become implicit in a raft of journalism and writing, and most books written on the Digital Revolution follow the theme.

Personally I could not agree more that much of "old" media will disappear or that there are many very novel aspects to the Digital Revolution. But the rhetoric does not do justice to the richness of the revolution. It creates a zero-sum game, with the "digital Taliban" (as John Hegarty says) on one side and latter-day Luddites on the other. But it is the zone in between that is fertile and rewarding.

It's also clear that if you are a client these days, the old rule of caveat emptor applies more than ever before. And that you need best advice to guide you through the rhetorical jungle with some sense of judicious, constructive scepticism.

Your only worry: shaken not stirred.

Your new puppy tends to enjoy chewing on things. Furniture, pillows, shoes... the works. Luckily, Dropcam allows you to check in on the little rascal to make sure he isn't getting into all sorts of trouble. So have another drink, or two. #NestAssured

Above *The much-hyped Internet of Things can still work well in channels that don't plug in. Nest found comfort in print advertising and analogue billboards when it launched its high-tech home security cameras.*

3 THE SHORT MARCH

I first went to work in China in the late 1990s. I was still there at the turn of the millennium when I was much taken by a very curious statistic, which makes for one of the more recondite crossover charts in history. It was the time when the number of internet users in China surpassed for the first time the number of troglodytes, or cave dwellers. The latter were (and are) surprisingly numerous, around 30 million, but after 2001 the surging number of Chinese netizens soon left them behind.

CAVE DWELLERS VS INTERNET USERS

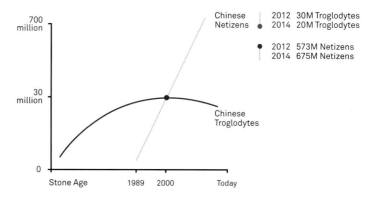

Above right *At the turn of the millennium in China, online citizens began to outnumber those who inhabit caves for the first time – now that's progress. Internet usage has increased dramatically since.*

This very Short March in China is a neat symbol for the force with which the Digital Revolution captured the world. It would be tiresome to repeat the statistics. But from the point of view of advertising, there will also be a critical crossover – the point when digital spending exceeds non-digital. It's coming soon.

Fragmentation

The impact on our world has been explosive. The orderly chain whereby manufacturers stimulated demand by creating brands, which addressed a mass audience with one message at one time, which drove them to the stores, was shattered into fragments.

You can see the fragments everywhere: fragmented shareholders and stakeholders; audiences splintered into hundreds of mini-segments; more

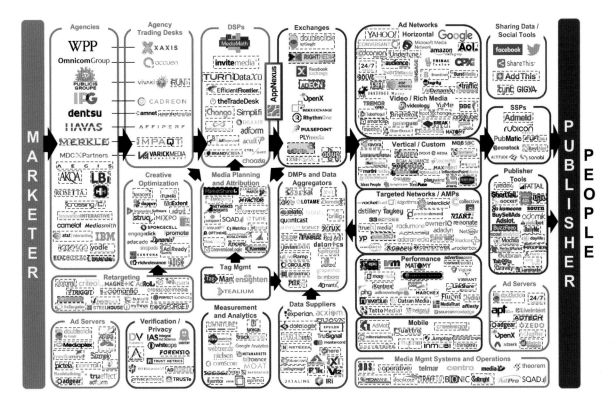

Above I keep this dinosaur, sculpted by Sui Jianguo and given to me by colleague TB Song. One of our (great) clients, Tony Palmer of Kimberly Clark, had described traditional agencies as dinosaurs, doomed to extinction. So, from 2008, it lived on my desk reminding me that this needn't be. Since then we became the world's largest digital agency network – and Kimberly Clark is an "at heart" digital client.

platforms and more touch points; supply chains and demand chains broken; more metrics and more things to say. And brands themselves fragmenting into hundreds of SKUs (Stock Keeping Units).

Shattered advertising agencies, too. The full-service agency network has new competitors in pure play digital agencies, social media groups, content shops, branded entertainment producers, and activation agencies.

Not only is there fragmentation, there is disintermediation as well. Amazon disintermediated the booksellers; Grindr, the gay bars; Uber, the taxis. Yes, they've all taken a hit, some more than others. But the story is always more complicated than it seems. And some of the disintermediators are less of a threat than they are a market expander. That seems to be the impact of Airbnb, for example.

Google was seen (and certainly saw itself) as the disintermediator of advertising. It has been joined in that doubtless pleasant illusion by Facebook. Hiring distinguished creatives; building a sales force which talks to clients directly; hiring from the clients themselves to make their pitch even more compelling; offering a range of services usually provided by advertising agencies: none of these could be construed as friendly acts. And yet this is a medium – digital advertising – that receives some $6.9 billion and growing a year from the advertising business worldwide.

I can remember, at various conferences over the past few years, all the polite denials from Google and Facebook speakers. "Some mistake, surely?"

Above *Orrin Klapp's writings on the gap between information and meaning, and the risks of social entropy from banality and noise, could hardly be more relevant to the Digital Revolution – despite being written before a single PC had hit the shelves.*

Well, at the time of writing, not one of the offerings proffered by the digital platforms competing with us has resulted in anything like disintermediation. The reality is that they have just not been able to demonstrate an ability to do what we do, which is to build brands on the principles of best advice. Meanwhile they do have a data reservoir, with all the pent-up leverage that brings, which we could never replicate. The truth is that we need each other.

The Digital Revolution is complex enough to require both them and us. We can and should try to work together. Around the world, I can see it starting to happen: as usual, the further from headquarters, the more there's real teamwork.

Cacophony

The unwanted child of fragmentation is cacophony. Noise, noise, everywhere. A few years ago I came across the writings of the now-forgotten Canadian sociologist Orrin Klapp, from the University at Western Ontario. They even smell slightly musty, as mine is a second-hand copy, but deserve to be displayed in neon now, because Klapp saw, with a clarity that still is scarce, exactly what would happen.

> Computers can speed the process of data, but give us little help in reading the meaning of the printout. Meaning has a reputation for arriving late – indeed the highest meaning, wisdom, is also slowest to arrive…. So society suffers a meaning gap, between input of factual information and the construction of common meaning. The paradox of the meaning gap generated by information overload is that ever more facts pile up, the credibility of which is unquestioned, but the overall meaning of the system is lacking and its rhetoric is rejected as hypocritical. The whole is less than the sum of the parts.[1]

There is a series of phenomena which has created a new dimension to what was never a very easy challenge – getting people's attention: information overload, distraction, attention deficit, and so on. As journalist John Lorinc put it in a piece in *The Walrus*:

> Digital communications have shown a striking capacity to subdue our attention into smaller and smaller increments; increasingly it seems as though the sheer glut of data itself has supplanted the hand of focused, reflective attention that make them useful in the first place.[2]

There are two great truths all of us need to remember:
1. We are designed to be selective.
2. We are designed to make patterns.

It seems to me at least that the job of agencies assumes a simplicity we often forget amidst the cacophony of our overloaded, multi-tooled lives: we are the meaning creators.

Lorinc quotes a puzzled participant in a technology conference asking: "If information is like the sea, what is seamanship?...We don't talk about 'human-wind interactions' – we talk about sailing."[3]

The tension between humans and information is not another either/or, a dichotomy which we observe but do not seek to influence: we need both sea and sailors, but it's the sailors who are vested with the task of deciding where to go and how.

This digital seamanship requires two things which are not generally deemed to be so important by quite a broad coalition of those which have led the Short March – from the new media, to the technology platforms, to the millions of applications.

It requires the ability to cohere, to bring together, to re-assemble the fragments, to make sense of them. And it requires some long-termism. The fragmentation has seen a descent into tactics as an end in themselves: any short-term program that can be measured suddenly gains respectability just because you know how many views or likes it gets. Someone has likened it to taking crack: instant hits are everything – and it is addictive.

There are voices of reason: bring on Melody Gambino, Director of Marketing at adtech firm Grapeshot.

It upsets me when I come across an all-too-prevalent mindset among the new wave of digital marketing technorati that glibly demeans the legacy of old-school Madison Avenue storytellers. Regardless of what some 'bro-geeks' who run ad tech companies might maintain, sacred advertising tomes like *Ogilvy on Advertising* still do matter:[4]

David Ogilvy, indeed, was slaying similar demons as far back as the 1950s. They don't go away: they just come back after a period of TV-imposed sobriety when mass media did develop some coherence, and they are now decked out in new, seductive clothes. In a speech to the 4A's (one of our premier industry trade groups) in 1955, he said,

It is my guess that 95 per cent of all campaigns now in circulation are being created without any real reference to long-term considerations.

They are being created ad hoc. Hence the oscillation. Hence the tacking. Hence the lack of any coherent personality from one season to another.

How tragically easy it is to stampede into change. But what golden rewards await the advertiser who has the brains to create a favourable brand image – and the stability to stick with it over a long period.

They still do.

Pages 26–29 *The short march of digital, from the mid-1990s to the present day. The advent of the Internet, access to broadband and adoption of mobile and has digitized global society. Digital advertising spend will surely overtake traditional by 2020.*

STARBUCKS

AGE OF INVENTION

Imagine yourself in a Seattle coffee shop in 1971, sipping a unique tasting coffee with a smooth, bold blend – a West Coast roast that makes regular coffee taste weak by comparison. Howard Schultz, who joined little-known Starbucks as Marketing Director a decade later, quickly saw potential in the brand's unique flavour to disrupt a lacklustre global coffee market. So he bought the company.

Alongside taste, Schultz envisioned bringing the Italian coffee-house tradition to the US. He focused on transforming the experience. The server behind the counter became a *Barista*, someone who cared so much about "customer intimacy" he or she took the time to ask your name and write it on your cup. Schultz created an employee culture of caring, and Starbucks was consistently rated as one of the best places to work.

The Starbucks experience was immediately different, more exotic, a place where customers willingly adopted a new lingo to order their "grande double skinny macchiato". And it was underpinned by quality – full control over the supply chain, from growers to roasters to distribution, all to ensure exceptional flavour consistency. The result? Explosive growth across the US, and internationally, from the late 1990s.

AGE OF APATHY

A marketer by trade, Schultz has historically been dogmatic about not spending money on advertising; success had been achieved through word of mouth, and that was to continue.

When Starbucks announced itself as "the third place", a destination between work and home open to everyone, the brand's efforts to refine experiential branding – at the exclusion of other marketing activity – became an obsession. Data showed that the average Starbucks customer already visited about six times a month, so resolutely focusing on in-store activities was, perhaps, a forgivable folly. But an ideological opposition to advertising caused the brand to suffer.

Instead, local charity-giving programmes, continued service improvements and (failed) music distribution partnerships were weak substitutes. And seeking expansion through grocery retail, alongside increasing store footprint to 15,000 outlets in 50 countries, compromised the brand's local feel. In 2009, Starbucks began closing stores, letting go of one third of employees from its headquarters and 2,000 in total. The company's "if you build it, they will come" philosophy had failed. And the Starbucks experience became as vanilla as one of its lattes.

Opposite top *Founders Jerry Baldwin, Zev Siegl – an English and History teacher respectively – and Gordon Bowker – a writer – named Starbucks after a character in Moby Dick. An updated version of their original "Siren" logo, a woodcut depiction of a mermaid with two tails, still represents the brand today.*

Opposite middle *Howard Shultz famously said he does not believe in "advertising", but over the years his thirst has grown – starting with promotional ads, then partner ads, through to tactical ads that have a little more flavour, like this one.*

Opposite bottom *Shultz's advertising awakening! "Meet me at Starbucks" was the first global brand campaign to bring the warmth of Starbucks to life in film. A valiant effort to capture the feeling of Starbucks outside of its locations, and timed (albeit a little late…) to fend off competitors both large and small.*

Right *Starbucks opened in 1971 as a single location in Seattle that sold only roasted beans. It took Howard Shultz joining to transform those beans into a global brand. He invented the idea of "the third place", a hub for friends, colleagues and communities to gather away from home or work. The formula worked.*

AGE OF COHERENCE

With Dunkin' Donuts and McDonald's upgrading their coffee offering in the US, copycat coffee chains expanding around the world, and the rise of boutique coffee shops on the corner of every hipster neighbourhood, Starbucks was forced to rethink.

Schultz began with rebranding – a new logo emblazoned on every store and cup around the globe. But he knew that the product would no longer be enough. An earlier test of TV commercials, developed with Pepsi to advertise a range of ready-to-drink Starbucks beverages, had been both well received and, importantly, increased sales. And so, time for the unthinkable – advertising.

In 2014, Starbucks launched its first major advertising campaign – with an anthemic brand ad called "Meet Me At Starbucks". Shot in 59 stores across 28 countries over 24 hours, the ad went back to the brand's origins to project Starbucks as a place to connect, face to face, in the warmth, comfort and diversity of its coffee shops. The brand was still underweight on digital advertising and overweight on product (rather than masterbrand) advertising, but was learning fast.

Schultz once said that "Our stories are our billboard". But those stories also seem to translate well as TV commercials, YouTube documentaries, print ads, and across a host of other channels too. Having developed a taste for advertising, Starbucks is now ranked by Fortune as one of the world's most admired companies.

TIMELINE OF THE DIGITAL REVOLUTION

Early 1900s

Enigma machines developed, with first models appearing after **WW1**. Looked like large portable typewriters in wooden boxes. First electromechanical computers, used to encode information to protect commercial, military and diplomatic communications.

1940s

Team led by Alan Turing, English mathematician and pioneering computer scientist, develops a device to crack Nazi messages encoded using **Enigma** machines. Credited with creating the first "universal machine", a mathematical tool equivalent to a digital computer.

1950s

Development of digital networks by government-funded, largely defence-related, projects in the US, UK and France. Early networks transfer "**packets**" of information, laying foundation for email.

1960s

Computer scientists and Pentagon employees create **COBOL**, or Common Business-Oriented Language, a computer code devised for utility companies to track usage but adopted quickly by many businesses. COBOL is still widely used today.

```
IDENTIFICATION DIVISION.
    PROGRAM-ID. HELLO-WORLD.
*
    ENVIRONMENT DIVISION.
*
    DATA DIVISION.
*
    PROCEDURE DIVISION.
    PARA-1.
        DISPLAY "Hello, world.".
*
    EXIT PROGRAM.
    END PROGRAM HELLO-WORLD.
```

1961

IBM introduces the 1400 series, replacing cumbersome vacuum-tube technology with **transistors**, shrinking the size and cost of computers.

1968

IBM breaks new ground again with CICS (Customer Information Control System) **transaction-processing code**, replacing batched punch-card tallying. Companies use CICS to store customer information and conduct online transactions.

1969

ARPANET (Advanced Research Projects Agency Network) launches a data communication system funded by the US government, which forms the basis of the internet. Connects research centres at UCLA, Stanford, University of Utah, and University of California, Santa Barbara.

ARPANET uses IMPs (Interface Message Processors), a network of small computers similar to routers. Based on **packet switching** – disseminating one bundle of data to multiple IMPs at once, rather than circuit switching linear data transfer, like a telephone call. Later develops the TCP/IP (Transmission Control Protocol/Internet Protocol), enabling simultaneous multi-directional data communication among a network of computers – the basis of the internet.

> **"SENDING ELECTRONIC MAIL OVER THE ARPANET FOR COMMERCIAL PROFIT OR POLITICAL PURPOSES IS BOTH ANTI-SOCIAL AND ILLEGAL."**
>
> According to a handbook published by MIT, whose AI Lab later hooked into the network.

1971

Students at the Stanford Artificial Intelligence Laboratory and MIT arrange a **pot sale** via ARPANET. Is this the first online sale? The ARPANET users simply arranged a meeting over the network.

> **"THE SEMINAL ACT OF ECOMMERCE"**
>
> John Markoff, in his book *What the Dormouse Said.*

1972

The term "personal computer" is coined. Refers to the Xerox Alto, whose **graphical-user interface** (GUI) provides inspiration years later for Apple Macintosh's and Microsoft Windows' operating systems.

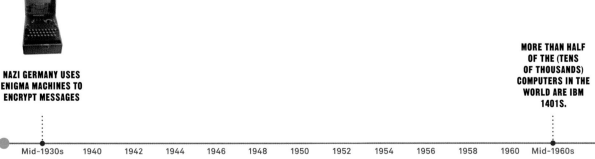

NAZI GERMANY USES ENIGMA MACHINES TO ENCRYPT MESSAGES

MORE THAN HALF OF THE (TENS OF THOUSANDS) COMPUTERS IN THE WORLD ARE IBM 1401S.

Mid-1930s   1940   1942   1944   1946   1948   1950   1952   1954   1956   1958   1960   Mid-1960s

1974

Early laptops and mobile

IBM Los Gatos Scientific Center develops a **portable computer prototype** called SCAMP (Special Computer APL Machine Portable).

Motorola begins a run of firsts in the mobile market, including the 8000 series, aka the Brick Phone.

"JOEL, THIS IS MARTY. I'M CALLING YOU FROM A CELL PHONE, A REAL HANDHELD PORTABLE CELL PHONE..."

First words on a mobile phone call from Motorola researcher and executive Martin Cooper to chief competitor Joel S. Engel of Bell Labs, in New Jersey, 3 April 1973.

1976

First incidence of spam when marketing director of computer manufacturer Digital Equipment Corporation (DEC) sends message **promoting sales events** for its latest models to about 400 users of ARPANET. Draws sharp criticism from the connected community but generates sales among the target audience, in Southern California.

1979

English inventor Michael Aldrich, working for Redifon Computers, creates R1800/30 Compact Office System. The *Times* reports it enables users to "place orders for goods, obtain information, and undertake programmed learning courses." Aldrich touts the "place orders for goods" part, and claims to have originated **ecommerce**.

1981

IBM rolls out first integrated-component personal-computer system, takes ownership of the acronym "**PC**". The 5150 computer includes a monitor, stand-alone keyboard, printer and paper stand. Also this year, Thomson Holidays UK installs first B2B online shopping systems.

1982

France Telecom introduces nationwide online-ordering system, **Minitel**. Ecommerce is becoming a thing.

1984

Apple launches Macintosh with **$900,000 Super Bowl** commercial that reaches 46.4% of US households. Compuserve launches Electronic Mall in US and Canada, a major step in the development of B2C (business-to-consumer) ecommerce.

Mid-1980s

In an early form of **digital marketing**, ChannelNet (formerly SoftAd Group) places reader-response cards in magazines, sends respondents floppy discs with car-model information and test-drive offers.

1992

SMS messaging arrives on heels of 2G mobile network expansion and sharp increase in cell-phone use.

1993

Clickable web ad sold by Global Network Navigator (GNN) to law firm Heller, Ehrman, White, & McAuliffe, linking directly to firm's website. Questionable whether it was a "clickable banner ad" or just a link. Publishers such as Condé Nast and Time Inc. ramp up website development.

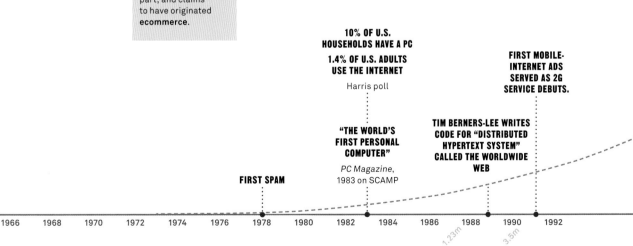

10% OF U.S. HOUSEHOLDS HAVE A PC

1.4% OF U.S. ADULTS USE THE INTERNET

Harris poll

"THE WORLD'S FIRST PERSONAL COMPUTER"

PC Magazine, 1983 on SCAMP

FIRST SPAM

TIM BERNERS-LEE WRITES CODE FOR "DISTRIBUTED HYPERTEXT SYSTEM" CALLED THE WORLDWIDE WEB

FIRST MOBILE-INTERNET ADS SERVED AS 2G SERVICE DEBUTS.

| 1966 | 1968 | 1970 | 1972 | 1974 | 1976 | 1978 | 1980 | 1982 | 1984 | 1986 | 1988 | 1990 | 1992 |

1.23m   3.5m

1994

First web magazine, **HotWired**, launches and becomes first site to provide ad clients with traffic reports, the first internet metrics. Coins the term **"banner advertising"**, and creates modular spaces on web pages akin to newspaper and magazine pages. Posts the **first clickable ad** from AT&T.

Vibe magazine's website emerges as a favourite among advertisers. MCI Communications, Jim Beam, General Motors, and Timex pay Vibe $20,000 for homepage ad positioning. Spending for online ads already tens of millions of dollars. CompuServe, AOL and Netscape debut.

US **government promotes ecommerce** by moving web hosting from NSFNET to commercial network providers, including MCI and AT&T. Uptick in digital ad spending the following year due to the transfer of hosting from the government to business. Yahoo! and AltaVista **search engines** launch. Oregon-based Multi-Media Marketing Group (MMG) is founded, credited with coining the phrase **Search Engine Optimization** (SEO). SEO ranking becomes an important measure of the marketing power of a brand.

1995

Nokia introduces first **smartphone** series, the Nokia 9000, a folding-notebook-style unit with internet access via WAP and a full QWERTY keyboard. DoubleClick founded, an early Application Service Provider (ASP) that serves ads (primarily banner ads). IPOs two years later as a Top 10 internet site.

1996

First **DVRs** introduced at Consumer Electronics Show, raising spectre of ad-skipping, the TV equivalent of ad blocking in digital media.

1997

Number of people using the web, and search engines, reaches **70 million**, up from 16 million just two years earlier.

FIRST CLICK-THROUGH BANNER AD

Have you ever clicked your mouse right HERE? → YOU WILL

"HAVE YOU EVER CLICKED YOUR MOUSE RIGHT HERE? YOU WILL."

AT&T was right: the click-through rate was 44%. Users who took the bait enjoyed a tour of seven museums around the world.

1998

TV ad revenue hits $8.3 billion. **Google** and MSN search engines launch. Google develops PageRank, measuring quality and strength of inbound links to determine relative value of sites. GoTo.com launches bidding for higher placement in search results.

2000

500% increase in the NASDAQ index shows technology companies performing at an all-time high. 10 March 2000: NASDAQ peaks at 5048 and the **tech market collapses**. Internet enters a new phase of information sharing, user-centred design, and collaboration.

Consumers engage with brands in a more organic, personalized way. Marketing embraces the concept of **"creating value for customers"**. Shift away from simply pushing advertising to customers online, towards delivering ads better suited to their lifestyle, personality, demographics, wants and needs.

2001

3G mobile connectivity debuts. Launched by Japan's NTT DOCOMO, in same year that the first **branded-content campaign** goes live. It is a series of short, dramatic video clips by A-list directors called "The Hire". BMW pays for the series and its cars are featured in each episode.

2003

Site-targeted advertising debuts. **Google AdWords** allows ad placement via keyword, domain name, topic, and demographics. Quickly becomes Google's main revenue source. Branded Content Marketing Association founded. Study shows consumers prefer native ads over traditional ones.

President George W. Bush signs into law the Can-Spam Act (Controlling the Assault of Non-Solicited Pornography and Marketing Act).

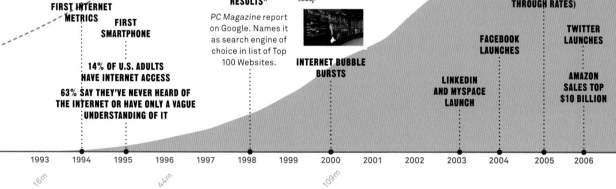

FIRST INTERNET METRICS

FIRST SMARTPHONE

14% OF U.S. ADULTS HAVE INTERNET ACCESS

63% SAY THEY'VE NEVER HEARD OF THE INTERNET OR HAVE ONLY A VAGUE UNDERSTANDING OF IT

"AN UNCANNY KNACK FOR RETURNING EXTREMELY RELEVANT RESULTS"

PC Magazine report on Google. Names it as search engine of choice in list of Top 100 Websites.

MARCH 10, 2000: POP GOES THE NASDAQ!

INTERNET BUBBLE BURSTS

GOOGLE INTRODUCES DIGITAL AD-RELEVANCE RANKING AS PART OF ITS PRICING MODEL, BASED ON CTR (CLICK-THROUGH RATES)

FACEBOOK LAUNCHES

TWITTER LAUNCHES

LINKEDIN AND MYSPACE LAUNCH

AMAZON SALES TOP $10 BILLION

| 1993 | 1994 | 1995 | 1996 | 1997 | 1998 | 1999 | 2000 | 2001 | 2002 | 2003 | 2004 | 2005 | 2006 |

16m   44m   109m

2005

Google offers **personalized search** results informed by user's search history; launches branded version of Analytics.

2007

Programmatic ad buying debuts. Ad exchanges sell ads in inventory with multiple ad networks and are bought via real-time bidding on a per-impression basis. Subscribers to 3G networks worldwide reach **295 million** (just 9% the of global subscriber base). Music and video streaming booms.

2009

Google Instant offers real-time search results. **Ad.ly** in-stream advertising service pays Kim Kardashian $10,000 per tweet, a test of promoted tweets. Facebook self-service ad buying offers **targeted advertising**, allows targeting by **geo-location** and language. Amazon sales reach $25 billion.

2010

Twitter introduces **Promoted Trends and Promoted Tweets**. The first Promoted Trend is Disney's *Toy Story 3*. Virgin America, Starbucks and Bravo also pay for promotional placement.

2011

US internet advertising revenue reaches **$7.68 billion** in the second quarter (24% increase from the second quarter of 2010). **Digital video** ads account for just 6% of all internet ad revenue in first half of 2011, but effectiveness leads to growth of in-stream advertising, such as TV advertising.

Ad-blocking software debuts.

Mozilla announces that its Firefox web browser will include ad-blocking capability. Microsoft Internet Explorer, Apple Safari, and Google Chrome browsers follow suit. 42% of US households now own a DVR, with primary purpose of **skipping TV ads.**

2014

Ad-bots create **"fake traffic"**. Study finds that advertisers spend "billions of dollars on online ads that real consumers never see" because of automated ad counters, or ad bots. Bots create "fake traffic", which undermines reliability of publishers' audience metrics.

2015

Real-time bidding takes off, enabling real-time buying and selling of ads on a per-impression basis. Winning bids instantly display on publishers' sites. Auctions mimic **exchange mechanisms** used in financial markets. It's a $15 billion industry, projected to grow by 65% by 2020 (Business Insider).

Global ad revenue reaches $17.08 billion (70% from mobile ads). **Amazon.com** accounts for more than half of all ecommerce growth, selling nearly 500 million SKU's in the US. Yahoo! confirms that it "punishes" users who employ ad blocking by holding back their personal email.

2016

Ad spending on social media campaigns projected by eMarketer to reach $23.68 billion, a 33.5% increase over 2015. US Government formally accuse Russia of **state-sponsored hacking** intended to interfere with the outcome of the US 2016 election.

2017–2019

By 2017, social media ad spend forecast to reach $36 billion, or 16% of all digital ad spending. Worldwide digital ad spending to grow from $226.7 billion to **$283 billion**, which translates to 35% and 39% of all media ad spending (eMarketer).

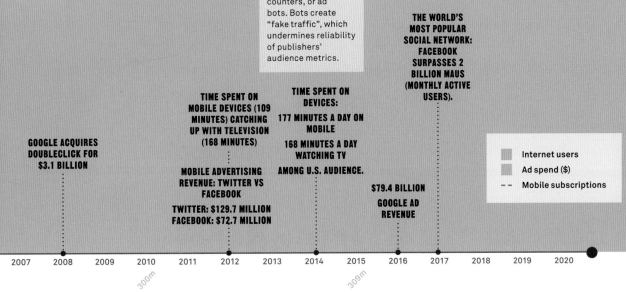

GOOGLE ACQUIRES DOUBLECLICK FOR $3.1 BILLION

TIME SPENT ON MOBILE DEVICES (109 MINUTES) CATCHING UP WITH TELEVISION (168 MINUTES)

MOBILE ADVERTISING REVENUE: TWITTER VS FACEBOOK

**TWITTER: $129.7 MILLION
FACEBOOK: $72.7 MILLION**

TIME SPENT ON DEVICES:

177 MINUTES A DAY ON MOBILE

168 MINUTES A DAY WATCHING TV AMONG U.S. AUDIENCE.

THE WORLD'S MOST POPULAR SOCIAL NETWORK: FACEBOOK SURPASSES 2 BILLION MAUS (MONTHLY ACTIVE USERS).

$79.4 BILLION GOOGLE AD REVENUE

Internet users
Ad spend ($)
-- Mobile subscriptions

2007 2008 2009 2010 2011 2012 2013 2014 2015 2016 2017 2018 2019 2020

300m

309m

4 THE DIGITAL ECOSYSTEM

Knitted together in the right way, the fragmented new media world gives us the sort of creative opportunity David Ogilvy could only have dreamed of. It's a dazzling ecosystem of opportunity if – and not because – you are sceptical in swallowing its own well-crafted hype.

What success means in this ecosystem deserves some forensic probing. Who's doing really well, and who's not? Who's making money, and exactly how? It is strange, but in all the flood of journalistic commentary on the subject, it is impossible to find a simple, and systematic, set of comparisons to help answer these questions. Well, there's one specially constructed on the following pages.

There are two big and simple things one learns from doing an analysis like this:

• For an advertiser, there's no one-stop shop. Most of these media complement each other in various ways. Which and how depends on our strategy, not theirs.
• Is is a race of algorithms in which profitability is the prize, not mere scale. It's not won yet.

Right *Seemingly invincible social platforms have quickly succumbed to fitter successors. Six Degrees had a short life, and barely made it to the start of the twenty-first century. Next, Myspace and Friendster appeared, and then moved aside for Facebook, while Xanga gave way to YouTube. Orkut, until recently the most popular network in parts of the world, has largely disappeared from sight.*

This is an ecosystem that is still evolving. My colleague Zach Newcombe, a partner at our global consulting network OgilvyRed, describes this as being a "Cambrian" moment: a point in time where the sudden arrival of maximum connectivity is spawning an explosion of new life forms. The question is, which are the fittest and will survive?

In 2011, Friendster failed because it missed the social interaction part of being a social network. It was like reading your résumé at a cocktail party. There will be other Friendsters. The American social media life forms shown opposite may not have the best possible business model. Later on I will describe how life on the Chinese internet has evolved. It could have better evolutionary potential.

But what is obvious is that there is an emerging "big three" of digital life forms – Google, Facebook and Amazon – of which two have paid-for advertising very much at the heart of their algorithms, Google and Facebook. In the case of Google, it is not surprising. But it only took Facebook a few years to move from a quasi-altruistic social network to an aggressive media owner. I remember being criticized for saying early on that they were the biggest direct-marketing database in the world, but did not deign to recognize it. Now there is no compunction, and the combination of mobile access, accurate targeting, rate-card savviness and an increasing ability to generate a direct response makes it a highly attractive component of any media plan.

Together this is beginning to look like a duopoly. Google and Facebook account for some $36 billion of the $69 billion digital media spend in the US. 52 per cent! When Theodore Roosevelt took on Standard Oil in 1906, it accounted for 70 per cent of the oil and kerosene market. Will our view of monopolistic trading change when Google and Facebook reach the same level? And will we have any Theodore Roosevelts around to slay the dragons?

Below *Facebook used to be all about its ads, confident in the allure of its huge audience to advertisers. Then marketers discovered the platform's more powerful function – social CRM. Now, Facebook is less of an advertising platform and more of a CRM vehicle, allowing brands to generate leads highly efficiently – for example, to launch new products like this campaign we did for Philips. Budgets are rightly being reallocated to capitalize on the effectiveness of this kind of social CRM.*

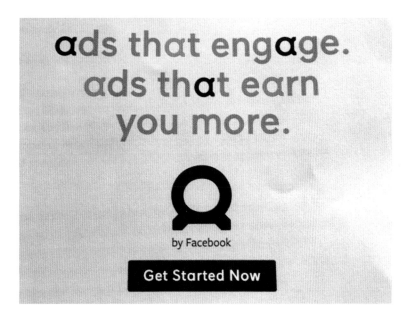

THE DIGITAL ECOSYSTEM

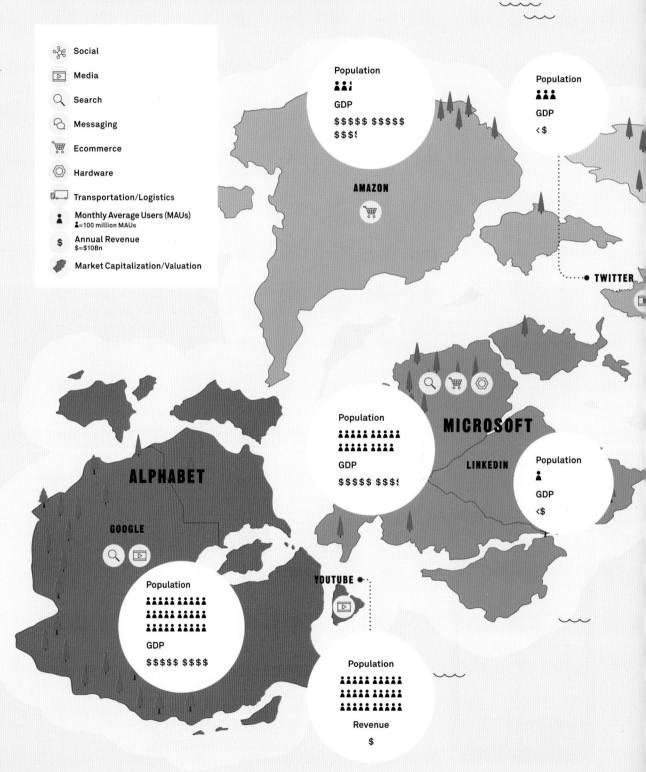

Social

Media

Search

Messaging

Ecommerce

Hardware

Transportation/Logistics

Monthly Average Users (MAUs)
=100 million MAUs

Annual Revenue
$=$10Bn

Market Capitalization/Valuation

AMAZON

Population

GDP
$$$$$ $$$$$
$$$$

Population

GDP
< $

TWITTER

MICROSOFT

LINKEDIN

Population

GDP
$$$$$ $$$$

Population

GDP
< $

ALPHABET

GOOGLE

Population

GDP
$$$$$ $$$$

YOUTUBE

Population

Revenue
$

Welcome to the digital ecosystem – a land grab akin to the game of Risk, still to be played out.

Advertisers must understand the new terrain well and place the right strategic bets. Unlike the evolution of land masses, these are fluid territories. They change in size, splinter off and new ones still emerge.

Start-ups appear with the potential to dominate the landscape, using algorithms as their armory. Smart though machine learning and AI may be, the biggest players now have such powerful network effects and sticky suite of features that it will take much more than it has before to conquer their territory.

APPLE

Population
🧍🧍🧍🧍🧍🧍 🧍

GDP
$$$$$ $$$$$
$$$$$ $$$$$
$$

Population
🧍🧍🧍🧍🧍🧍🧍

GDP
$$

WECHAT

INSTAGRAM

FACEBOOK

Population
🧍🧍🧍🧍🧍 🧍🧍🧍🧍🧍
🧍🧍🧍🧍🧍 🧍🧍🧍🧍🧍

Revenue
$ $$

BAIDU

Population
🧍🧍🧍🧍🧍 🧍
GDP
<$

SNAPCHAT

PINTEREST

Population
🧍🧍🧍🧍🧍
🧍🧍🧍🧍🧍

GDP
$$

Population
🧍
GDP <$

YAHOO

Yahoo sale of Ali Baba stake

Population
🧍🧍🧍🧍

GDP
$ $$

ALI BABA

Verizon sale

Population
🧍🧍🧍

GDP <$

Population
🧍🧍🧍🧍🧍 🧍🧍🧍🧍🧍

Revenue
<$

The Death of Everything?

Meanwhile, what of "traditional media"? The pull from the duopoly has sucked the revenues out of it, especially in the press medium, and to some extent television. The "digital exclusivity" narrative has played this as the "death of…" The death of television, in particular, is given centre stage. The admirable journalist Bob Garfield has been a leading proponent – even having a chapter labelled "The Death of Everything" in his book *The Chaos Scenario* (2009). I think even Bob would admit that the revolution has been rather less apocalyptic than his prophecies.

It is not a new claim. In 1996, Nicholas Negroponte, the author of *Being Digital*, wrote that "Television will macdisappear in less than ten years". In the same year, the chairman of the BBC, Sir Christopher Bland, said: "TV sets across the world will be jettisoned within a decade." More recently, it is the New York University academic Scott Galloway whose thesis has become somehow more ideological. He sees the death of TV as that of "the advertising industrial complex", the conspiracy of TV and advertisers which has been artificially sustained by big brands – in fact, the death of branding as we know it. This is also not a new angle. In 1994, Professor Ronald Rust and Richard Oliver prophesized exactly that in "The Death of Advertising", published in the *Journal of Advertising Research*.

What has actually happened since then? It is informative to look at the table of measured media investment between 1999 and 2017 prepared by my colleague Adam Smith of GroupM. It shows that linear television (or non-time-shifted broadcast of cable viewing) has maintained a strong position in a market much expanded by digital. Its share of around 40 per cent is the same as it was in 1999. TV is not dead!

The reason for this is that people's viewership of linear TV still holds up, despite the surge in digital media. Of course, the real story here is that digital has gained at the expense of the press medium. There was a death of classified ads, and direct response has shifted en masse to digital. Even the press medium is not completely dead. It can be resilient in places where strong content is justified by journalism of quality and consumed by an audience elite of sufficient scale or sufficient specialism. Then it still is a model sustainable by advertising – especially if circulation can be charged for. If any one of those parameters breaks down, the commercial model breaks down, too.

So TV is *not* dead: though it is changing beyond recognition, it is more useful than ever before. "Cord-cutting", "TV Everywhere", and "OTT" (over-the-top) are roiling the TV landscape, but they are hardly fatal illnesses. In fact, they are heralding the age of greater TV consumption. The pay TV industry is adapting to new viewing patterns with multi-channel on-demand subscription services and consolidation. TV advertising, popularly thought to be a declining force, is thriving and growing fast in broadcast and digital. Television content is better than it ever has been before – more varied and of higher quality – but the audience is fragmented across different media. We don't know yet how to measure these audiences particularly well, and that (not cord-cutting) may be the biggest threat to TV of all.

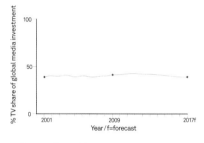

Source: Group M

Above *Graph showing that TV's percentage share of media investment over the last 16 years has barely changed, and remains at around 40%.*

There is no doubt that the "TV is dead" argument has led clients into a splurge of hypertargeting. My own belief (and it is only based on experience with real clients, nothing more) is that brands, having experimented, are now searching again for the fundamentals. What gives your brands the reach they need? What gives you the combination of greater reach and greater impact?

In the long term, where there is demand, supply usually configures itself to match it. It seems at least as likely that the media industry will conform to this and find new ways of delivering a total aggregated audience. Who knows, this might even pose an interesting challenge for the digital mass media: do they enter television or seek to slay it? My purpose in saying this is not to indulge in any wild prediction but simply to inveigh against the excesses of the blind anti-TV prejudice. TV is alive and well in developing markets, and alive in many developed markets.

6 reasons why TV is not dead

1. It offers the safest way to scale with net reach, which remains unobtainable in any other way.
2. It does not suffer from ad fraud, which might taint up to a third of digital investment.
3. Because TV content is consumed on devices other than TV, the TV audience is significantly underestimated. When the view numbers become "real", ad spend will increase.
4. TV remains unquestionably the best vehicle for communicating emotion; brand platforms require emotion.
5. There is a weight of econometric evidence which shows – conclusively – that cutting TV budgets damages sales.
6. Online itself is sustaining TV: it has become the second largest spend category.

The Ghettoization of Digital

This is a phrase used by my client on Dove for many years, one of the great contemporary marketers, Steve Miles. Yes, it is true: "ghettoization" is the unfortunate offspring of unthinking reverence. We revere, then we separate. We separate, then we erect silos to affirm the fact and protect the territory. And then we justify it by describing it as "pure" play.

As Steve says, there is no such thing as digital marketing or digital advertising; there is just good marketing and good advertising. As he puts it: "If Dove is good at digital, then what makes it good there is exactly the same as what makes it good anywhere. It is the fundamentals of marketing."[1]

The digital guru whom Nestlé hired to digitalize its marketing, Pete Blackshaw, uses almost exactly the same words: "The 'fundamentals' remain fundamental."[2]

> "There is no such thing as digital marketing or digital advertising; there is just good marketing and good advertising."

So much that is digital starts from the opposite view point. It is incidental not fundamental. It elevates the media platform above the brand platform. And, it is not scaleable.

It's in this light that I have my own take on the famous (or infamous) Super Bowl 2013 Oreo tweet (see overleaf). It was the tweet that really registered for the first time the potential of being always-on – of exploiting a moment in time.

An Australian academic, Professor Mark Ritson, has done us all a service by dissecting the realities behind this tweet.

By dissecting the actual number of Oreo followers, the click-through rates, the amplification (re-tweets), Ritson shows that the tweet reached a mere 64,000 people – or 0.02 per cent of Oreo's customer base.

It's a point well made, and done in an amusingly irreverent way. But maybe its merit is more as an attack on the cult around the tweet, the silo triumphant, an easy dragon to slay, rather than what that tweet really betokened. So, ultimately, there's a bigger point. I've had the good fortune

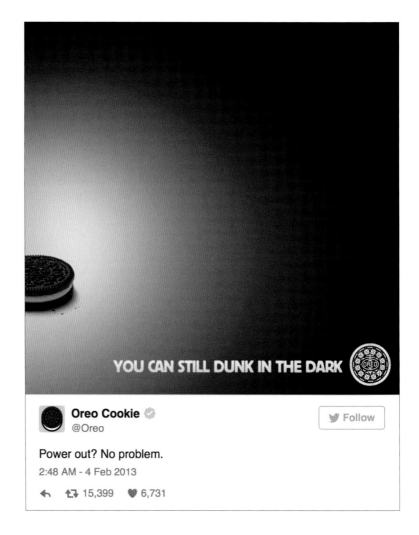

Right *A social media team at the 2013 Super Bowl had the nerve, the agility and the creativity to take advantage of a blackout with this tweet, and then hyped it indefatigably. It provoked headlines such as "How Oreo's Blackout Tweet Trumped Million-Dollar Super Bowl Ads."*

Above *Our agency John Street in Toronto has always realized that when it comes to predicting the future of digital, there can be a humour deficit. Their antidote has been hilarious videos such as this one to satirize the ability of cats to generate huge views, and poke fun at the advertising industry in the process.*

"It is easy to pull by pandering to the lowest common denominators of crowd culture: we would just put a cat in every video."

to run an advertising agency and a public relations agency. Those who hyped the Oreo tweet as an advertising breakthrough really did it a disservice. It was a brilliant piece of public relations, which spoke to a range of stakeholders, from staff to inventors. But it was "ghettoized" as a new formula of digital advertising, which it did not have the scale or replicability to be.

In the end, though, it made Oreo famous; it made Twitter famous; it made Mondelez (Oreo's parent company) famous; and it made the people who designed the tweet famous – and it even made the academic who "umasked" it famous.

The problem comes when new social media seeks to claim as a silo the credentials of the old. Quite simply, they don't work very impressively in a silo. They can work very impressively as part of a whole.

We have become victims of our desire to show ourselves to be successful. I plead guilty of signing off case histories where the measure is "views", as if views are all that matters. They do matter, because they show that what you do has got pull, that consumers enjoy it. But pull has to have conscience. It is easy to pull by pandering to the lowest common denominators of crowd culture: we would just put a cat in every video.

The ghettoization of digital leads to claims that are easy to attack. Branded content has been subjected to such attacks simply because it does not stack up the same viewing figures as online video creators do (see tables overleaf). How could it? It still has a branding or a selling purpose that necessarily constrains. No professional marketer is interested in views as a simple objective: the digital component is part of a gestalt. It often

Rank	Video	Views All Videos (Millions)
Most Viewed Creators (vlog-style)		
1	Pew Die Pie	13,411
2	The Diamond Minecart	8,196
3	PopularMMOs	6,605
4	Smosh	5,930
5	Vanosgaming	5,818

Right *Look at the total views creators such as PewDiePie and Smosh get. Brands envy that, but those views are dependent on building – even pandering – to an audience built over years of daily video production. That's not something particularly useful for a brand.*

Rank	Video	Views (Millions)
Most Viewed Brand Videos		
1	Akira: Shakira La La La	561
2	Android: Friends Furever	201
3	Dove: Real Beauty Sketches	139
4	Evian: Roller Babies	133
5	Metro Melbourne: Dumb Ways to Die	114

Right *These are rather more valuable numbers. These videos garnered these views because they were part of coordinated promotion campaigns that had commercial objectives.*

Rank	Video	Views (Millions)
Most Viewed Videos		
1	Psy: Gangnam Style	2,600
2	Wiz Khalifa: See You Again	2,000
3	Mark Ronson/Bruno Mars: Uptown Funk	1,900
4	Justin Bieber: Sorry	1,800
5	Taylor Swift: Blank Space	1,800

Right *Music videos routinely dominate the top views-per-video chart. This is because music is consumed via free media and streaming services. This doesn't represent the triumph of a few great artists so much as it does the total disruption of the music industry.*

operates at the level of agenda setting, which is exactly what it does well. And we have a mountain of evidence that suggests it works best in concert with traditional media.

Overclaims for social media give the (mainly academic) critics easy game to shoot out. It's damned as "hoopla"[3]; or as "a bullshit wagon"[4] Fair enough. But blanket criticism would be as misplaced as the exaggerated language of the ghettos and silos. Amplification and advocacy are real gains for any marketer. They happen not to be simplistically measurable in views.

Here's the nub of the issue, for digital apologists and digital detractors alike. Both use the language of *advertising,* and tend to think in advertising terms – reach, frequency, creative, consumers, advertising, brands and so on. It's hardly surprising: the title of this book also perpetuates the use of the term.

But advertising in the digital world is no longer *advertising.* The disciplines (and the very word speaks to a controlling desire to keep them as separate as possible) of advertising, public relations, direct marketing, sales enablement, and others, too, are truly collapsing; they no longer live apart. Much of advertising is public relations; much of public relations is direct marketing; much of direct marketing is advertising. Yet the debate is couched in advertising terms, while the real battle is about how well you integrate and the extent to which, by treating digital and traditional media as additive, you can be a better communicator.

Before the Digital Revolution, the situation seemed quite clear: the media earned its revenue from a combination of what advertisers paid them

Below *We have, perhaps unwittingly from the user's point of view, signed a new social contract in the digital age. Platforms, advertisers and users exchange value as a mix of data, dollars and engagement. More complex than the previous model – where media owners simply sold advertising or subscriptions – the new dynamic becomes more valuable to everyone as platforms grow and network effects kick in.*

THE DIGITAL SOCIAL CONTRACT

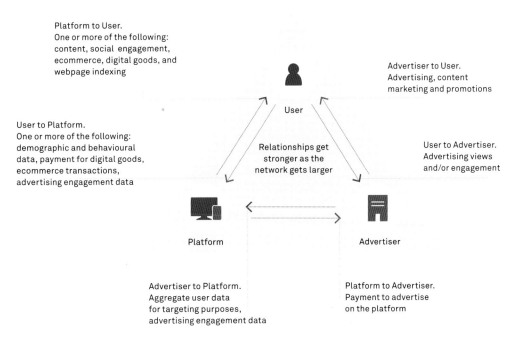

Platform to User.
One or more of the following: content, social engagement, ecommerce, digital goods, and webpage indexing

Advertiser to User.
Advertising, content marketing and promotions

User

User to Platform.
One or more of the following: demographic and behavioural data, payment for digital goods, ecommerce transactions, advertising engagement data

Relationships get stronger as the network gets larger

User to Advertiser.
Advertising views and/or engagement

Platform

Advertiser

Advertiser to Platform.
Aggregate user data for targeting purposes, advertising engagement data

Platform to Advertiser.
Payment to advertise on the platform

for placing ads and consumers paid them on the cover price or subscription.

Now there's a different type of relationship, a rather more subtle and less visible "contract" between the parties: the media owner, the advertiser, and the consumer.

The Age of And

I've been describing the digital world more as this *and* that, rather than this *not* that. This is no accident. When it comes to digital advertising we use the word "and" quite a lot. It's a word that has attracted attention before, especially by business theoreticians. Notable among these was Jim Collins in his book *Built to Last* (2005). "Embrace the genius of 'and' … a truly visionary company embraces both ends of a continuum, continuity and change."

Since he wrote that, the zero-sum game has become more not less obvious – forcing artificial polarities on us.

So I would go a step further and say this should be the "Age of And".

To some extent, it is inevitable in all revolutions that there will be zealots versus resistors, taliban versus dinosaurs. The tensions are there: but perhaps we are getting to a point where we can see the benefit in recognizing that they are additive and complementary:

> analogue *and* digital
> integration *and* specialization
> slices *and* scale
> maths *and* madness
> form *and* content

We'll meet them all in this book.

In *Ogilvy on Advertising,* David supplied a list of his favourite words. Let me add one of my own. There's an American word that describes a state of harmonious well-being, a word that somehow bubbled up from uncertain origins in the 1920s: copacetic. The answers lie in the harmony you find in-between – in the *copacetic consensus.*

It's worth singling out one "zero sum" here that has bedeviled our world since well before *Ogilvy on Advertising* was published, and that is the slogan of Marshall McLuhan that the "medium is the message" (1964), which was given new digital life in a myriad of ways. I believe it to be wholly wrong. In this case the "and" is very subdued indeed: the message is the message – even though it can be influenced by the medium.

David's surviving colleagues remember his advice: "It's what you say, not how you say it." It's advice needed now much more than ever it was before.

The Coming War: YouTube and Facebook in Video

Some colleagues, a senior client and I recently spent a day meeting the two rivals, Google and Facebook, one after the other. It's a very special experience – like visiting Athens and Sparta in the same day.

To my colleague Rob Davis, who runs our video practice, it made concrete a general sense of impending battle.

Rob has started to distinguish the video networks between those that are "ephemeral" and those that are "archival".

Ephemeral networks achieve maximum impact in the moment. They are designed for interaction. Video viewing is just one feature the network's community uses. They have little search value, as they don't prioritize the archiving and storage of video. Facebook, Instagram, SnapChat and Periscope are all examples of ephemeral networks. This category is growing fast.

Archival networks give a place to host and arrange content specifically for the video viewing experience. These networks are designed for watching video. They have tremendous search impact and serve as the go-to place for someone seeking video. YouTube, Vimeo and DailyMotion are among the remaining archival networks. Most others have ceased operation.

By late 2014, YouTube touted the delivery of 4 billion video views per day. No other platform came close. Facebook was delivering about 25 per cent as many videos. But by the time YouTube reached its 10th birthday in February 2015, something had changed. Facebook claimed it earned as many views as YouTube and would soon release data showing it had eclipsed YouTube's daily viewership.

Facebook's dramatic increase in video views was driven by technological tweaks rather than a groundswell of viewership. They introduced auto-play videos, which would start playing as the user slowly scrolled over them, and began counting these automatic engagements as a "view", a sleight of hand that immediately doubled the daily view count. In contrast, YouTube only counted a view when the user clicked the play button. The new strategy essentially doubled views overnight.

What we saw during our visit to Google was an archival network struggling with the difficulties of maturity. During its rise, YouTube's influence defined the entire video marketplace. Unfortunately, YouTube also struggled with its identity. Every 18–24 months, the site would go through major changes: was it a content platform, a social network or a hub

"The message is the message – and it can be influenced by the medium."

Below *One of the most enduring online video brands, The Young Turks network has become a media entity in its own right.*

for interactive experiences? Clarity was achieved about two years ago when the ability to customize YouTube was eliminated. From that point on, it has been about delivering a standard video experience. The business model is based upon pre-roll advertising and a new ad-free subscription service, YouTube Red.

The PewDiePies and Young Turks of the world form the basis of YouTube's cultural relevance, and drive the platform's traffic (along with music videos, which still make up a huge portion of the totals).

Unlike YouTube, Facebook started without any focus on video. Initially, users were encouraged to embed videos from other networks into their Facebook posts. Facebook eventually added their own video service. Since then they have aggressively promoted distinct features in support of their version of viewability, which sometimes run counter to what we would recommend for YouTube or websites in general.

For instance, like most of its ephemeral network cousins, Facebook is a scrolling experience. Users thumb through, scrolling until something interesting catches their attention. We like to say content that works on Facebook "stops the thumb". Much of the advice we heard from Facebook during our visit was about thumb-stopping, but Facebook is also intent on delivering messages via the video asset even if the user does not choose to watch the video, creating a unique set of circumstances for brands and creatives.

Thumbnails (the static images which appear before a user plays a video) are what FullScreen calls "the book covers of the online video world". We know from experience outside of Facebook that video thumbnails should be attention-getting images that accurately portray the content within a video. Accepted best practice suggests never featuring products or logos within a thumbnail, as users are less likely to watch videos they think are overt advertising.

However, Facebook's advice runs counter to this. They suggest thumbnails with product imagery and text. Why? The user who slows their scroll to read text or look at a product thumbnail will trigger the auto-play function, which counts as a view of the video.

As Facebook and YouTube continue to slug it out, other ephemeral networks are making inroads. Vine introduced the idea of a short "loop" video while Periscope and Facebook Live, the live streaming networks, caught the imagination of a public looking to broadcast. YouTube and Facebook have both recently instituted live capabilities.

In the long run, there must be a question about YouTube's ability to retain market share. Creators are in love with ephemeral. They are not giving up on YouTube, but it is becoming their library and search-target. The sharing and interactions are happening on other channels.

With Facebook expected to announce a full video library capability, they may be poised to take away YouTube's one main advantage.

5 lessons for leaders in the digital age

However fast-changing the digital ecosystem, the essence of leadership doesn't change one jot, though the levels of noise, obfuscations, hype and novelty do sometimes overwhelm us. These are the five things that seem important to me after 20 years of driving a digital agenda. I don't believe they're taught in any business school.

1. Do keep asking the question "but why?" insistently, repeatedly, like a curious 5-year-old. "Why" is the only word that cuts through the fog, gets to the real problem and helps distinguish between the means and the end. Why? Why? Why? I even run training courses entitled "The Power of Why".

2. Don't fetishize certainty. The ready availability of a slew of measures doesn't mean they are useful. Treat all KPIs (Key Performance Indicators) with caution, and the singular KPI with as much reserve as a plague spore. It could infect your whole organization with a distorted sense of priorities.

3. Do programme yourself to total openness. You have a unique opportunity to break down internal silos. And you need the collaboration of a wider range of attitudes than ever before. Playing your cards close to your chest has become a loser's stratagem.

4. Do avoid the divas when hiring. They abound, and they can easily dazzle, only then to disappoint. As one of my clients once said: "Talent is a mere commodity, only perseverance differentiates." When I've repeated this to graduates, they tend to gasp, but it's never been truer than now.

5. Do relish dualism. The tensions of the digital world can push you – or those around you – into zero-sum games. But success lies in managing the tension rather than clinging to the "either" or the "or". It's also more fun.

DOVE

Tim Piper was a young Australian who had washed up in our Toronto office. As much a film director as a traditional writer, in 2005 he had written and directed a 30-second TV commercial called *Broken Escalator* for Becel Margarine. The escalator breaks down and the unfit passengers caught on it scream for help. He felt compelled to shoot a longer version. The Creative Director of OgilvyOne saw it, and told him about this

Above Evolution *was a viral hit – created by Tim Piper, his unwitting girlfriend, and our resourceful production team in Toronto. It was shot on a shoestring, and initiated a campaign that added $1.2 billion to Dove's brand value and increased revenue by $500 million.*

"thing called YouTube". It was posted, and to everyone's surprise, got 50,000 views almost immediately.

The next year, the agency received an open brief on Dove to amplify the Campaign for Real Beauty. Tim presented a series of emotionally driven short-film ideas, including *Evolution*. This is a tribute to the entrepreneurial creative culture fostered by Creative Directors, Janet Kestin and Nancy Vonk, who empowered creators to present anything they were passionate about. The clients loved the idea of emotional short films, but preferred the other concepts to *Evolution*, which seemed slightly off-brief. But Tim had a gut feeling that there was, as he puts it, "some freak visual factor", which would make people want to share this one.

There was no money allocated for the *Evolution* video, so with the help of the director filming the approved films (Yael Staav) and agency producer Brenda Surminski, Tim was able to make Evolution off the back of another production, though he was sensible enough to let the client know. It was time for favours. He enlisted a local fashion photographer, make-up artist,

post-production house, and even his girlfriend to be the talent. Tim wrote and art directed the spot with creative partner Mike Kirkland. The clients loved it.

It was posted with no distribution plan as such. But it just "went" – and became the one of the early branded viral sensations of the internet. Some lessons are salutary: because there was no budget, it was never submitted to a market-research testing regime. The real learning was that if you can find something that creates visual resonance, that captures a brand's values in a concrete way, you've found a way of using video that people will not just notice but care about. You care, you share.

But let's go back to the very beginning. With David Ogilvy's help, Lever Brothers launched Dove in 1957. Differentiated from the outset as a beauty bar, it replaced the "squeaky clean" feel of typical soaps with moisturising cream, and featured accessible female celebrities of the era, such as Jean Shy and Pearline Watkins, in its ads. Dove has always been an authentic brand. By the early 2000s, in a crowded category fragmented by private label and online, our client asked us to transition Dove from a singular product to a portfolio of offerings.

I've always believed in the notion that brands have Big IdeaLs™ (see page 60) as well as big ideas. So our solution was to develop a cultural point of view that would be profitable while influencing society for the better. And if someone was to ask what Dove's was, I'd say: "Dove believes the world would be a better place if women were allowed to feel good about themselves." It's a powerful organizing tool that relates back to the brand's best self. As Steve Miles, responsible for Dove globally, put it, "Brands with purpose are not just socially beneficial, but are the pathway to superior growth".

The beauty industry operates from the unquestioned assumption that beauty is something positive and pleasurable. So we were shocked to find out that a staggering 98 per cent of women did not feel happy with the way they looked. We envisioned a world where women believed that beauty is a source of confidence, not anxiety. And Dove was the brand to make that statement, with the launch of the Campaign for Real Beauty. It was to be a defining moment for Dove,

and for the potential impact of a consumer brand's communications on culture.

But by the early 2010s, the Campaign For Real Beauty had become a victim of its own success. Real women were suddenly everywhere – the beauty industry was cleaning up its act, and teenage girls wanted to see real women in magazines. So we set to work re-evaluating our earlier insight, which while no longer disruptive, revealed a deeper layer. As 96 per cent of women still claimed to dislike the way they looked, the problem was no longer unrealistic beauty ideals. Our research found a new cause was women's internal monologue: 54 percent of women considered themselves their own worst critic and a third said their biggest anxiety was the "pressure I put on myself to be beautiful".

Above Sketches *is the most shared ad ever and one of the most watched videos of all time. It exposed women's overly critical assessment of their own beauty compared to the more generous appraisal of a stranger. Simply put, the film communicated that you are more beautiful than you think.*

Dove understands that to keep mattering brands must continue to evolve, so over the next three years we kicked off each spring with an annual "hero" campaign, *Sketches* in 2013 (see page 82), and its successors *Patches* in 2014 and *Choose Beautiful* in 2015. They earned 14 billion global impressions in the three years from 2013, and a media value of over $90 million from coverage in *Huffington Post* to *Today*. Most of those impressions were digital. Today Dove is valued at over $5 billion, with more than 40 per cent of brand value attributed to advertising, according to WPP's BrandZ study. And Dove's own econometric modelling has eliminated price, confidence in the economy, distribution changes and media spend as the source of sales growth – proof that harnessing purpose in advertising can drive a brand into the heart of culture.

Others have tried to create a similar evolution for their client's brands as Tim started for Dove, but they so often miss the point. As Tim intuitively understood from his desk in Toronto, Dove doesn't prey on women's anxieties, it voices them. It turns them into a public issue that women unify against. Dove is an empathetic leader, an ecosystem for the digital age. Its voice is the internal voice of women everywhere, what women would like to say if society would let them. That millions of women have finally acknowledged their own beauty is perhaps the best success metric of them all.

5 TO BE OR NOT TO BE A MILLENNIAL

If you would believe some pundits, journalists, marketers and sociologists, Millennials represent a distinctive and unified tribe, the agents of an unprecedented transformation in the world. Well, I have been as guilty as any of them in bandying about the word "Millennial". The thing about labels is that we use them because they are easy.

We've been through Generation X and and now we have Generation Y, otherwise known as Millennials. Next to come are the Centennials. Oh, and to complete the collection, we should perhaps label older people as Generation S. Needless to say, each of these cohorts are different in certain key respects. I guess if one were to be even slightly cynical, that is hardly new or surprising. And various commentators have pointed out how much of the language used by Gen X to derogate Gen Y has in turn been used by Gen S to do the same to Gen X.

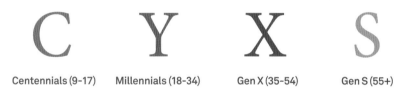

C	Y	X	S
Centennials (9-17)	Millennials (18-34)	Gen X (35-54)	Gen S (55+)

Right Labelling generations is useful only if it serves our understanding of each cohort. Millennials grew up amidst a Digital Revolution and have defined their lives differently as digital natives. Gen C, who are hot on their heels, were "born digital". We're yet to see the impact they will have on the world.

But what does make Millennials very different is that they are the generation which has coincided with the Digital Revolution. They are the first digital natives. Well, not even that really: at the upper end of the age spectrum, their experience might have been denominated by a Sony Walkman (the iteration that played CDs, not cassette tapes) or dial-up internet access. They were in at the primitive beginnings; and it's the Centennials – born after 2000 – who represent the real natives.

In fact, just as it is difficult to pin down Millennials in any useful way as one digital cohort, so it is also challenging to see them as homegrown in other respects. The first thing we tend to do in a presentation on Millennials is to deny that there is such a thing as a Millennial. We are, after all, talking about 38.1 per cent of the world's population – and there's little in common between Pakistan's 99 million Millennials and the US's 91 million. Confining ourselves to the US, it is quite difficult to talk of a homogeneous group when, for instance, income disparities between rich

Above *Generation me? I simply don't agree. Our research suggests Millennials are more altruistic than their parents. They certainly seem to care more for people than things.*

Millennials (most often the poster boys and girls for the tribe) and poor ones are so large.

The early characterizers of Millennials seem to me to have had some kind of perverted, vested interest in stigmatizing them. Of course, horror fascinates – and the picture painted was horrific. I call it the great "narcissism calumny": that this is a uniquely self-obsessed, me-loving, ruled-by-impulse generation. I just don't believe it. The academic research on which it was based has been widely criticized. And when Ogilvy & Mather did its own research, we found the exact opposite. They actually tend towards altruism – much more caring and giving to those less fortunate than their elders were.

A built-in sense of entitlement is another alleged hallmark of Millennials, but it just doesn't wash. In fact, compared to Gen X, they have a greater propensity for saving money and possess a sense of frugality, by, for instance, patiently recognizing that there is a "point of readiness" at which you can buy a home.

Meanwhile, Centennials show a more extreme development of the same responses. They're much less inclined to see themselves as "about fun", or to do anything risky. And they are already and actually worried about the future, in particular, the environment.

So this is the American Millennial challenge: just being one coincides with a period in history when the good times are running out. And that does mean the emergence of distinct characteristics. They are much less likely to own homes, or to use credit cards, or to buy or drive cars, or to get married at the same age their parents did. They are much more likely to share. And to value diversity, and to believe that all lives matter – black, gay, white, straight. Thank goodness for Millennials.

But then there's a great danger of stepping into a second fallacy. It's the great millenarian fantasy that the social equivalent of a Second Coming is nigh. But most Millennials are not millenarians. Most do not believe that they will usher in a golden age where people don't have to work, where they trade in homegrown vegetables, and where they all live together in emancipated bliss. That dewy-eyed commentary is based on some exaggeration from quite minor trends. "Normcore", for instance – the fashion for wearing only commonplace items, bought from Walmart or LL Bean – does not seem to me likely to destroy the world's fashion industry. (And Normcore is hardly new: I have practised the extreme form of it – wearing second-hand clothes – with great satisfaction in the past without ever inciting a Second Coming.)

Of course, Millennials don't have the same view of work, as anyone who employs them – and Ogilvy & Mather employs them in the thousands – knows. The old view was linear and compartmentalized. A Millennial is, in my experience, much more demanding – and rightly so – of how work fulfills his or her potential. That means more sideway shifts, more path changes, more of a link to personal interests, more opportunities to take a break and do something else. It may be difficult to manage, but who can deny that it is more civilized? And, again, we have to be careful. We are not about to witness the complete reform of organizational structures or the abolition of hierarchy. Rather, the system adapts – if it is intelligent enough.

MILLENNIALS ARE HARD WORKING, ENTREPRENEURIAL AND NOT AFRAID OF RISK

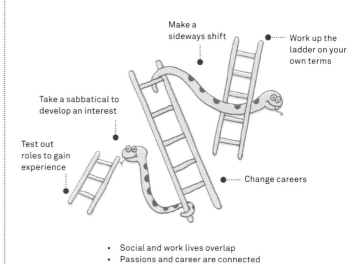

TRADITIONAL CAREER

Get promoted and manage people

Work your way up the ladder

Enter as a junior

- Social and work networks are kept distinct
- Passions are focused on a hobby outside work
- Social life runs parallel to career

MILLENNIAL CAREER

Make a sideways shift

Work up the ladder on your own terms

Take a sabbatical to develop an interest

Test out roles to gain experience

Change careers

- Social and work lives overlap
- Passions and career are connected
- Side projects are commonplace

Above Millennials are no longer faced with a simple career ladder – more like a game of snakes and ladders! They frequently make sideways shifts, take temporary breaks, and reach up and across to more technical challenges. When they fail, they dust themselves off and try another ladder. I admire both their effort and bravery; it must surely make for some interesting experiences along the way.

Many of these views about Millennials, whether of merit or not, are influenced by perceptions of technology, and the impact it exerts on them. And here is the crux: a conflation of the digital revolution with the idea of generational change.

But are they one and the same?

In one sense, undoubtedly, yes. The great gift of the Digital Revolution is connectivity, and none have received it more than Millennials – or, to a larger extent, Centennials. The mobile phone is so important as the vehicle for digital access that lack or loss can produce identifiable anxiety syndrome. We all get it, but they get it worse.

The statistics I love most come from a 2016 AT&T online survey of 2,000 US citizens asking what they would sacrifice instead of giving up internet access for the rest of their life. Forty per cent said they would rather lose the sight in one eye, and 30 per cent responded that they would rather chop off one of their fingers. Bravo!

Connectivity certainly becomes a cause of dependence, and spawns a series of behaviours, of which multitasking is the most ubiquitous. But, beyond that, we have to be careful not to assume that everyone exhibits the same attributes in response to the use of technology. I've not seen a shred of evidence to suggest they do.

For instance, demographic segmentation studies can often be soulless affairs. While they are capable of shedding light, they ought to be treated with caution, not least from giving one the false illusion that their

Would you rather...?

| Give up _____ | OR | Give up the Internet |

Chocolate	87%	13%
Sight in one eye	40.5%	59.5%
All of your hair	36.4%	63.6%
A finger	30.1%	69.9%
Your sense of taste	29.2%	70.8%
Your dream job	23.5%	76.5%
Love	19.1%	80.9%
Human interaction	16.9%	83.1%

KEEP CALM YOUR INTERNET'S ON

AT&T Internet

Above *For digital natives, the internet has truly become an extension of self. In this AT&T study from 2016, almost a third of the US digital native respondents surveyed claimed they'd prefer to chop off a finger than lose their phone.*

"segments" are real people. That said, there are a few (surprisingly few) significant segmentation studies that have been conducted on the impact of digitalization. They all, of course, construct and label their segments differently. Take your choice between Techno-sploiters and Mouse Potatoes, Techno-gamers or Gadget Grabbers. But there are some conclusions that can be safely drawn from them:

- Humanity does not have a common set of attitudes toward technology.
- A decrease in technophobia, which is real, does not infer that techno indifference is also on the decline. In fact, the latter is rising.
- Even digital natives exhibit different attitudes dependent on the degree to which they are socially engaged. In other words, connectivity is not a constant; rather, it is a variable that manifests itself in different ways for

MILLENNIALS ARE MOST ENGAGED ONLINE, BUT THEY ALSO ENGAGE WITH ALL ADVERTISING FORMATS IN SELECTIVE WAYS

Brand sponsorships

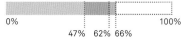

0%   100%

47% 62% 66%

Branded websites

0%   100%

55% 70% 75%

Editorial content such as newspaper articles

0%   100%

58% 68%
     66%

Consumer opinions posted online

0%   100%

53% 69% 70%

Ads in magazines

0%   100%

48%   62%
         61%

Ads in newspapers

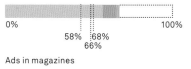

0%   100%

54%
    62% 62%

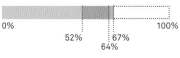

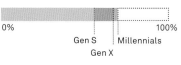

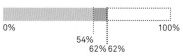

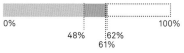

Recommendations from people I know

0%   100%

80% 85%
    83%

Ads on TV

0%   100%

52%   67%
       64%

KEY

0%   100%

Gen S   Millennials
Gen X

Source: Unilever-Kantar.

Above *When it to engaging with a broad set of advertising formats, Millennials show remarkably similar tendencies to previous generations, albeit with more emphasis on the influence of friends, forums and familiar brands.*

AN AMERICAN DIGITAL NATIVE IS MORE LIKELY TO BE

1. Ethically conscious
2. Caring about self-image
3. Culturally blended
4. Committed single
5. Mobile

different people. It sounds so obvious, but digital zealotry doesn't always put it that way. The reason, of course, is that in technology the "leading edge" is both an end and a means in itself. As a means of pushing boundaries, it is highly effective; as an end it has to be controlled, or it can control your thinking. "It's leading edge or it just doesn't matter" is a dangerous default option in digital advertising as much as it is in analogue advertising. Centennials themselves prove the point in perhaps a surprising way. They use social media differently than Millennials do. They don't use Facebook so much. They prefer instead small ecosystems such as Snapchat, which are more private.

- Centennials are more sceptical and wary. Two thirds prefer to interact with friends in person, as opposed to 15 per cent who would rather do so online. A majority prefer to make purchases in brick-and mortar shops rather than online.

- Research conducted by J. Walter Thompson shows that Millennial views about technology are much more nuanced than they are often portrayed. In fact, they fear being trapped by it.

- Millennials show a disturbing tendency not to follow the rules set by those who first tried to define them. For instance, they read. A study by Pew Research in 2015 showed a surprising pattern in book reading, with those aged 18–29 more likely than their elders to have read a book in the last 12 months. Now many of them are still students, but the point stands. Fully 80 per cent of the youngest group had read a book, compared to 71 per cent of those aged 30–49, 68 per cent of those 50–64 and only 69 per cent of those 65 and older.

- Millennials continue to engage with traditional advertising formats more than Gen S, in fact. Of course, they often do so in a different way.

- Millennials are "meshers". They use second devices to complement the content they're accessing on the first. And they're "showroomers", meaning, they research their purchases in the virtual universe, and then buy.

- As they buy, Millennials are waving a big yellow flag to all of us. They tend to be under-indexed in many of the big brand franchises. The reason for this is revealing: putting affordability aside, this so-called narcissistic generation actually searches for something beyond mere gratification. They look for authenticity, and for brands that behave well. The same is true for Centennials, but even more so.

5 MYTHS ABOUT MILLENNIALS

1. They're technophiliac.
2. They're narcissistic.
3. They don't read.
4. They don't visit stores.
5. They don't consume advertising.

I'll get into that in greater depth later. For now, it's worth rubbing salt into what I hope is an open wound. Nothing exhibits more the danger of simplistic generalizations than the topic of Millennials. They are not what they are said to be. They are neither digital victims nor digital fanatics. As a result, they are both more complex – and more interesting.

Above *Coca-Cola showed how readily Millennials will engage in television-like content with their #CokeTV Moments campaign. A series of shows, hosted by Millennials on a dedicated YouTube channel, bubbled with youthful candour as participants engaged with challenges and topics. It may be online, but CokeTV has all the hallmarks of teen-oriented television shows of old. Millennials are multi-channel thinkers and active participants, but they still like to lean back and watch too.*

Opposite bottom and above *Millennials share something in common with every generation of young people – a reluctance to plan for the distant future. When it comes to retirement savings, however, starting early can have an outsized effect, something Prudential demonstrated in partnership with Harvard University psychologist, Dan Gilbert. In order to show how even tiny inputs can make a massive difference over time, Prudential and Gilbert erected a succession of dominos of increasing size and set them toppling. Even though they began with a normal sized domino, the last one to fall was 30 feet in height, setting a new world record in the process.*

6 THE POST-MODERN BRAND

Above *The origin of brands is commonly attributed to the marking of livestock to denote ownership. We don't keep cattle at Ogilvy, but we've built on the legacy of this early form of branding, through trademarking to trust building and beyond.*

For as long as I can remember, brands have been in crisis. It used to be the threat of retailers' own labels, which, supposedly, would drive brands from the world. Now, in the digital age, they're apparently in mortal danger. Just scan the headlines: "9 Iconic Brands That Could Be Dead"; "Is Brand Loyalty Dying a Slow and Painful Death?"; "Are Corporate Brands Dead?" It's a pundits' paradise, and, as one put it rather more romantically, we must surely be seeing the "Twilight of the Brands".

Of course, we can see the reason why brands might seem threatened. In a world of apparently perfect information and peer-group reviews, why do you need a brand itself to tell you it's good?

But don't write off brands. Far from dying, I believe they will survive in the digital age.

Attempts are sometimes made to classify the history of branding in phases. It's risky to try to be too neat, as history textbooks are wont to be. But it is also tempting to try and label the great waves of branding – if for no other reason than to understand where brands have come from and where they might be headed next.

It all started with a red-hot iron – "that's my steer" – and then evolved into "trademark branding". The brand was a trademark of quality. Brands moved next into the era of hard facts and pointed argument: how to make our product different, at first with rational pitches. But then TV brought sound and moving pictures into consumers' homes, and we entered the era of brand image, of emotional branding. Each phase has tended to be accretive, overlaying and sometimes co-existing with the one that came before.

And that's where *Ogilvy on Advertising* stopped: at the high tide of the hard facts era of branding.

Then the digital world started to kick in, and the idea of "brand", apparently defined in stone by gurus such as David Aaker or Philip Kotler, started to seem very old fashioned. We started to see the emergence of the post-modern brand.

Culture Vultures

The word "culture" does not appear in *Ogilvy on Advertising*. But in the 1980s, brand owners started talking about culture as an asset that could be owned. The poster child for this was generally regarded to be Nike,

WAVES OF BRANDING

1850s ·· ● 2015 +

	Trademark Branding	Rational Branding	Emotional Branding	Cultural Branding	Brands that DO
WAVE	Trademark Branding	Rational Branding	Emotional Branding	Cultural Branding	Brands that DO
ROLE	Guarantor of quality	Product differentiation	Brand bonding	Cultural relevance	Create value and be useful
		m&m's PLAIN "THE MILK CHOCOLATE MELTS IN YOUR MOUTH-NOT IN YOUR HAND"	Do you know these people?	**JOHNNIE WALKER.** KEEP WALKING.	*Dove*
TERMS	Trust Claims Salesmanship in print	USP Features Product demo Big idea	Personality Brand pyramid Brand image Promise	Movements Manifestos Share of culture Purpose	Transformation Brand action Engines of engagement Behaviour Experience
MEDIA	Point of sale Mail order Print	TV	TV	Paid, Owned, Earned	Content

Above *Branding has moved through a series of waves. In the original* Ogilvy on Advertising, *David showed himself to be the inventor of emotional branding – he certainly had a big idea or two. Now, digital is forcing a return to the tangible. It's still grounded in the purpose and emotional promise of the preceding eras, but it's a new era of* behavioural *branding – what we like to call "Brands that DO".*

which found a rich cultural seam in the narrative of competing through brute willpower, a battle of the individual against the world, the victory of inner strength over physical prowess. "Just Do It" preceded the internet, but upon the slogan's arrival in 1988 and thereafter, the addition of "owned" and "earned" to paid media became a powerful enabler of cultural cues. It created destinations for the brand to invite people into. As culture generated a shared system of meaning, it allowed brands to "start a movement". Before long, the phrase "share of culture" replaced "share of market" as an objective – and brands fought for their share like vultures fighting over meat.

Champions for culture assailed the preceding era for its superficiality. The academic Douglas Holt, a pioneer of cultural branding, called it the "commodity emotions trap". Coupled with the bureaucracy of large companies, culture had tended, at its worst, to result in meaningless abstractions. Holt gives a hilarious account of one such, which all of us in the business must recognize:

> They started out with the brand vision: this drink was to "Enable a life lived absolutely, completely, and totally fulfilled". The core proposition was "A new thirst-quencher that empowers you to achieve far more than you ever thought". But some managers disagreed; they did not think that this was quite right. So more research was commissioned

and the brand vision changed. Now the brand would champion "Up for Adventure". And in the next iteration, they moved on to "Refresh Your Day". Then to "Refueling Vitality", "Refreshment for an Active Lifestyle", and "Fuel for Life". The company's management eventually settled on "Refresh for Life".[1]

At its best, however, culture helped power brands to success. Holt, again, makes a crucial point: "Nike's famed shoe innovations happened early on and do not coincide with the brand's takeoff. Nike succeeded with innovative cultural impressions, not innovative products." Nike launched its "Word of Foot" campaign featuring the personal stories of regular, everyday athletes. That set in motion over four decades of marketing dedicated to the idea that everyone is an athlete – not to mention the ubiquitous acceptance of athletic shoes as everyday footwear.

The culture vultures were certainly onto something. And nothing summed up a cultural aspiration more than a manifesto. Suddenly it seemed that we were awash with them; and manifesto writing became as much as an art form as the advertising that emerged from them.

We might call this progress. And "progress" was precisely the idea claimed by Johnnie Walker, one of the more successful examples of a brand undergoing the manifesto treatment.

At the turn of the twenty-first century, Johnnie Walker was stalling under market share pressure in both established and new territories. It would take a spirited combination of insight and iconography to ensure the brand's status into the next millennium.

This would be the role of the manifesto. In line with the changing values of twenty-first-century men, the brand came to understand that the notion of success was shifting from the material to the motivational. In essence, success was becoming defined not by what a man had, but what he might achieve and the direction in which he was heading. The brand's owner, Diageo, articulated the idea as "Johnnie Walker inspires personal progress", which was eloquently distilled down to the line, "Keep Walking".

Johnnie Walker's manifesto cleverly reached into the brand's history to map its future. This trick is best illustrated by a new logo that heralded the brand's transformation. Initially sketched on a restaurant menu in the early

Right *Johnnie Walker's iconic Striding Man was flipped, literally, to point him in the direction of the future rather than the past.*

1900s, the brand's iconic Striding Man was flipped, literally, to point him in the direction of the future rather than the past.

Where the protagonists of culture have been less successful is turning their views into a system for working. Culture as something to tap into can be magical; culture turned into a "model" is a death trap. It either produces "step processes", which become pedestrian, or results in briefs of the "please design me a provocative cultural expression as a counterpart to the rise of 'Trumpism'": interesting clothes for a brand to borrow, perhaps, but not rich as a brief to a creative team. It's an ingredient of the brief, and it might be the intent of the work, but it's not a brief any creative would understand.

It is an annoying fact that explicitly cultural language is better for describing post-hoc what has happened that it is for provoking the happening in the first place.

Authenticity

However, the accelerating Digital Revolution started a new, fertile strand of thinking. It has brought with it an unprecedented pressure for transparency.

Put simply, there is no longer any hiding place. The bracing wind of transparency has blown through corporate corridors in a way that defies resistance. Yet there were still – and probably always will be – attempts at resistance. When Toyota first started to receive reports of accidents in the US in August 2009, and there were credible attributions of those accidents to unintended acceleration, their first reactions were slow. As the truth emerged, it seemed that it had to be dragged out. Now I do not believe there was any willful conspiracy not to be transparent; rather, the culture and politics of a conflicted organization just never put a premium on transparency as a value, and hundreds of small decisions added up to an overall behavioural trait. The learning came the hard way, and Toyota's brand suffered as a result.

The good news is that when it comes, transparency can heal. It has redemptive power. Toyota was able, after a while, to stimulate supporters' groups on Facebook in the US who felt the process of vilification had gone too far.

However, how to avoid being there in the first place? Enter the Arthur W. Page Society of the US, who published a defining document of the digital age in 2007, "The Authentic Enterprise". As it says:

> In such an environment, the corporation that wants to establish a distinctive brand and achieve long-term success must, more than ever before, be grounded in a sure sense of what defines it – why it exists, what it stands for and what differentiates it in a marketplace of customers, investors and workers. Those definitions – call them values, principles, beliefs, mission, purpose or value proposition – must dictate consistent behavior and actions.
>
> In a word, authenticity will be the coin of the realm for successful corporations and for those who lead them.[2]

"The bracing wind of transparency has blown through corporate corridors in a way that defies resistance."

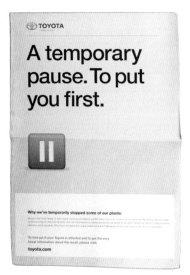

Above *Toyota issued a mea culpa when it came unstuck due to a defective accelerator pedal, but the company took far too long to calm its critics.*

Opposite top IBM's proof of authenticity lies in its belief that the world's serious problems, in healthcare and security, cities and global commerce, can be resolved through humankind's unique ability to "think". This billboard dispays icons from IBM's Smarter Planet campaign, in which intelligent solutions contribute to smarter cities. And it shows how design can express a powerful idea in the digital age.

Opposite bottom Dove re-establishes the relationship between women, their inner selves and their outward representation in media and advertising, exposing the rhetoric of the cosmetics industry. The poster's message? You don't have to conform to a stereotype to be beautiful.

Above More than any other brand that has tried to do so, Coca-Cola has occupied the territory of "happiness" by tapping into emotions that go so much deeper than the bubbles.

In place of the voice of authority, stakeholders in the digital world demand "proof of authenticity". Are you who you claim to be? And, who do you claim to be?

One of the co-authors of this white paper went on to become the IBM CMO, Jon Iwata. Jon is a remarkable client who helped reinvent traditional notions of marketing and public relations. He has an instinctive dislike of what he calls "campaignery", which has inspired his own work at IBM over three different interactions of the brand's public presentation of itself – in other words, its platform. A quotation from Abraham Lincoln is much in use at IBM: "Character is the tree, reputation is the shadow." Is advertising in the digital age a player in the shadows, or a builder of character?

In working with clients such as IBM, Dove and Coca-Cola, we learned there was a simple way to capture their deeper values, so that IBM's proof of authenticity lay in its declaration that all the world's problems, from healthcare to security, and cities to global commerce, can be resolved through humankind's unique ability to "think". Dove's lay in re-establishing the relationship between women, their inner selves and their outward representation in media and advertising, thereby exposing the rhetoric of the cosmetics industry with the radical ideal that beauty is more than skin deep. And Coca-Cola's lay in acknowledging the common human need for authentic enjoyment, enhanced through our shared experiences, and expressed over the years with beautiful simplicity as "open", "real", "happiness", "enjoy" and "feeling". In each case the corporate values and the product values meshed together.

We have found it very useful to express this in terms of a Big Ideal – one step on, if you like, from a Big Idea. What exactly do you stand for?

A Big IdeaL™

A Big IdeaL is a type of positioning, but not all positionings are Big IdeaLs. A positioning can be based on a purely functional benefit: Brand X washes whiter, or is more refreshing. But a Big IdeaL is about having a worldview or a purpose that goes beyond a simple functional benefit, even though it should be supported by the functional aspects of the brand.

And it's not a shallow emotional benefit: it touches culture. It's a belief system which drives everything that a brand does and helps it to attract widespread support. It's something to be voted on by consumers and stakeholders who have a bigger vote than ever before. For these reasons, at Ogilvy & Mather we have never written Big IdeaLs like "normal" positionings. We wanted to find a simple way of capturing a brand's Big IdeaL that would force the writer to express the brand's point of view on the world, or on life, or the country in which it operates.

So we developed a form of words which could work as a summary of a brand's Big IdeaL. In practice we find that completing this phrase forces the writer(s) to focus quite hard on what the brand's worldview really is. The phrase is deceptively simple because it could be completed in 30 seconds, but doing the necessary thinking to get it absolutely right could take months. The phrase is:

> "It's a belief system which drives everything that a brand does and helps it to attract widespread support."

Brand X believes the world would be a better place if ....

Try completing the sentence for brands you are familiar with, brands that have momentum and a clear sense of identity. It might take a little while but the chances are you can come up with something that feels interesting, maybe even provocative, and quite specific to that brand.

We have found that the best Big IdeaLs seem to exist in the intersection between two realms of thought and experience.

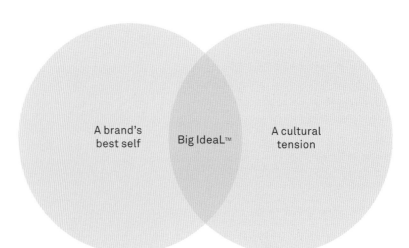

A brand's best self   Big IdeaL™   A cultural tension

They connect with the brand's "best self". This is not always exactly how the brand is right now, but how it is as its best. Clues to the brand's best self may be found in its heritage – those moments when the brand was most successful, or in the relationship that the brand's most loyal users have with it, or maybe in its visual identity. Bear in mind, however, that brands only exist in context: if the brand's greatest hour was in 1964, we need to reinterpret what made it great back then for a contemporary context. Big Ideals need to connect not just to a list of brand benefits, but to the little pieces of magic that comprise that brand's current or potential claim to greatness.

Big Ideals also connect to a cultural tension. This is where we claim culture. "Markets are conversations", according to *The Cluetrain Manifesto* and leading brands need to be interesting conversationalists. They are worth listening to when they have a valid point of view that resonates within culture. Coca-Cola's famously utopian "Hilltop" advertising was conceived against the backdrop of the bloody Vietnam War, when "community" was tensely pulled against notion brands.

Together these two things amount to what the brand believes in.

There are other ways to reach similar conclusions, and I have always been careful never to insist on this approach as a formula, or even necessarily to share it with clients even as it was guiding our work. It belongs to the kitchen not the front parlour.

Below *Chipotle is the most striking example of how important it is in the digital age for a brand to actually do what it claims. Having set out its stall under the banner of "food with integrity" and won over mainstream fast-food customers, it suffered a sucession of embarrassing food-safety scandals. While the brand's ambition to serve fresh, locally sourced, high-quality ingredients is a noble one, the company's inability to deal with these crises has seriously undermined that promise.*

"The danger always is of being seen to buy authenticity."

Others in the advertising industry have been addicted to the word "purpose". It also works; although I feel sometimes it has led to an artificial leap into CSR (Corporate Social Responsibility). This brand has a purpose of X; therefore we need a CSR programme of Y to demonstrate it.

Chipotle has recently been burned by this trend. Having set out its stall under the banner of "food with integrity", and won over mainstream fast-food customers in the process, the brand suffered a succession of embarrassing food-safety scandals, including a serious outbreak of *E. coli* and norovirus. While the initial ambition of fresh, locally sourced, high-quality ingredients was a noble one, the company's inability to consistently deliver on its promise has undermined the integrity of its brand positioning. The punishment? A double-digit decline in stock-market value.

The danger, always, is of being seen to buy authenticity. It's not tradeable. One of the more ill-conceived attempts, and much maligned in the media, is that of Pepsi and the Kendall Jenner ad in 2017. The ad rather crassly traded on protest and tensions surrounding the police in America, two touchy subjects, and implied that all we needed to solve police violence, racial tension, and political anger was an ice-cold Pepsi. The backlash was immediate, multi-channel, and nearly universal. And it was deserved, too. Pepsi has used generational change to underpin its efforts to dethrone Coca-Cola, but greatly missed the mark this time.

From Authenticity to Belief

We can convincingly demonstrate the power of *belief* through research. In a study done at Ogilvy & Mather, we compared sets of brands and sorted them into two groups: those with a higher point-of-view rating and those with a lower one. In other words, those that had a belief about the world, or stood for something, and those that didn't so much. The research supported the notion that belief mattered, since consumers sorted them very clearly via their buying decisions.

So we know that if a brand is seen to have a strong point of view, then its consideration, or its likelihood of being among a consumer's group of possible choices, is heightened. Brands with stronger points of view also rank higher in consumer perception. We created an algorithm and applied it on a larger scale to WPP's Millward Brown BrandZ database, one of the largest sets of brand data available anywhere. We found that the best-performing brands for point of view outperformed the lowest by 2.2 times in terms of their likelihood of future market share growth. Predictive methodology like this can't prove a relationship between ideals and business. Nor is there any business index I know that does so retrospectively. The macro evidence is prima facie; the micro evidence tends to require confidential company information, however convincing it may be. In other words, it could pay to believe.

So what makes this so powerful for the digital age? One very important thing: it provides a means by which a brand can organize itself amidst the digital chaos that surrounds it.

Above *American Express created OPEN forum, an online community sharing business advice between peers, leading entrepreneurs and industry bloggers. OPEN forum gives them greater exposure, business development tools, and an opportunity to build credibility for their business.*

ARCHAEOLOGY OF MATTERING

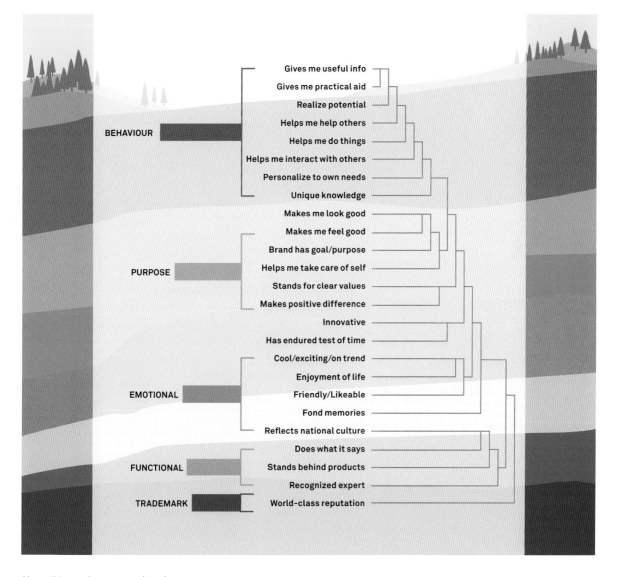

BEHAVIOUR
- Gives me useful info
- Gives me practical aid
- Realize potential
- Helps me help others
- Helps me do things
- Helps me interact with others
- Personalize to own needs
- Unique knowledge

PURPOSE
- Makes me look good
- Makes me feel good
- Brand has goal/purpose
- Helps me take care of self
- Stands for clear values
- Makes positive difference
- Innovative
- Has endured test of time

EMOTIONAL
- Cool/exciting/on trend
- Enjoyment of life
- Friendly/Likeable
- Fond memories
- Reflects national culture

FUNCTIONAL
- Does what it says
- Stands behind products
- Recognized expert

TRADEMARK
- World-class reputation

Above *"Mattering" requires more than a logo, a use case, or even a purpose. This cluster analysis of people's response to brand attributes reveals a new hierarchy for the digital age. It shows behavioural attributes rise to the top, far more important to people than the ones lower down in the sub-strata. Brands matter today because they behave in a way that helps people accomplish what they want to do. So, brands that are useful, practical and personalized are the ones that "matter" most.*

This is the role of post-modern brands: to define their own space within the internet – their own ecosystem – which they populate with their own content. Brands act as editors, keeping what is good, junking what is bad; brands act as curators, exhibiting information in a way that is ordered and compelling. It is brands that re-assemble our attention, that provide a resort for those who are interested; it is brands that act as enablers of culture, watering holes for the herd; an enclave within the landscape of interruptions.

The Well-Behaved Brand

For some while now – about the past five years – we at Ogilvy & Mather have been noticing something else. Brands may not be about to die but they are having to work harder to matter to people. If people are asked whether brands matter, more than half in developed countries and still more in developing countries say "yes". "Mattering" is quite a high bar, so these figures seem significant to me. However, our research shows that consumers are demanding much more from their brands: a logo, a reason why, an emotional promise, a cultural belief – all these may no longer be enough.

If you really get into what matters, an interesting picture emerges.

The things that matter group into those that are concerned with trademark, those that are functional, those that are emotional, those that are to do with belief – and then those that are to do with behaviour, what a brand does in order to matter to you. Think of it as a kind of "archeology of mattering" (see table on page 63). Today, the top layer is about doing: what does a brand offer by way of service? These are some of the things that matter to people .

In plain words, fewer empty promises, please. Show that you mean what you say by doing something. In the digital age brands that behave well have the edge.

Many brands require significant transformation. In the past, putting a flag out, often with a new tagline or positioning, was the way to begin to make that happen. But in a world where few taglines are memorable or meaningful anymore, actions that demonstrate new points of view are a better way to drive change in perception.

The Philips of today is a cutting-edge example of behaviour branding with an anthropological, design-led approach to innovation that engages the brand's key audiences in a deeper way and shows – rather than tells – how Philips thinks and acts as a business partner in healthcare and lighting.

Opposite and right *It would be easy to assume that you don't reach business decision-makers through emotion. But nothing could be further from the truth! In a series of digital documentaries for Philips, we showcased the brand's innovation and leadership in infrastructure, healthcare and lighting in a more illuminating way. Our "Breathless Choir" film, which told how Philips' healthcare technology helps individuals with respiratory illness achieve fulfilling lives, was breathtaking. The jury at Cannes agreed – it won a Grand Prix award.*

PHILIPS BREATHLESS CHOIR

When Philips set about relaunching itself on the basis of "Innovation + You", it had a distinctive point of view – that innovation should be built not for its own sake, but around each of us. While other technology companies might focus on how they "invent" or "think different", the company founded in 1891 in Eindhoven in the Netherlands would be absolutely people-centric. And in doing so, it would shift from being seen as a consumer lightbulb brand, to a business-to-business company expert in lighting, healthcare and infrastructure technology.

But how to get there? Philips is a company that lives and breathes innovation. It tackles problems with an anthropological, design-led approach – but it's a culture that hasn't been exposed well. So, we helped Philips take a bold leap of faith, and use emotion to persuade even the most rational of business decision-makers.

Together we created 'Breathless Choir', a film exploring how Philips' healthcare technology helps individuals with respiratory illness achieve fulfilling lives. And we did it with a level of emotion, authenticity and belief rarely evoked by B2B brands.

We enlisted the help of one of the foremost leaders of music - Gareth Malone – already well versed in assembling unlikely groups of people to transform their collective voices. Yet this would be his most difficult challenge –helping people with respiratory problems sing together. Like Claire, a cystic fibrosis sufferer, or Lawrence, a 9/11 first responder who lost a third of his lung function – and others with severe breathing issues.

It started very gently, some spoken words, a focus on the breath. And with patience, and practice, the group became one. Amazing! After a few days they started to believe in themselves. Finally, they put their belief to the test in a performance at the Apollo theater in New York City – and the result was breath taking. No matter who you are, the delight of seeing people exceed their limitations is powerful, and it changes your view of Philips.

We needed more than a 30-second spot to tell such a transformational story, and our choice of longer form content drove engagement and online sharing behaviour well above benchmarks across twenty plus markets. *The Economist*, MSNBC, *The Wall Street Journal* and LinkedIn – the business media carried an unusually emotional film for their audience.

Authentic and unexpected, "Breathless Choir" showed how Philips innovates differently. How it solves problems around real people, how it thinks and acts as a technology partner, and how it holds a set of human beliefs that touch everything it does.

Claire

Lawrence

Day 5
Apollo Theater, Harlem, New York City

The Inclusive Brand

David Ogilvy did write: "the consumer is not a moron, she is your wife". It's disappointing, then, that 40 per cent of women typically do not recognize themselves in the advertising which is directed at them.

In the digital age, this is as little tenable as it is right. Sexism is an instantly shareable vice. As the activist Cindy Gallop puts it rather eloquently, "Social media is a whole new way for us to do what we've been doing since the dawn of time: share the shit out of things."

The biggest advertiser in the world – and the biggest to address the

problem – is Unilever. It had the courage to look into its own data and to confirm the stereotyping across its (and Ogilvy & Mather's) work: the really compelling thing about #Unstereotype is that the data showed that progressive portrayals of women were not just more enjoyable (how could they not be?) but more impactful. It's a business case, not just a moral case.

The devil is in the details of how to do it. "Femvertising" has become a not very helpful catch-all phrase, and a veritable bandwagon of hashtags – #thisgirlcan, #inspireher, #girlscan, #likeagirl, #notsorry. It does not do the overall cause any good to assume that they are all equally well grounded. Pantene backed away from #notsorry, which encouraged women not to apologize when they've done nothing wrong in difficult social situations. "Be strong and shine", they said – but what on earth is the connection with shiny hair? Not surprisingly, there was no business lift to this campaign. It's borrowing an agenda: it's not rooting one in the brand.

A shift seems to be taking place where the centre of the debate is moving from "feminism" to "soft feminism" to "girl power" to "deeper fulfillment. The more it shifts, the more likely you are to look for work that gets deep into the real desires of women. When Under Armour says, "I will what I want", it reads that women are now surrounded by a lot of superficially "empowering" messages which in reality disempower, because they generalize the person. If sports products enable you to do what you want, they celebrate strength not weakness. Lesson number 1 in brand building: always go back to the product.

Above *Pantene backed away for #notsorry, which encouraged women not to apologize when they've done nothing wrong in difficult social situations. "Be strong and shine," they said – but what on earth is the connection with shiny hair? Not surprisingly, there was no business lift to this campaign. It's borrowing an agenda: it's not rooting one in the brand.*

Opposite top *Always #LikeAGirl campaign was a hit with the judges at Cannes, and it garnered significant press and social attention. This is firmly in the girl power mode, but does it lack a connetction to the product, and a nuacnced expression of the needs of women?*

Opposite bottom *"I will what I want" – a truly empowering phrase that supports a deeper fulfillment of womanhood in a world that constantly seeks to undermine women.*

There's a big issue, of course, at work here: and that is the mindset of the advertising (and marketing) business. This is the direct result of an inbuilt diversity issue. Put simply, there are not enough women in positions of management or in creative departments. And this reflects a broader issue in anything to do with STEM (Science, Technology, Engineering, Maths). So digital technology and creative advertising together don't make a diverse marriage: the opposite. It was depressing in writing this book that, for instance, the founders of the internet I selected, as well as the greats of Chapter 14, were all male. This, alas, was not unconscious bias.

It won't improve in the advertising business until there is much closer parity between men and women in technology. And that will bring other benefits. As Shirley Zalis, the woman who did more than anyone to pioneer online market research, and who founded "The Girls' Lounge", a kind of pop-up workshop that combines activism with manicure, says, "the social norm just becomes more nurturing, and nurturing companies are likely to be more successful". Shirley popped up for us at one of our events at Cannes in 2016, and also emphasized that this whole debate is not just about women, it is about gender. It's about how men are portrayed also.

When Guinness ran an ad featuring the Welsh rugby player, Gareth Thomas, who had come out in 2009, it rang a bell with me. Fourteen years earlier, Ogilvy & Mather lost the Guinness account in large part due to the uproar (especially among licensees) caused by the first gay Guinness commercial, in 1995 (certainly it was ahead of its time). That was a brave and lonely attempt to show gay normalcy by a brand known for its masculine qualities. A social revolution in 25 years has caused what seemed unacceptable to become not just normal but normal in the most apparently extreme redoubts of masculinity.

So one further communications impact of the digital world has been the opening of social silos. Brand owners have quickly realized that the targeting efficiency of the internet allows them to reach discrete groups, and, more importantly, to become accessible through relevant content to them. But then the lids have come off all together: slipstream is turning into mainstream.

Above *Honey Maid Graham Crackers featured a gay family in "This is Wholesome", a moving TV commercial that evoked the parallels among wholesome families and wholesome foods. It aired in March 2014, at the height of the same-sex marriage debate in the United States and provoked an outpouring of praise. And, sadly, derision. Rather than crumble in the face of virulent opposition, Honey Maid reaffirmed its values in "Love", which clapped back at critics by showing artists spelling out the word love using printouts of online hate mail and comments the brand received.*

Opposite top *Red Label tea, a staple in India and Pakistan, put a transgender band as ambassadors for its product, making a strong cultural statement in the process.*

Opposite middle and bottom *With the Proud Whopper, Burger King showed that the LGBQT community are the same on the inside as everyone else. How? Same burger, different wrapper.*

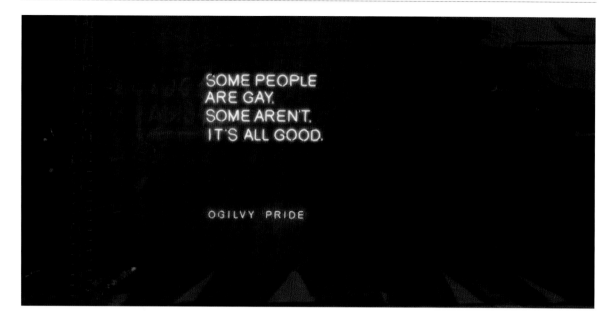

Above *A very high proportion of our staff are Millennials. So it's not only a matter of belief in what's right, but also a question of what's important to them that we support the LGBTQ community, and have been doing so proudly for a decade.*

It had become clear that this was not just about quick access to the commercial power of diverse audiences, but about the brands adapting in terms of their behaviour. Brands that do believe in diversity at their core.

LGBTQ mainstreaming has made this very clear. Tiffany & Co. is often perceived as epitomizing the traditional, but the brand challenged the norms of its category when it honoured tradition while celebrating modern love. The definition of timeless love has not changed, of course, but it has expanded, encompassing wider acceptance. Tiffany met this head on, and just two and a half years after same-sex marriage was legalized in New York, the brand included a gay couple in its advertising. It was a statement that this brand, a stalwart of the storied tradition of luxury gifting, endorsed the gay audience as mainstream.

And when we launched Ogilvy Pride in 2008 it seemed entirely reasonable for it to identify with the LGBTQ constituency at a time when it was severely challenged. In fact, we know that almost 50 per cent of Millennials are more likely to support a brand after seeing a LGBTQ-themed ad.

Our Ogilvy Pride network now operates in multiple markets, opening the eyes of staff and clients to the LGBTQ mainstream. And we count Stonewall as an Agency partner. I'm proud of that.

Back in 2010, I founded an Islamic consulting unit within the Agency. We called it Ogilvy Noor, meaning "light". Its aim was very simple: to cast light on another constituency, grossly neglected by the West, both by many western companies selling in Islamic countries or in respect of the ignored (or sometimes shockingly stigmatized) Muslim constituency in the West. I keynoted the American Muslim Consumer Conference in 2010. It's fair to say that there's little one could have done to have appeared more out on a limb than this: but this is a constituency that is mainstream. Let's remind ourselves that some 23.2 per cent of the world's population adheres to Islam as of 2010, which will rise to 29.7 per cent by 2050 (Pew Research Center). And that the vast majority of Muslims living in the West see themselves unequivocally as mainstream.

Muslim values are not un-modern: far from it. Shelina Janmohamed, our leader of Noor, is helping us understand the new Muslim Futurist: young; proud to be Muslim; trend and fashion conscious. But the vast majority feel that brands don't understand them. Being "halal" is not a question of narrow compliance to a formula; it's a matter of recognizing the deeper Islamic values and that recognition cannot be faked.

Last, but not least, ethnicity is a denoter of the inclusive brand – especially in the US. Here's a country with multiple ethnic divides: Caucasian, Hispanic, Asian and African American. When I first moved to New York, I had a mentor, Jeff Bowman, an African American. Actually, I was supposed to mentor him, but it worked out the other way round. Jeff has gone on to make a career out of the Total Market thinking. This rejects the old American world where General Market agencies abandoned the segments and clients and used specialist, Black, or Hispanic, agencies to reach them – literally, as races apart. That made sense for a quite a long while, but changing demographic realities call this structure into question. These minorities, taken together, form the majority.

Jeff calls this the New Majority. By 2044, the majority of the population of the US will be composed of ethnic and racial minorities. The old General Market/Multicultural Market segmentation no longer makes perfect sense when the General Market is itself multicultural. First, the multiethnic population is growing fast; second, the US population is increasingly cross-cultural in its tastes; and third, fragmented multicultural budgets are never large enough (even when demographically appropriate) to make the impact that a total market budget can.

A total budget which is ethnically conscious and responsible is more likely to be effective than a small "ethnic budget" which is always vulnerable to being cut or to making false choices between various minorities. This means not going to the default position of only planning advertising to an audience of non-Hispanic whites.

Digital media can become a way in which mainstream messages can touch and acknowledge ethnic context or product preferences. But they are being delivered as part of a holistic communications strategy and not from some parallel tactical universe.

If anyone doubts this, they should look for a moment at African American millennials. Thanks to A.C. Nelson and its seminal report, *African American Millennials: Young, Connected and Black* (2016), we have a clear view of them as tech savvy, articulate and at the leading edge of digital advancement – a good antidote to the old formula of "will it play in Peoria?"

7 CONTENT IS KING; BUT WHAT DOES IT MEAN?

"Content" is one of the most used, reused, misused and abused words in the practice of marketing communications. It is associated, both consciously and subconsciously, with the phrase "Content is King", which is the title of an essay Bill Gates posted on the Microsoft website on 3 January 1996. "Content is where I expect much of the real money will be made on the Internet, just as it was in broadcasting," Gates wrote.

Content was not a word in David Ogilvy's lexicon, although he might have recognized "contents" very readily.

When it would become a singular noun applied to media, it started to morph into many meanings. "Branded content" has become, perhaps, the most enduring of these.

Branded Content

Branded content – communications contributed by brands within a vehicle whose primary purpose is to entertain rather than to sell – originally developed as a sub-discipline of the advertising business, with its own approaches, intellectual ethos and agencies. The role of the brand was essentially that of sponsor, whether it be of a whole property or as part of the entertainment narrative.

"The vast majority of content produced on the internet remains unread, unwatched, unseen and unheard."

Then we had the Digital Revolution. "Branded content" broke large with BMW's "The Hire", a series of eight short films produced for the internet and DVD in 2001 and 2002. Notable directors and actors were hired to make the 10-minute narrative segments, which showcased the performance benefits of BMW automobiles. This was a seminal example of content being enfranchised in a broader role.

The dramatic disintermediation of media opened up the means to create and distribute material to everyone. Absent a better term, the digital world glommed onto an amorphous, inoffensive one. Content started to be applied to anything that was produced and lived on the internet, from blogs to websites. It became short form and long form. It became client-sourced and crowd-sourced. And as it spread out in cyberspace – formless and fissiparous – we eventually realized we had to tame it. Brands and agencies evolved the concept of "ecosystems of content", which at least a brand could stake as its own digital territory, where the parts were actually linked, and where the sum of the parts created some value for the user.

Above right BMW Films got a head start on branded content with "The Hire", a series of short films featuring screen actor Clive Owen and shot by Hollywood directors such as Ang Lee. Distributed online and on DVD, each placed the car as the hero of a larger story.

The vast majority of content produced on the internet remains unread, unwatched, unseen and unheard. In 2014, Spotify released data indicating that only 80 per cent of the music-streaming service's songs has been listened to. That means 20 per cent of the music – some 4 million songs – had never been heard. A new service, Forgotify, sprang up to rectify what it deemed a "musical travesty", delivering playlists of "neglected songs". It has inspired other services as well. No Likes Yet supplied Instagram photos that hadn't received a single like, as the name suggests. If unseen video is more your thing, navigate over to Petit Tube where you can view the internet's most unpopular clips.

And that's not even the ads. Once you factor in the number of lonely, unseen advertisements, the results grow more discouraging. Google says that 46 per cent of paid video ads are never viewed. For display ads, the number is even higher: 56 per cent of them go begging.

Above right *This is the image I use in presentations as a warning: avoid the landfill. Advertising must not become a dumping ground for content. As practitioners we must recognize content as something people chose to engage with, not discard.*

"It is *content* that we will produce in the future, not advertising, direct-mail pieces, or whatever."

This has made content a rather dirty word – hardly kingly at all. In internal presentations, I use this image to stigmatize it – as so much digital landfill.

How, then, to avoid the call of the dumpster?

It helps to have a sound definition. This is mine:

content

noun

Communication so good you want to spend time with it or share it.

That's a high bar. It means that something worthy of being called content must so capture you that you choose to watch, read or listen to it. It must spur you to vouch for its value as you repost it on to your friends.

The parts agglomerated in these ways: what the brand *paid* for, what it *owned*, and what it *earned*, known as P-O-E (see page 134). POE starts to define content in a more rigorous way, as something that is planned for.

But the question still remained, why consume the content?

When we want clients to understand what content can be, we show a film clip from the early 1980s of David Ogilvy.

What, really?

Yes, really.

"It seems to me that [print] editors must know how to communicate [better] than we admen," he says. "We admen have an unconscious belief that an ad has to look like an ad. Ad layouts signal to the reader, 'This is only an ad, skip it.' So always pretend you are an editor."

This is the mindset that is required for content online. In 2010, Ogilvy & Mather began hiring journalists, people who understood how to engage content beyond the confines of 30-second TV spots, not just in length but also in depth. Journalists expand investigation into a subject; the traditional creative team (a copywriter and an art director) compresses it. These are two very different things.

And then we started looking for people with curatorial skills: collecting, re-presenting, showcasing, and acknowledging the source of material we did not originate ourselves – and doing it with pride. These skills are not common. They require subject matter speciality, even scholarship, combined with a generalist bent, as well as a broad network of other curators and experts to call on. Curators are, in the ponderous words of the American Alliance of Museums, "information brokers who, through learned and creative interpretation, create meaningful experiences for people".

All this betokens a shift in the business of agencies, which is still not recognized or even expected – namely, they are becoming publishers. It is *content* that we will produce in the future, not advertising, direct-mail pieces, or whatever. As such, agencies will – or should – cease behaving like agents (who used to get paid by the media in a system invented in the mid-eighteenth century) and act more like the media itself. We have, if we want it, the chance to break the shackles of our past.

And brand owners also need to think of themselves as publishers.

Perhaps the first to do this overtly was Red Bull. When a beverage brand launches a global print magazine in a supposed post-print era, and then rapidly reaches a circulation of over 3 million monthly readers, it signals a readiness for consumers to accept the dominance of brand over product. It's part of a strategy that has redefined Red Bull as a publisher, specializing in categories favoured by aspirational young males, such as sports and music, and injecting the brand with an enviable dose of rocket fuel.

The brand is defiantly not engaging merely in "content marketing", but rather has teams in markets across the world, selling media to other brands, but scarcely mentioning Red Bull.

Thinking About Content

Having defined content, we can now start to attack it in a more structured way. To do that, we need to think about its properties.

In Ogilvy & Mather's experience, sometimes content is *magnetic*, it attracts people; sometimes it is *immersive*, you get embedded in it; sometimes it is *smart*, enabling you in some way; and sometimes it is just downright *practical*.

Of course, like all self-respecting business people, we have a natural tendency to like four-quadrant grids. Our content grid is shown overleaf, spanning from breadth (broad and mass) to personalization (personalized and individual) on one axis, and from utility (useful and informational) to entertainment (entertaining and emotive) value on the other.

Like all such constructs, these quadrants are not hard and fast. There are overlaps and grey areas.

Information, for instance, can be highly entertaining; and many great pieces of content have provided it in documentary formats that entertain. Nonetheless, teasing out differences helps give a more thoughtful approach to this amorphous thing, content. But the differences are all more or less,

Below Logistics is a complicated but indispensable part of modern life. Through brand journalism we've helped educate UPS's business customers on the importance of logistics for future growth and profitability. Armed with more knowledge, they've been motivated to buy UPS services as a result.

CONTENT FROM OUR SPONSOR

UPS

Stop Owning Your Supply Chain
Companies that collaborate across the supply chain can...
More >>

Best Temperatures for Short-Term Refrigeration Storage
Temperature standards for shipping perishables — from biological samples to... **More >>**

Does Trade Actually Help Developing Countries?
How trade can be a powerful force for good if certain conditions are... **More >>**

Turning Congestion Challenges into Operational Opportunities
Congestion in the United States costs nearly $80 billion a year in wasted time and... **More >>**

3 Ways for Any Business to Avoid a Misstep
Taking care of your supply chain, community, and employees can pay... **More >>**

○ SEE MORE ARTICLES

The Wall Street Journal news organization was not involved in the creation of this content.

THE RED BULLETIN

FRANCE

HORS DU COMMUN

RAD COMPANY
LE VTT EN MODE
BLOCKBUSTER

PARIS LA NUIT
Expérience VIP
dans les clubs
de la capitale

24
HEURES DU MANS
LA GT ACADEMY
RELÈVE LE DÉFI

ROPE
JUMPING
18 hommes
en action
pour un
saut record

OUTDOOR
Un monde
fou attend
dehors

LENNY
KRAVITZ

MUSIQUE, CINÉMA, AFFAIRES
LA SUPERSTAR FAIT LE BILAN

PHOTOGRAPHIE DE MARK SELIGER

THE CONTENT MATRIX

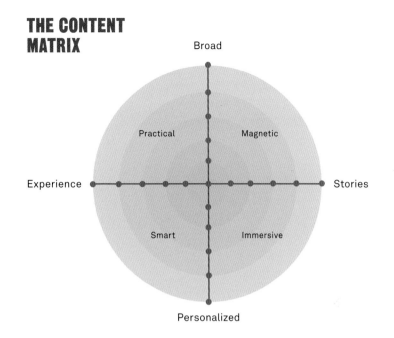

Above right *The Content Matrix. Sometimes content is magnetic; sometimes it is immersive; sometimes it is smart; and sometimes it is practical.*

Opposite *Red Bull has become something of a media giant (one that sells beverages). Record-breaking stunts, a winning Formula One team, global flugtag contests and box-cart races, music studios in major cities – and a magazine with one of the largest circulations among young males.*

rather than either/or. Another helpful way of using this content matrix is to see it as a playground in which two great dividends can be looked for: creating experiences and creating engagement.

The digital world has put a premium on design: experimental design has become a critical pillar of the digital world.

Enjoyment, however, comes through the power of stories.

Neither designing experiences nor narrative enjoyment are remotely new concepts, but in the digital world they have both exploded in importance. They bring the "content" to content.

Planning for Content

One way of planning for a strategic approach to content would be to consider each of the four quadrants of our matrix.

1. Magnetic Content

How many times have clients in the last few years said at the end of a brief, "…and please will you make it viral." That's not something we like to hear. Not only do we mistrust "virality" itself – Ogilvy & Mather's own video practice has officially banned the word from all internal discussions – but the degree to which a piece of content is magnetic or not is often difficult to plan for or predict.

And our understanding of the root causes – what makes for the magnetism – is only recently developing.

The magnetism of a piece of content is linked to arousal. Arousal is a state of heightened emotion, drawing people to share information or material. In short, it is what guides our fingers to the share icon.

The apogee of experience design – so far at least – may be The Museum of Feelings. Glade transformed more than 5,000 square feet (465 square metres) of Manhattan space into an immersive pop-up experience to appeal to its visitors' senses of sight, sound, touch and importantly smell. More reminiscent of an art installation than a marketing event, the space was designed to help people recognize how much our external environment affects our internal emotions. On the outside, the building would frequently change colour to reflect the emotional state of its surroundings, triggered by a sentiment analysis of New Yorkers' social media feeds. Inside, rooms were themed around five specific emotions: exhilaration, invigoration, joy, optimism and calm.

In the final room, visitors used polygraph-like machines to measure their biometrics, heart rate and skin salinity, which alongside external cues like building temperature and Twitter sentiment would combine to layer a corresponding colour over a user's selfie. This "MoodLens" transformed a simple selfie into a living work of art that was far more reflective of a visitor's emotions than a standard profile picture, laying bare an individual's genuine emotional wellbeing directly on social media.

"... the degree to which a piece of content is magnetic or not is often difficult to plan for or predict."

When I first wrote a speech on this subject, my working title was "Techniques of Arousal". That seemed too redolent of that naughty old sexologist Dr Ruth Westheimer. But arousal is, in fact, a respectable academic study. It was recognized a long time ago that some television programming can create arousal very effectively, but the sharing impact of the internet has led to increasing study of the phenomena.

You can read the research of Taylor, Strutton, Thompson, Cushman, Earl, Binet, Field, Neba-Field, Riebe, Newstead, Mulkan, Berger. Certainly, you might have heard of Jonah Berger, Associate Professor of Marketing at the Wharton School at the University of Pennsylvania. He wrote the book called *Contagious* (2013), which is useful.

In sum, all of these experts demonstrate that it is heightened emotions that drive people to share information.

Berger has tended to emphasize the arousal of the subject (for instance, email sharing is boosted by the good feelings following physical exercise) as opposed to the emotional content of the message. He doesn't really study film. However, as practitioners, we know that content itself creates the context, and, therefore, the arousal. And other academics who have studied film confirm that social transmission is affected by emotional content.

- Arousal is caused most by *positive* content.
- The emotion has to be *highly* arousing.
- Arousal has a disinhibitory effect, which results in greater sharing.

Stimuli that provoke high arousal also trigger a high reminiscence effect: we remember them more. The more the emotion reflects the self-concept of the subject, the more likely sharing will take place.

And, finally, our academics confirm for us that successfully designing high-arousal content is rather difficult. And they find something else to be critical: a sense of surprise, of the totally unexpected. As MacDonald and Ewing note in *Admap* December 2012: "The key emotional driver of sharing turned out to be a surprise."

What happens then is that a ripple of creative joy starts to spread. In fact, what happens is physiological. The neuro-transmitter dopamine starts working; and the synapses in the brain start firing.

So the key to understanding the internet is not technological; it's chemical.

And the positive release which comes from arousal actually replicates the processes used in therapy. The social sharing of emotion produces immediate benefits, a therapeutic effect.

What arouses us to share our happiness? We can discern a clue from one of the most successful promotions of all time. When Share a Coke was developed by our Sydney office, we had no idea that it would prove utterly magnetic and that it would generate billions of shares. Wherever it has run – and that's most places around the world – it has helped reignite the relationship of young adults to one of the world's most iconic brands.

Share a Coke aroused the sense that being socially connected is fundamental to our social and psychological well-being. Young adults tend to spend less and less time with family and more with peers, and these peer relationships become more intimate the more experiences are shared. We have always shared, but the internet allows us to share more. As futurist Stowe Boyd puts it, "I am made greater by the sum of my connections; so are my connections."

That is one reason why I do not like the word viral, and try to use it as little as possible. I understand the analogy; but to me there is something malign about the word. When the research clearly tells us that internet sharing is the sharing of hedonic value, talking about making things viral somehow feels inappropriate.

Another word to be careful of is meme. Richard Dawkins, the ethnologist and evolutionary biologist, coined the term in his 1976 book *The Selfish Gene.* He described a meme as the cultural equivalent of a gene in biology.

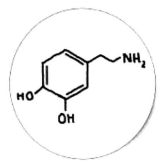

Above *This is it – dopamine: the creative molecule. Food, sex, exercise – and even advertising – can trigger a release of dopamine from nerve cells (neurons) to other parts of the brain through the tiny space (synapse) in between. A spike of dopamine acts as a "reward", signalling pleasure, motivation, and most important of all, salience – alerting the brain to pay attention to whatever stimulus activated it.*

"I do not like the word viral, and try to use it as little as possible."

Above *What arouses us to share our happiness? We can discern a clue from one of the most successful promotions of all time. When Share a Coke was developed by our Sydney office, we had no idea that it would prove utterly magnetic and that it would generate billions of shares. Wherever it has run—and that's in most places around the world—it has helped reignite the relationship of young adults to one of the world's most iconic brands.*

The latter self-replicates by a chemical process, while a meme undergoes the same process through cultural repetition and interpretation. Examples include a melody, line of poetry, fashion, and learned skills.

Ironically, his idea became memetic itself. And now in the digital age it defines anything that spreads. But Richard's original meaning had much more to do with deeper "transmitted code", like the heroic codes of, say, Beowulf, than it does with bits of internet flotsam and jetsam, like bulldogs on skateboards.

And my colleagues at Social@Ogilvy, Ogilvy's specialist social media practice, would argue against viral for very different reasons, believing that once there is the intrinsic surprise and charm in a piece of video – the preconditions – then social design kicks in, and through a whole series of interactions, optimizes the spread.

In internet terms, magnetic often means the wild and the wacky. This is the world of scary raptor reptiles, of carrot-eating contests, of mutant poodles. In fact, I once sat down and identified four types of humour that will – if done well – invariably spread.

Above A skateboarding dog? An archetypal example of the absurd form of humour.

Below *Our Paris office aided and abetted Europcar in a mischievous prank to publicise the company's new on-demand car rental service. How? We crushed people's cars. Well, we pretended to! Unsuspecting members of the public returned to the car park to find the remnants of what they believed to be their vehicles, with their reactions broadcast live on the radio. When they called the parking helpline and it was recommended they seize the opportunity to rent a car to get home, exasperation quickly turned to expletives. The prank not only generated laughs among listeners – and eventually the victims – it doubled subscriptions.*

1. **Jocular**: and the joke is often against someone, as it is with the enduring genre of fail videos.

2. **Pranky**: the "lost" bikini top that turns into shark's fin as a guy retrieves it.

3. **Cute**: a computer mouse dangles on a cord that a cat holds in its mouth. "They told me it was a mouse. They lied."

4. **Absurd**: a bulldog riding a skateboard.

There is no doubt that humour like this can help create magnetic content. And Ogilvy & Mather have used all of these forms of humour to do so.

Here's a prank.

We had to publicize a new car rental service: a flexible multiple subscription allowing one to use a car on demand no matter when or where.

Our Paris office tricked a few unsuspecting members of the Parisian public into believing their cars had been crushed into blocks of scrap metal. We captured the ensuing drama, including the car owners' expressions of anger, with hidden cameras. Actors posing as police officers stepped in and offered a telephone help-line number. Those who took the bait and made the call were patched in to a national radio broadcast, during which many cursed profusely while receiving advice to rent instead of owning a car. More expletives were broadcast before Europcar was revealed as the prankster. (Of course, we didn't broadcast anyone without their permission.)

The message got through; subscriptions doubled.

But yes, this was my car,

But there is another story at work here. All this reminds me of the great nineteenth-century showman, P.T. Barnum, who understood exactly how to attract people to the circus. He drew in thousands by exhibiting a taxidermized monkey's torso attached to a fishtail. "Roll up, roll up – see the mermaid!" This is a crude form of arousal.

The art of arousal today has to aim higher. If we are going to entertain, we must do better. We have to tell stories. That bulldog riding a skateboard is a curiosity; it is not a story.

A story requires structure, theme, mood, plot and characters rather than caricatures.

Dove's Real Beauty *Sketches* film (2013) is a fine example of advertising as storytelling, and vice versa. It embraces the power of narrative, of viewer engagement, of appealing directly to a woman's sense of empathy. We invited women to sit for a forensic artist and asked them to describe themselves. Their replies exposed a skewed appraisal, one that emphasized their perceived physical flaws. Strangers were then invited to describe the women to the artist, and the appraisals were much more generous, framing the subjects' looks more holistically and using details other than purely physical.

When the two sketches were revealed to each participant, the contrast between their negative self-perception and favourable external view could hardly have been more stark, surprising both to the women and the viewer. The emotional power of that reaction explains why the film has become one of the most watched pieces of advertising in the world.

The surprise here is shocking: the difference between how women see themselves, and how others see them. But it's also profoundly moving. It is dopamine rich.

2. Immersive Content

Zen and the Art of Marketing Communications may seem a long way apart, but the Digital Revolution has brought them closer together than you might think.

Digitalization had always carried with it the promise of a two-way communication. You, the individual, can be isolated. You can be invited to participate in the dialogue. And then you can join it. And, in joining, you can literally both find yourself and lose yourself.

To illustrate, I'll return to Dove. Imagine that you, a woman, were given the power to change the harmful female stereotypes that had become rote in digital media as much as in old media. We did not endear ourselves to Facebook when we created an application for Dove that did just that, using Facebook's own algorithm.

We invited women to expose the problem of negative advertising capitalizing on and directly targeting female insecurities using the "Ad Makeover" tool, a web application designed to subvert Facebook's own advertising marketplace and give women direct control over the ads. Typically used only by marketers, we connected the Facebook advertising auctions platform to a simple consumer interface, allowing women who

> "The art of arousel today has to aim higher. If we are going to entertain, we must do better. We have to tell stories."

Sponsored	Create an Ad ✕
Muffin Top?	It could get worse! Lose it with these spa tips.

Sponsored	Create an Ad ✕
The perfect bum is the one you're sitting on	Tessa and Dove displaced a feel-bad ad with this positive message. Send yours.

Sponsored	Create an Ad ✕
Jelly Rolls?	Reduce your belly fat with this one old trick.

Sponsored	Create an Ad ✕
Every body is beautiful	Elena and Dove displaced a feel-bad ad with this positive message. Send yours.

Sponsored	Create an Ad ✕
Need a bigger bust?	This miracle cream will enhance what you want.

Sponsored	Create an Ad ✕
Think of your cups as half full	Sarah and Dove displaced a feel-bad ad with this positive message. Send yours.

Above *In "Ad Makeover", by turning Facebook's algorithm against those disreputable marketers who pray on women's insecurities, we empowered women to trade humiliation for admiration by replacing negative messages with ones of mutual support.*

visited the site to replace crude associations like "Thunder thighs?" with positive messages such as "The perfect bum is the one you're sitting on".

Or consider the deep engagement UPS sought during the peak-shipping season. Parcel deliveries through the 2015 holiday season (from the day after Thanksgiving to Christmas Eve) accounted for about 60 per cent of all deliveries made that year. When our client UPS wanted to underpin its promise of a hassle-free holiday (after a difficult holiday season in 2014, due to atrocious weather) we guaranteed that we could deliver not just gifts but also wishes. Through the Wishes Delivered campaign, UPS invited package recipients to post a wish on UPS.com, or via social media using #WishesDelivered, and for each wish donated $1 to the Boys and Girls Clubs of America, The Salvation Army, and the Toys for Tots Literacy Program. One of many wishes fulfilled resulted in the delivery of a truckload of snow to school kids in Texas who had never seen the frozen white stuff.

Such programs create personal engagement at a very high level. Implicit in them is an element of play. Can I beat the system and change the Facebook algorithm? Can I make a wish that will be fulfilled against all apparent odds?

But what happens if the play becomes explicit? Enter the world of gaming, the point where content moves far beyond engaging and mildly immersive to being absorbing and completely immersive.

Above *UPS used crowd-sourcing and a donation scheme to create a programme which solicited wishes for the holiday season. "Wishes Delivered" generated a cash contribution to charities for each approved wish. It was throughly engaging, but what really made it immersive were the stories. Stories like that of Carson, (the child in the middle), a young boy who formed a fast friendship with, and deep admiration of, Mr Eddie, his regular UPS driver. In fact, Carson had his own UPS outfit and enjoyed making his own packages. When the holidays came around, Mr Eddie arrived with more than just the usual deliveries. He had something far more special for Carson: his own child-sized truck and a day to be a real UPS driver, just like his hero.*

Academic studies of video gaming define immersion as the state where gamers are so involved in the game that they become lost in it.

The evidence does, in fact, show that immersion exists on three distinct levels: a level of engagement, a period of adaptation and learning the controls; engrossment, where those controls become invisible; and total immersion. On this level you are cut off from reality to such an extent that the game is all and everything. In the words of one research study, it's "a Zen-like state where your head just seems to know what to do, and your mind just seems to carry on with the story".[1]

This is what psychologists call "spatial presence". You create a model in your mind of the "space", but then move on to favour that "space" over real space, encouraged by cues that create a consistent sense of being "there". The environment has to be rich; that is to say, it has to dominate you with sensory stimulus. As Jamie Madigan writes: "The more senses you assault and the more those senses work in tandem, the better. A bird flying overhead is good. Hearing it screech overhead is better".[2]

In its purest form, immersion requires skill sets which mesh ideation and technology together. The combination is not easily found.

Games are important for commercial advertisers, not because a content program would be deficient without one, but because they contain ingredients and approaches which can be inspiring – and entrancing.

And what successful games like these have in common is that they are all good stories. So let's not forget that a story in itself can entrance. Gaming psychologists call this "flow". It's when the interface between you and the story – game or novel – disappears. And it happens with full-blooded immersion. What the Digital Revolution has done is to make it possible for those stories to have an interactive component. At one extreme you can actually join up and become the storyteller.

Right *With the launch of "Farmed and Dangerous", a satirical four-part comedy series premiering on online platform Hulu, Chipotle shunned product placement and chose instead to engineer its values directly into the show's DNA. Armed with an original script and a herd of exploding cows, the show was anointed "one of the funniest things I have ever seen" by media pundit Jim Cramer. Unfortunately a promotion is only ever as good as a product, and an E.coli outbreak ended much of the good work.*

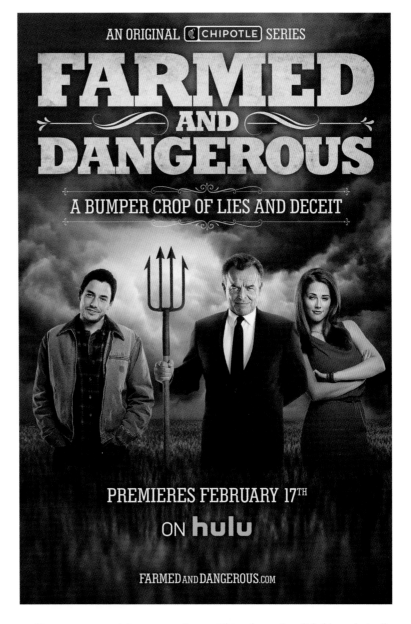

Or, you can participate as a viewer. Chipotle, again, did this technically very well, aggressively slaying agri-business in "Farmed and Dangerous".

The word not to forget in designing communication in this quadrant is "entrancing". Does the content reward you as it engages you? Otherwise it will become as quickly expendable as the vast mass of unconsumed content.

3. Smart Content

There's been a lot of "smart" around in the last 20 years: smart cars, smart phones, smart carts, smart homes – and smart arses into the bargain. So, why trot it out again with content?

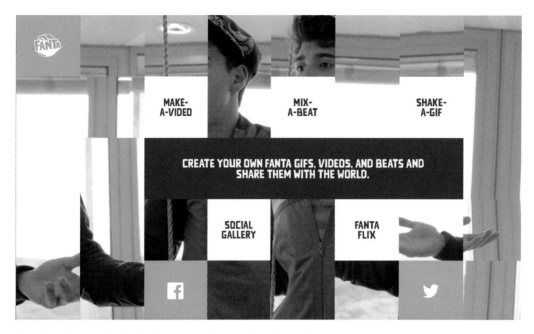

Above *Participatory gaming is at the heart of the next-level brand experience our sister agency, David, created for Fanta. Rather than create a highly-scripted environment, Fanta offered its audience a full palette of tools and material to create gifs, videos, and beats to share with the world. Fanta expertly and helpfully inserted itself into a range of fun behaviors that its audience was already engaged with.*

Below *For Perrier, we invited people to enter* Secret Place *and be a part of the best party ever. In a 90-minute feature film that worked like a video game, visitors have experienced 100,000 hours of play and have lived over 4 million lives.*

Above *Nestle's Devenir Maman keeps track of a pregnant woman's milestones, deploying smart content to engage and inform.*

Because at its best it signifies the point at which you can design your way into a better experience of life. This is not content which is there to entertain, but to help you, and in a very personal way.

You're a committed Amazon shopper, and you're looking for a home automation solution. The Amazon Echo is reasonably priced, highly interconnected with other technology, offers exclusive deals on Amazon, and voice recognition shopping.

That's smart.

You're an expectant mother in France. You're a little anxious and feeling insecure. You have so many things to keep track of and learn, and making sure that you (and baby) eat right, get enough rest and are progressing properly through pregnancy is a little overwhelming. Nestlés Devenir Maman has you covered, keeping track of pregnancy milestones and helping you make the best choices for you and your baby.

That's smart.

What's the psychology here?

It's all about being in control. Scientists now believe that control is a sum of different influences on personality, not just social learning but biological influences also. As one group of Dutch researchers has put it, "feeling in control represents a blend of socially desirable traits that are all related to psychological well-being and successful performance." It is a direct enabler of self-regulation of behaviour, and that's exactly where content comes in as an enabler – a stimulus for, or a reinforcement of, that self-regulation.

What is at work here is the power of design – integrating information and experience.

At an extreme, this leads to the phenomenon of "self-quantification". Individuals have never before been able to record the metrics that measure the routines of their life which affect their health and well-being. Now they can. Not just for the sake of losing weight or improving their fitness, but for a whole range of indicators, from sleep behaviour to work/life patterns to mood changes.

Not everyone, myself included, wants to be self-quantified, or "body hacked"! But the general principle of enablement, in a personalized way, is a very powerful one. It goes to the heart of the choices one makes as an individual, and how we can make better choices.

Digital content is a precursor to making better choices. For instance, Nestlé Milo paired an activity bracelet with a unique exercise and meal-planning app to help kids better understand the link between their diet and physical exercise. By combining challenges, video, avatars and real-time data, we appealed to their love of technology and games. So rather than force them outside to play, users were encouraged to take more steps each day in order to top the leaderboard among their friends, and follow tips and tricks to become "champions" in their chosen activity. They could see how much energy they burned in the process. Alongside, they could view their meal choices in terms of energy consumed, giving a quick indication of their progress towards a more balanced diet and exercise regime. By using more carrot and less stick, we gave kids an opportunity to actively enjoy being responsible with their health, and they jumped at the chance.

It's perhaps worthwhile to remember the second meaning of "smart": it is not just an adjective, it's an acronym – Specific, Measurable, Attainable, Realistic, Timely.

These are no longer goals for career-builders in business. The ordinary person has been enabled by the Digital Revolution to apply them to himself and herself, too.

4. Practical Content

Our final type of content is very practical. It sounds quite flat, but in fact it is empowering. It is content which helps elevate and enhance the collective experience of individuals, communities and businesses. This type of content puts resources in your hands.

Right *Milo's activity bracelet and accompanying app combines exercises, meal planning tips and online games to keep kids healthier and more active offline.*

The first resource is knowledge. Companies have always seen this as something to be shared. Some audiences have been catered for more than others. One thinks of motorists, for instance, for whom the Michelin Guides were created, or classics that have passed, such as the Shell Guides to the English countryside.

In the digital age, that knowledge can be distributed more accurately, in a more timely way, and also completely specifically to where you are.

When Google wanted to showcase the capabilities of its new Chrome web browser, its Labs division reached out to Canadian Indie band Arcade Fire to help develop a new take on the music video for their single, "We Used to Wait".

The interactive short film *The Wilderness Downtown* conceived by artist, entrepreneur and director Chris Milk, brought the user directly into the storyline. Unbeknownst to them, by inputting their name and the address of the home they grew up in, over the course of 5 minutes they would be taken back to their hometown. Guided by a teenage version of themselves, they would run through familiar streets and end up circling their childhood home to the sound of the band's atmospheric track.

Chrome has since grown to be the dominant browser, and Arcade Fire one of the biggest bands in the world.

Right *In* The Wilderness Downtown *the iconic indie band Arcade Fire's latest single, "We Use to Wait" was chanted in the background as Google's Chrome browser quickly transported people to the neighbourhoods of their youth. A Google Labs experiment, it helped launch Chrome to become the world's most popular browser by combining a lightning fast experience with an incredible interactive video – an unusually immersive way to showcase a new product. Rarely is such emotional content so inherently practical too.*

Under an editor's hand, knowledge brings a competitive edge. It expounds and justifies a point of view or positioning. But not just as a white paper, but rather as a dynamic program.

Ogilvy set up just such a program, the IBM Newsroom, to deliver rich, editorially driven content. Launched in 2014, the IBM Newsroom creates a wide range of properties: articles, videos, infographics, ebooks, SlideShares and more.

When a brand delivers truth, it earns credibility, and with credibility comes consumer trust. As such, the Newsroom aims to deliver information its audience needs, not just content to promote the brand. In this way, Ogilvy helpd IBM join the conversation – not preach from the pulpit.

Qualcomm dominates the OEM (Original Equipment Manufacturer) market, powering about two-thirds of all smartphones, but the consumer

Right *In 2012, Qualcomm microchips dominated their market, powering two thirds of smartphones. But the brand was not well known among consumers. Our agency was given a brief that paralleled the famous "Intel Inside" program of the 1990s – familiarize consumers with the underlying technology and establish a powerful ingredient brand. This time it was smartphones rather than PCs, and we called our solution Spark. Powered by a hub on the Qualcomm website, we re-imagined the future of communication and technology with stories of inventors changing the world. We hired industry veterans from* USA Today *and* PC Magazine *to steer an editorial team, who developed branded content. It all seemed to spark a lot of interest.*

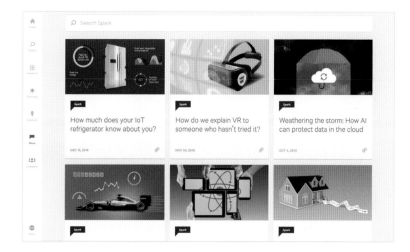

Above *Barneys New York zeroed in on the sort of journalism their audience wanted – and wanted from Barneys. The Window is an online lifestyle magazine-cum-ecommerce site that works well.*

side had been a low priority for them. Their task was to familiarize consumers with the underlying technology and establish Qualcomm as a powerful ingredient brand.

Spark was the result. By hiring industry veterans from *USA Today* and *PC Magazine* to steer a team of editorial staff, developing branded content on sites such as Mashable, exploring syndication opportunities, and using tools such as Stumbleupon, Spark focused on generating and distributing highly practical, interesting and engaging content to early adopters and tech-savvy users – all of which was clearly attributable to Qualcomm.

News is a resource that's freely available – but its over-availability creates an opportunity for curation. Let's aggregate and assemble the news that will appeal to our audience and distribute it to them as packaged content.

This is a space where success and failure are still being tested out. Big ambitions have bitten the dust.

Consider GE, which sought to become a major news provider with properties such as "Pressing" ("raising the national conversation, right, left, center") and "Mid-Market" ("the goal is, this is someone's Monday morning destination"). Neither has survived. While its GE Reports site continues to produce excellent feature-style journalism that relates to its business, in these two they misread their audience. They aimed to fill what seemed to be a news void, but it was one that readers did not care to see filled – at least by GE.

Practical content can become activist: it provides platforms for empowerment. It does not just provide contextual information but also a sense of inspiration within a community as well. This is exactly what our client American Express seeks to do with its OPEN Forum.

Practical content can also be incredibly useful, especially for an audience at the start of a steep learning curve, such as new mothers. What do contractions feel like? How accurate are ultrasounds? What music is best for my baby? These are the questions – among many, many others – that run through a woman's mind moments after finding out she's pregnant. And it's not just the next nine months that makes her anxious – it's the next few years!

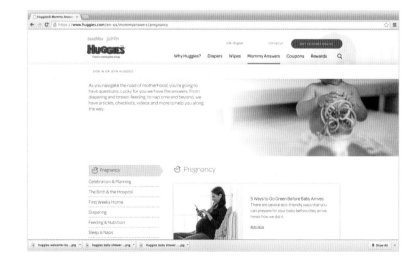

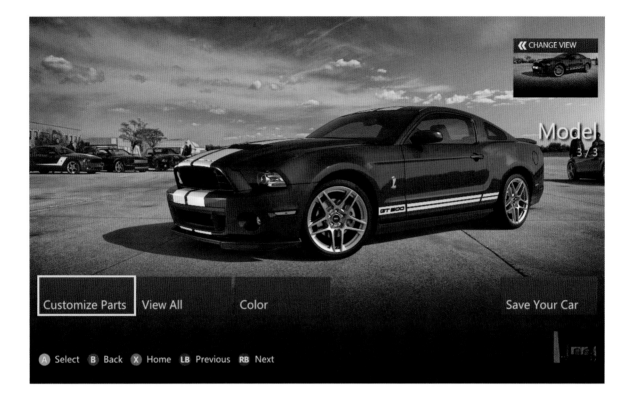

Above *Ford invites customers to dream up their perfect Mustang – and build it too. Customers use its website or mobile apps to configure a bespoke vehicle.*

A final play, not as broad but still capable of scale within a defined audience of higher value customers, pushes empowerment into the physical space: the content becomes a utility. Yes, tools are also content. This is where digital design most influences experience.

How, for instance, to design a tool which enables you to configure a vehicle?

Or to guide you through your menu choices.

In essence, digital enables companies to contextualize their products and services through information at greater scale than ever before.

It all starts with an idea. But an idea today has no wings unless it explores some of these digital dimensions. At its best it will play freely among them.

When we created a program for Coke Zero in the US, the idea was that you wouldn't know it until you tried it. Armed with the research-driven knowledge that 85 per cent of Millennials had never tried the Coke variant, but knowing that half of them would become monthly drinkers once they did, we deployed digital technology in some rather impractical places to achieve some very practical results. A billboard that dispensed the drink, a TV commercial which viewers could Shazam for a sample, and other "drinkable advertising" got people trying and then buying Coke Zero.

Above *For Coke Zero we asked ourselves, why imagine the taste when you can try it for yourself? So we created the first drinkable advertising campaign, offering free samples through unexpected channels – including a twist on the classic billboard.*

Opposite bottom *The tool can be an object in itself. Ogilvy & Mather were asked to help Vittel publicize the case for regular hydration. Proving that smart technology doesn't always require the internet to power it, we put a twist on the everyday bottle top by integrating a simple mechanical timer into the cap itself. Turn the cap at the start of the day and at regular intervals a little flag would pop up to alert you to take a sip.*

Organizing for the Content

So does King Content have feet of clay? Not if it looks to what it can do at its best: to arouse, to entrance, to enable and to empower.

But there is one caveat. How to organize for it?

As it happens, that's not as easy as it sounds. Not only do we need to help brands and media partners work together in new ways, we ourselves in the advertising industry needed to find new structures. With anything new and complicated, it is easy to get caught up in the planning and strategy. Those elements are crucial, but when it comes to any kind of creative work, what matters in the end is the doing.

I was once asked to paint a slogan on a slogan wall at one of our offices in China on the subject of strategy. Over-sated with several days of strategic discourse, I wrote the words "superior execution is the highest form of strategy". It was greeted with a certain surprise.

But never is that truer than in the case of content.

And the battleground here is the Content Studio.

Of course, they are not universally called that. There are kitchens, centres, newsrooms, hubs, shops, story labs – you name it.

But let's call them Content Studios. By the beginning of 2016, Ogilvy & Mather were operating some 126 of these for our clients around the world. And the demand is increasing exponentially.

CONTENT STUDIO: SEVEN BASIC APPROACHES

What do they do? There are seven basic approaches:

Right Content Studios need to do seven basic things well: foster community, develop an editorial lens, forge partnerships, be both curators and collaborators, act in real-time, be ready to manage crises and activate in a responsive, always-on manner.

Not every studio performs the same functions. And, in some, particular functions are more important than others.

But in doing these things any Content Studio worth investing in has to justify itself in two ways.

1. It has to have as its central guiding purpose the creation of a Content Calendar. It is this calendar which defines the whole rhythm of the studio. The inventor Robin Sloan borrowed a term from economics, and did us all a favour when he popularized the idea of "stock and flow". Stock is the bedrock, what you have to have all the time. But then:

> Flow is the feed. It's the posts and the tweets. It's the stream of daily and sub-daily updates that remind people you exist. It's the content you produce that's as interesting in two months (or two years) as it is today.[3]

In fact, our social managers prefer to subdivide "stock" between "hero" content, planned annually and produced quarterly; and "proactive content", planned weekly and produced weekly. All the rest is real time.

So a perfect Content Studio's flow looks like the diagram opposite.

2. It has to be dedicated to a second big purpose, which is to measure how effective all this is, and then not just measure but optimize.

Initially it worried me that there were no tools available for assessing the effectiveness of different types of content. But then a brilliant young analyst in our New York team developed a system that can sort pieces of content by their performance against different metrics, including those that link directly to sales. She called it "Pulse".

HOW THE CONTENT STUDIO WORKS

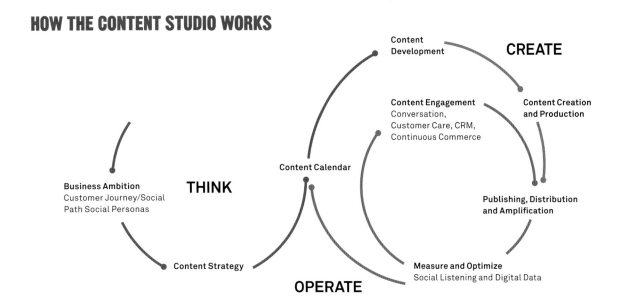

Above *The workflow that lies behing the Content Studio, where the client's content strategy comes alive as a content calendar. It doesn't just happen: there has to be an engine that drives the development, distribution, and effectiveness. It's the same in principle whether you are Mastercard, with an audience of 30 million people a week across its digital and social properties, or a local restaurant chain, drumming up a customer base in the hundreds. The mantra is "think, create, operate".*

At the end of the day, it's keeping a finger on the pulse like this that holds King Content true to his promise.

I do firmly believe in that promise. The concept of brands and agencies as publishers marks the first real change in our business since the invention of the commission system in the coffee houses of eighteenth-century London. It anticipates the final demise of that commission system, even if the industry is still at a very early stage of feeling comfortable with "content".

8 tips for content

1. Don't try to be a mainstream news provider.

2. Don't compromise on quality: journalism is a craft not a commodity.

3. Scale! Be willing to promote your content, to make sure it interrupts the interruptions. Don't be foolishly purist and expect you can just build it and they will come.

4. Recognize that you need an engine to drive it.

5. Don't forget why you are doing it. You are creating your own "walled garden" which people have to enjoy. Enjoyment has been proven to enhance not impede information processing.

6. Make it sticky: link a lot; balance stock and flow; create series and sequences; build loops.

7. Don't forget why you are doing it: who is the brand custodian and where is the brand conscience?

8. Personalize. And use higher cost content as a reward for loyalty.

CADBURY

One of the defining images of the digital age is a gorilla hammering drumsticks. How did that happen? Cadbury Dairy Milk's 2007/08 marketing programme has assumed mythical status. The actual history is sometimes difficult to disentangle.

It began in a dire period for the brand: a salmonella scare leading to a recall of over a billion chocolate bars. And, generally, this was a brand which no longer enjoyed universal brand preference. It was highly polarized by age. Anyone over 35 considered it to be the best chocolate, and those under 35 did not.

So a brief went out with two components: to "get the love back", and at the same time, to remind younger consumers, in particular, that Cadbury chocolate is actually made with milk. There was a codicil given by the new Marketing Director, Phil Rumbol, who was insistent that the advertising should be as enjoyable to watch as it is to consume the product. What an exciting brief for an agency.

Unfortunately, great briefs are never easy, especially if you sometimes know too much. The incumbent agency could not crack it. Phil gave the brief to Fallon, went to Australia on a business trip, and came back a week later to find there was a small raft of work to see.

There was one campaign idea out of them which seemed to answer the second part of the brief: Glass

Above *Like a disappointing movie sequel, a second film,* Trucks, *didn't live up to expectations. It lacked the sheer joy and exuberance of the bar set by* Gorilla. *Glass and a Half Full productions was looking half empty, not half full.*

and a Half Full productions, a flexible enough device for understanding milk content, and with that were four executions, among them *Gorilla*.

It was the very antithesis of linear, persuasive advertising, and the reactions up the line in Cadbury were of bemusement not amusement. Phil recalls it was something like: "Let's get this right: You want to make an advert two times longer than a normal ad. It's got no chocolate in it, and it's got no message. Are you mad?"

What follows was a masterful exercise in stakeholder management. Phil persuaded his superiors at least to make the ad. Then it was shown to the senior management team, one of whom said: "You are never showing that ad."

Phil then requested, "Can I ask for one last favour? Please take it home, watch it with your family over the weekend and see how they react." Of course, on the Monday the positive calls came in – yes, it had made them smile.

Then came the meeting with Todd Stitzer, the CEO. Again, the blanket refusal. In this case, the marketing team answered the CEO with the standard defence: research. They did their research pre-tests. The results were not promising. It "could be for any brand", it "didn't tell you anything new about the brand". Of course, these were the answers to the wrong questions. The question which the "old model" research should have asked was "does this, aspirationally, feel like something Cadbury Dairy Milk would do?". By then

Above *Cadbury's famous* Gorilla *commercial featured Phil Collins' track* 'In the Air Tonight', *which added an air of drama before the sticks came crashing down. He had been waiting for this moment, and it showed.*

the CMO was onside, and the 10 or 20 last pretests of Cadbury ads, when plotted from worst to best on the standard nine box matrix, had provided some permission to believe that this one was relatively "airable".

At the end of the day, an edit of respondents' reactions on video, moving from smiles to big, big smiles was what won the day. It was aired on 31 August 2007.

The impact was instantaneous. YouTube and Twitter were barely a year old, but the views and posts became an avalanche. With them came the spoofs – the tribute of the digital audience to something which engages them. So what was the idea?

It's been constructed in Cadbury culture as being about "joy". A latter-day Phil in Cadbury, Phil Chapman, was one of the most articulate explainers of this kind of joy: a world away from "happiness", something vital and visceral; in the case of *Gorilla* something that even comes close to anger, letting feelings out of the system. Defining the idea is important. Cadbury, during the time between the two Phils took something of a wrong turn into a zone which was called joy (Joyville) but which was actually joyless. And Glass and a Half Full's immediate sequel to *Gorilla, Trucks* is a laborious sequence of airport trucks "fooling around" where joy seems almost completely

Above *And with a bold and beautiful vibrato – the joy was back! Triplets evoked the essence of Gorilla, its indulgent irreverence, by way of three unborn babies singing acapella in their contented mother's womb.*

absent. Much, much later I remember Phil and his boss, Cadbury President Bharat Puri, saying of a South African script featuring a woman pregnant with triplets, as he signed off on it, " with joy, you have to sniff it". A lot has to do with charm, and craft plays a role here. The Italian Art Director Juan Cabral, who made *Gorilla*, made it look wonderful – even adding the gold tooth which gives his scowl so much charm when the camera moves too close to him.

Back in 2007/08, the sales decline went into reverse, and Cadbury posted a 5 per cent increase in revenue. Todd Stitzer stood up at an analyst's presentation in early 2008 to talk about the teamwork. He did it with a reasonably straight face.

8 CREATIVITY IN THE DIGITAL AGE

"GIVE ME GOLD"

David Ogilvy both managed his agency and acted as its creative director; and there have been others like him. But if you're a "normal" adman or woman working up the ladder by handling clients and running offices, you need a creative partner.

I was lucky to have Tham Khai Meng as mine. A charming, quiet and understated Singaporean who was passionately obsessed by the quality of the work, he had led our Asian network, creatively predominant, for 11 years. So when I asked him over dinner in the unlikely venue of the Andaz restaurant in Lahore, kebabs in front of us, and the lowering mass of the Badshahi Masjid behind, to join me in New York, I had three fears.

The first was that I was deliberately flouting the conventional wisdom that we needed a big-ticket name. Or, worse, that an ethnic Chinese just would never pass muster in New York. And the third was that he would not come. But I knew that he was the one.

He came. We then shared a desk in New York, a completely alien notion there, but one which demonstrated that we could not be divided, and that our agenda was common.

In June 2008, we inherited a very average performance, winning some – but not many – awards at the Cannes Festival of Creativity. Ogilvy & Mather languished in the third division, and had done for years because, for many good reasons, award-winning creativity had not been an agency priority for some time. At one point Khai leaned towards my half of the table and said: "I hate it. I can't work in a place that meekly accepts being slightly above average."

So we agreed to set out to become number one – "Network of the Year". We set five years as the time frame; we created a programme throughout the agency; we treated it like a combination of a military mission and a political campaign. The cry went out: "Give me Gold". It seemed crazy and impossible, but rather to our surprise, we achieved in it in two years.

A central part of this has been the Cadre system, bringing together our best creative people once a year to talk about and improve the work. They're only invited if their offices are admitted to the Cadre; and that is calculated on points earned from awards won. We try to meet in interesting places. I have addressed the Cadre from a baroque pulpit in Cuzco, Peru, a tent in the Maasai Mara, Kenya, and a hotel saloon in Inverlochy, Scotland.

Above *The desk I shared with Khai at Ogilvy's global headquarters in Manhattan: a common work surface for a shared ambition – that we should strive for creative excellence and the utmost effectiveness.*

Above *Developing advertising that challenges the creative convention is the work of artists, and a skill we've continually refined. When Khai declared, "Give me gold!", our creative teams across the world responded with work that set a higher bar.*

Below *David was sometimes enamoured and often sceptical of advertising awards, and rightly so. In the years since his wins creative award shows have become big business.*

Creative awards are a dangerous thing in our business. They only represent excellence inasmuch as the juries who decide them can recognize it, or, in the politics that go with jury service, are prepared to reward it. David Ogilvy did not feel comfortable with them, although he was not alone in enjoying the lustre they brought.

But by the early part of this century, three things had changed since he received the Clio shown in this picture.

First, the clients themselves had started attending Cannes in droves, attracted in a brilliantly successful strategy by the owners. It started with Procter & Gamble; and then the rest followed. For those clients, it became of a way of improving their own creativity, which in turn helped them achieve competitive advantage.

Individual clients come and go, but collectively they changed Cannes from something self-indulgent into something more missionary, concerned with the value of creativity in business. The categories for entry expanded into effectiveness, technology and other disciplines beyond advertising. And, of course, there's nothing a client who attends Cannes likes more than to mount the stage in the Palais, or feel their choice of agency vindicated by its performance there.

Secondly, the economic justification – to us at least – had become very clear. This is a business where success is directly related to the extent to which one's share of the best creative talent is disproportionately large, and Cannes is where you find them. I don't think there is any other business except for professional football where this is the case. Cannes provides a perfect recruitment mechanism. The stars in our business want to work in a company that takes creativity seriously, and where winning is seen as core to the purpose, not as an expendable luxury.

Thirdly, the arrival of the big holding companies – and the institution of a Holding Company of the Year award – meant the competition was featured in their annual reports. Performance was used by financial analysts hunting for any alchemical symptoms which might indicate underlying strength or weakness. All this happened at a time when bloggers were being critical of BDAs (Big Dumb Agencies), and the business model had to show itself to be as sexy as it was efficient.

So it was that when the 100th anniversary of David's birth had to be celebrated, we decided to take it (against the conventional wisdom) to Cannes. On 23 June 2011, people woke up to a gigantic red carpet spanning the entire length of the Croisette, which we subsequently cut up into small pieces and turned into David Ogilvy Red Carpet insoles, and used as a New Year's direct-mail piece sent to clients and friends. That year, we came second.

By mid-afternoon of 23 June 2012, the following year, it became clear that we were edging towards victory. A congratulatory text from my counterpart Andrew Robertson of BBDO, a typically generous gesture, confirmed it: their tally of points was at that time more accurate than ours. A few hours later, our teams invaded the stage in triumph. Since then, we've won four times more. Of course, we will not win forever, and rightly so.

But wanting to win, and working to win, has become a part of Ogilvy & Mather's culture. It taught me that my biggest battle was against our size. Big we were, and dumb we would be unless we *behaved* as if we were small, as if every last prize mattered to us as an issue of life and death, because it

Below *The first time we de-camped to Cannes we proudly came second and cut up the red carpet as a celebratory direct mailshot. We won first place the following year.*

Above *Proof that agencies can be big without being dumb. The moment of victory is precious but fleeting; the greater value comes from the culture that winning creates.*

"Big we were, and dumb we would be unless we behaved as if we were small"

reflected fundamentally on our worth as creators and as craftspeople.

And we never pursued Cannes in isolation. It was always twinned with winning the Effies, which measure pure effectiveness.

However, the acme of success must be to win both a Grand Prix at Cannes and a Grand Effie. This happened for the first time with our film *Evolution* for Dove, in 2007 (see Hall of Fame case, pages 44–45).

ART OR SCIENCE?

David did not like the word "creativity". He described it in *Ogilvy on Advertising* as "hideous". Rather, he saw himself in the business of inventing ideas.

I think this repugnance for a word, which has, after all, become so widely accepted as a description of what entire industries do, came from a very visceral reaction to the over-statement of those who have argued – then and now – that advertising is exclusively an art and not a science. This precious and self-indulgent mindset led to work which, while pretty and interesting and entertaining, just does not sell.

David was first and foremost a salesman. "We sell or else" was his motto; and, in origin at least, his salesmanship was founded on "scientific" principles, not least his admiration of the adman Claude Hopkins whose book *Scientific Advertising* (1923) still has its admirers.

The former advertising planner Paul Feldwick has written an original and

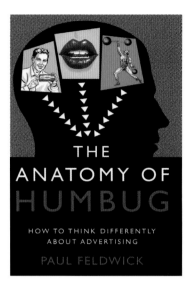

Above *In a unique take, Paul Feldwick turned his strategic planning sensibilities to the subject of how advertising works. Capturing a hundred years of ideas on the art vs science of advertising, the debate will surely run for at least another century.*

Above *Anacin pioneered competitive advertising, pitching itself to the headache sufferer as superior and different from the rest. In a US commercial from the 1940s, a confident spokesperson, talking straight to camera, directly compared the brand to Aspirin with Bufferin, which itself claimed to be twice as fast as Aspirin. To raise the stakes, he pronounced Anacin the "fast, fast, fast" remedy and likened it to a doctor's prescription – containing unique ingredients designed to remedy a headache without the typical side effects. To hammer the point home, an endorsement – that three out of four doctors recommend it. In fact, the main ingredient was just plain old Aspirin.*

intelligent history of the theories of advertising, *The Anatomy of Humbug* (2015). It is one of a kind, and it lays out the twists and turns of this debate over time. It has been an epic struggle between art and science.

On the side of art are Bill Bernbach and Charles Saatchi; and on the other side are the forces of science, where Claud Hopkins' mantle was inherited by Rosser Reeves and David Ogilvy.

This – the "great debate" of our business – is never ending but is now cast in a new light as we become more familiar with the digital age.

The sub-plot, though, has always been more subtle, and revolves around whether creativity is most effective as an appeal to reason or to emotion.

The apostles of reason argue that the fundamental purpose of advertising is to sell. Reeves' famous Anacin commercial is perhaps the best illustration of this.

Those of emotion suggest that its role in consumer behaviour is paramount. Emotions account for brand preference, they argue, and trot out fMRI studies and likeability measures to prove the point.

Then we saw over-emotional enthusiasts such as Kevin Roberts with his simple slogan of "love marks" ranged against the Australian academic Byron Sharp who believes that love is missing the point. We use our mammalian brain to decide, and it rewards simplicity and ease of remembering. It's an emotional decision but based on the simplest front-of-mind cues, nothing else. The fact that there are extremes in a debate is best adduced by the acerbic rhetoric as they slog about each other.

Things start to become more interesting when we add in the very real dynamic of getting advertising approved. For many clients, approving an emotive piece of creativity can be a frightening proposition. It is difficult to judge. It requires an emotional response in return. Are you prepared to lay bare your soul in discussing it; how do you know it will work? And, of course, how can you defend it within your organization to those who are even more proof-demanding than you are?

So, a third level of debate opens up, the sub-sub-plot. How do you measure creativity?

Of course, the scientists lean towards quantitative testing; and not just post-testing (which even artists might find difficult to argue with), but pre-testing. And, because no one will want to take the risk of spending millions of dollars in TV production before seeing those pre-test results, pre-testing with very inadequate stimulus material.

How can you hope to portray emotion in an animatic, or even a photomatic or stealomatic? They are crude proxies for film, but pre-tests thrive because they seem to provide certainty. I have known clients wait for a one-line email with the EI (a common testing measure) score in it, which would determine "go" or "no go".

Of course, the artists (and the pre-test companies) point out the absurdity of this, and explain that a pre-test should be used diagnostically and not as surrogate decision-maker. But we all know that organizational politics mean that a red preview from Millward Brown renders a decision to air the copy politically very dangerous. And that is despite the fact that some highly successful pieces of TV advertising have run regardless of the test results, based on just an intuitive decision, of which the re-launch of Old Spice was a defining example of the digital age (see Hall of Fame case, pages 104–105).

In the early 2000s, something funny happened: science came to the aid of art. The "Ah-ha" moment for me was in the unlikely venue of Changchun, in North Eastern China, in 2008. With temperatures of –20°C (–4°F), our planners were less than impressed by my choice of venue (chosen to emphasize all that we still needed to learn, because Changchun was the least well known of the planned cities of the twentieth century, as the sometime capital of the notorious Puppet Empire of Manchukuo). We had invited Dr Robert Heath, Professor of Advertising Theory at the University of Bath; and he gave a brilliant exposé of the newly mined and startling implications of neuroscience for market research.

Simply put, neural scanning demonstrates that brand preference has a physical basis. Just look at the image below of the brain, in a blind and branded test of Coca-Cola. The glowing zones which are being stimulated by brand Coke relate to liking and memory.

What Heath had succeeded in doing was to show how emotional content in advertising is often more powerful than rational messages; the latter can be easily filtered out by the brain, while the former can be processed even at low levels of attention, and then act as a kind of "gatekeeper" to the rational decision which all marketers yearn for. In other words, it may be easier to get positive test results or research validation for those rational campaigns that are solely product based, but the risk is that they will "pass like ships in the night". Logic persuades; but only emotions motivate. If people *want* to use your brand, they will find a logical rationale themselves – but the wanting comes first.

"For many clients, approving an emotive piece of creativity can be a frightening proposition."

Below *A neural brain scan shows how the brain responds differently to the Coke brand compared to its taste. In the blind test (top), parts of the brain triggered by taste are active. But introduce the Coke brand (bottom), with its imagery and associations, and areas relating to memory and enjoyment are illuminated.*

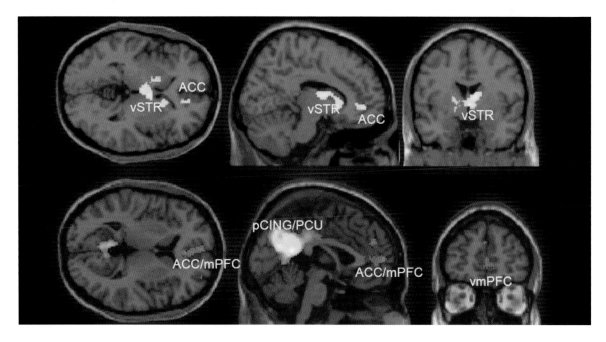

OLD SPICE

Like many others, my first tentative experience with aftershave was with Old Spice. The Beaujolais Nouveau of colognes, it was satisfying but shallow – a confection of nutmeg, star anise and citrus at the top of its perfume pyramid, with deeper, masculine notes below.

Launched in 1938, by the Shulton Company, it really had become grandpa's brand – the musk had become musty. It was fuddy-duddy and the very definition of uncool, a half-a-billion dollar business highly concentrated in a big and still-profitable foot-print. Then the axe fell: the relaunch by Unilever of a demographically interesting range of men's toiletries which had previously just jogged along. It was all the more dangerous because Axe had launched in the US a few years earlier. Axe's weapon was the oldest known – sex – and the Axe effect depositioned Old Spice even more. The Axe user became more attractive to women, as simple as that.

Above *The first attempt to refresh Old Spice looks a bit sour today. Although an important part of the journey, the Bruce Campbell campaign had the irreverence but not the style and demographic insight of the work that followed.*

By 2006, things looked grim: Old Spice needed a better strategy and a change of agency. In this case it worked – after a while. Weiden & Kennedy Portland started by immersing themselves in the history of the brand, and its cultural rating in a way which would have won the plaudits of the cultural strategists. They spent two days combing through the archives to under-stand the history. The result? A strategic refocusing of Old Spice from "old" to "experienced". We're not your grandfather; we're your elder brother. Or, as it was expressed, "experience is everything". It doesn't appear in case histories, and not many people remember the Bruce Campbell commercial which launched it. He strides around a wood-panelled library. It wasn't his fault, but my goodness it seems laboured to me now. They were meant to communicate a sense of old-fashioned charming innuendo. And this reframing was aimed at teens and twenties consumers.

But in 2009 something else happened in the marketplace which caused alarm, and I was to observe it from the other side. It became apparent that Unilever was about to launch Dove Men +Care, the male extension of its female beauty brand. In fact, we were developing a positioning around men who were comfortable in their own skin. We had a Super Bowl film about to go into production, the apex of a socially designed program built around the microsite dovemencare.com, and aimed at evoking consumers' unsung moments of manhood.

In the meantime, the client structure changed at Old Spice. P&G had acquired Gillette in 2005, and had run it as a standalone unit. But in 2009, a new male grooming unit was formed in Cincinnati, incorporating both the Gillette and P&G brands. One of the Gillette clients assigned to it was Rishi Dhingra. In the frenzied period before the anticipated Dove launch, agencies were briefed afresh. Rishi recalls that he told them, "We will give you the guardrails, but within that you have freedom". That was a very un-P&G way of doing things, and indeed was the beginnings of an Old Spice exceptionalism which allowed it to be highly experimental, to use phrases like "ridiculously masculine" to complement the official strategy speak of "help young men navigate to the stages of manhood". Ideation took place at a very rapid pace – the agency was adamant that it would not give a predictable solution. Throughout the whole process, they pushed back against any effort to control, over-rationalize, and in Rishi they had an enlightened client who empathized with them. Out came Isaiah Amir Mustafa, an NFL player and small-time actor, but an inspirational piece of casting, to bring to life the idea: "The man your man could smell like". The first television commercial was beautifully shot by director Tom Kuntz. It was a leap of faith. It had to be – the agency had insisted on a pre-nuptial which broke the

Above *Old Spice's The Man Your Man Could Smell Like campaign featuring Isaiah Mustafa cleverly played on commonly felt notions of desire, pride, jealousy and masculinity – all in a uniquely quirky way – to take a swing at Axe. It worked.*

P&G rule that all advertising would be susceptible to pre-testing. As Rishi says, "the true test was when the consumer reacted to it", which they did in their millions. It's probably the feeling of attractive rebelliousness which makes Mustafa so effective. But also the strategic thought behind him, which was that 60 per cent of men's body wash is bought by women. By saying as he did "look at your man, now back to me", he simulated – and created – a conversation between men and women.

By July 2010, with an eye still on Dove, the campaign changed into a more directly social gear. Mustafa filmed the so-called Response Campaign in two-and-a-half days, recording 186 personalized messages to Old Spice fans on Facebook, Twitter and YouTube. In 24 hours, with 6 million views, it became one of the most popular interactive campaigns in history, winning the online buzz war (capturing 76 per cent of it, in fact).

And the upshot? Dove Men +Care still established itself in the contested male grooming market, but Old Spice transformed its brand equity and returned to volume growth in its home markets, then set about a programme of global expansion. By the time it reached India two years later, pre-nuptial had been all but forgotten. The empire had fought back and pretests were the order of the day again. But when it tested with young Indian men it was a top scoring ad. Rishi believes that they had seen the US versions on the internet and were predisposed to like them.

Above *Visiting Changchun, one of the world's lesser known planned cities, with the late Tim Broadbent. Tim was a friend and ally in the pursuit of advertising effectiveness and the industry is indebted to his mastery of research – not least his warning that the stories we tell ourselves (and the market researchers) are not always to be believed.*

As the late Tim Broadbent, to whom we at Ogilvy & Mather owe so much of our own thinking on this subject, wrote:

> Mostly what happens is that we want something, and then we come up with a rationale to justify why we want it. The justification is not the same as the motivation, although conventional market research can confuse the two.[1]

So we learn about brands without being consciously aware that we are learning, which is why a narrow reliance on specifics such as the consumer recall of a selling point or a key visual contained in a pre-test misses the point. It is based on psychological models which long precede the digital age.

However, it is interesting to note that attempts by Heath and others to create a perfect pre-test have not met with great commercial success. Maybe the answer just lies in more intelligent use of the old studies?

Shortly after, the definitive proof emerged that emotive campaigns were twice as profitable as rational campaigns. It came to us courtesy of the study, "Marketing in the Era of Accountability" (2007). This should be on every student's digital bookshelf. Unfortunately, it languishes too much in the WARC archives, while the fruitless debate as to whether we are artists or scientists rages on.

Time out, please.

The answer is that we are both.

The science of advertising works because of the art of advertising.

Binet and Field show, definitively in a study of 880 campaigns, that it is *creative* campaigns that outsell, on every business metric.[2]

Of course, these findings circle back beautifully to the issue of creative awards. In Cannes, as a jury you are inclined to award creative campaigns. In so doing, Tim pointed out, "juries have been criticized – but their instincts are sound: …emotive campaigns are much more likely to strengthen the brand. They do better for the client. They deserve to win". Not only that, but, in the digital age, their fame is amplified as a result of social buzz, creating a positive cycle of advocacy and excitement.

In a study of Cannes award winners, their campaigns were shown to be 11 times more effective than work that had not been awarded.

Back to David Ogilvy. His first work in advertising was not to write an ad at all but to perform a consulting project. The report he generated is interesting for the pungency of its conclusions, so trenchant indeed that they resulted in Mather and Crowther being fired from the business (the famous work which later emerged came after a re-hiring). However uncomfortable the findings might have been to the client, they are rooted in observation, in evidence, in hypothesis – all the techniques which a little later led to David working for George Gallup as a researcher.

But, 25 years later, in 1955, it was the same Ogilvy who attacked the "hard facts" school of his friend and rival, Rosser Reeves, the founder of Ted Bates, in a famous speech in Chicago[3], and laid out a manifesto for brand image advertising. Suddenly he was joining the debate of what creativity is, and what it is for, from, apparently, the opposite end of the spectrum.

Or course, in reality there was nothing contradictory in his evolved position. It simply reflects the enduring dualism about creativity, that it is neither purely an art form whose exact workings in the marketplace cannot be forensically proven nor is it a rigorous science susceptible to explanation only by rules and proof through numbers.

At the end of Paul Feldwick's book, he poses an (un-answered) question about how the Digital Revolution affects the sorts of debates that have characterized advertising's past.

I think the effect is clear already. It is about the confirmation that dualism is not a "benign conspiracy", as Heath describes it, but is a far more substantive and holistic convergence of the two.

At its root, digital media tends to be processed in a high-attention mode. So for agencies who do take an integrated approach, and who think of digital not as something apart but as just a part of advertising, the complementarity of artistic, emotional messaging with scientific, rational arguments starts to become real.

David Ogilvy was, of course, at home with Direct Response – "his first and last love", as much as he was an inventor of "brand image". The digital age has a chance of demonstrating that there is no inconsistency between the two schools – unless there are other issues of politics, prejudices and preference which intervene.

I find it a pleasing irony that it is a binary system that is leading to a communications world which is more unitary than ever before.

PERVASIVE CREATIVITY

The "great fragmentation" both disfavours and favours creativity.

At its worst, it simply diminishes creative impact by allowing the parts – multifarious expressions in different media – to go their own way at the expense of the whole. Creative fragmentation follows on from industry fragmentation as a host of players and partners each struggle to find their own place in the sun.

But at its best, it reaches out into the world in ways that previously would have scarcely been imagined.

> "This is creativity which pervades the world, not recognizing any barriers, divisions or silos."

Right *David Ogilvy's "The Theory and Practice of Selling the AGA Cooker" is a masterpiece of direct marketing. Fifty years after its 1935 publication,* Fortune *magazine dubbed it the best sales manual ever written. It shows a keen knowledge of product and customer as well as the barriers and drivers to sale. David notes that, "The worst fault a salesman can commit is to be a bore," a peril he gives wide berth on every page of his entertaining manual. "The good salesman combines the tenacity of a bulldog with the manners of a spaniel," David writes. "If you have any charm, ooze it." Hunt this manual down online – it is easily found – and read it, even if you don't care in the slightest about cookery or appliances.*

When I asked Khai to provide an adjective to describe the newness of this creative opportunity, he went silent for a while, and then obliged with "pervasive". This is creativity which pervades the world, not recognizing any barriers, divisions or silos.

What I call "packaged" creativity, which delivers messages in neat bundles to interrupt your passive use of media, is essentially invasive. It seeks to intrude in defined spaces. It lobs carefully crafted missiles out into the world. But "pervasive" creativity spreads: it is essentially liquid. As Khai wrote:

> If you want a metaphor for Pervasive Creativity, think of water; it is both vital for life and unstoppable when in full flood. It flows through cracks too small to see. It's always flowing, moving, exploring, and getting into everything, never getting stuck. Pervasive creativity means having one's antennae tuned to channel MUSE, looking for inspiration in everything.[4]

In a sense, the digital age allows us to take mainstream something of the philosophy of graffiti. We can introduce messages in startling ways, just as an artist such as Banksy provokes by taking clean conventional messages in conventional contexts, and turning them on their head: "sorry, the lifestyle you ordered is out of stock".

Don't pre-select your silo!

Right *Banksy understands how to turn conventional formats, like a billboard, into an unlikely commentary on our lives. His lesson? Creativity doesn't care for pre-defined media plans.*

Right *Do you really want to wake up every morning and smell the bacon? The difference between pervasive and invasive is a narrow one.*

So, in the digital world, the demands on creativity to be excellent are greater than when it was only invasive. Sure, we can reach people when they are waking up in the morning, but can we do it in a way that is appreciated but at the same time surprising?

The boundary between creative and gimmicky is a narrow one here. One might think that Oscar Mayer overstepped it when it started with the thought: "What if smells could be digitized?" Nine months of research and development later, it resulted in a dedicated mobile alarm-clock app that wakes you to the sound of sizzling bacon with an accompanying bacon-aroma-emitting smartphone device.

The premium, then, is on inspirational thinkers, who can transcend the "bittiness" of the digital world, and then jolt us into seeing things differently, but without descending into silliness. Sadly they are scarce.

Right Raw: *pervasive creativity in Asia is a collection of striking everyday creativity, such as the type demonstrated by this man selling hand-decorated stuffed horses, found by street photographers along the roadsides and byways.*

Above *Coca-Cola showed that creativity can be just as fluid as a beverage with their Liquid And Linked concept of content excellence. The videos which articulate it were used internally, but are available on YouTube now.*

The good news is that pervasive creativity recognizes a reality of the world that advertising agencies had rarely been interested in – that consumers can also be highly creative. Some years ago, we collected examples of this in Asia, and published them in a book called *Raw* (2012).

So it's not now just a case that "the consumer is not a moron, she is your wife", but also of recognizing that she can be at least as creative as you are. Work which acknowledges this, and which allows that creativity to express itself, gains most from being pervasive. Now the consumer can even become a freelance copywriter.

Probably the manufacturer who best articulated for themselves the notion of "pervasive creativity" was Coca-Cola. They labelled it "liquid and linked". The concept of link expressed the belief that a media neutral idea, if sufficiently inspirational, could pervade but at the same time cohere: pervasive, but also cohesive.

So What is an Idea?

There is no doubt in my mind whatsoever that the digital age has hugely increased the importance of the idea in advertising, and yet the word is rarely given enough attention, let alone subjected to much analysis.

Ideas that "pass like ships in the night" were always to be dreaded; and "big" ideas sought for. But what makes an idea "big"? Why is that more important than ever now? And, indeed, what is an idea?

It is curious how infrequently the last question is answered, precisely, granted that this is meant to be a business fuelled by ideas.

One of my treasured advertising books is a dog-haired volume called *Practical Advertising* from 1909. It was published each year, in London, by our British antecedent, Mather & Crowther. It is their Mather in our name; and it was here that David Ogilvy came to work for his brother, Francis, in the 1930s.

One of the house ads in this book shows a client with a plump, well-fed face, in a winged collar, polka-dot tie and a pince-nez, scrutinizing a newspaper. The headline says, "Looking Twice". And the copy proceeds with a paragraph: "How often do you have to look twice before finding your advertisement? How many earned readers to you suppose will be equally diligent?"

How many indeed? And that, I suppose is a neat way of explaining why we need ideas. It's the ideas that make people notice things.

But have you ever been asked to define an idea? Please give yourself just 30 seconds – and pause without reading on.

Try it now, right now. So what *is* an idea? If you have pen and paper to hand, write your answer down.

It's not that easy, is it? And, strangely, not many advertising people have ever defined it very convincingly. Or, if they have, gone into print with it.

So we need to go to a philosopher to find the definition, not a blue-chip philosopher but a rambunctious, philandering, drunken, provocative

Right *Did you look twice? A reminder from 1909 and our predecessor agency Mather & Crowther, London, that an advert is only valuable if it attracts your attention.*

Looking Twice

How often do you have to look twice before finding your own announcement? How many casual readers, do you suppose, will be equally diligent?

℅ Even the best advertisement is the worst investment in the world—*until it is seen.*

℅ Mather and Crowther Service is the complete, practical, highly organised product of time, skill and vast experience. Avail yourself of that Service, and be your appropriation £100 or £100,000, your advertisements will be *seen—read—studied—remembered.*

℅ Considering we began this advertising business in 1850—considering we have been growing and developing ever since—considering our present equipment—considering our present output —and considering our methods—isn't it reasonable to suppose that *all other details* will be rightly handled too?

MATHER & CROWTHER SERVICE
10, 11, 12, 13, NEW BRIDGE STREET, LONDON, E.C.

Above *Arthur Koestler – philosopher, provocateur and proponent of the best definition of creativity I've heard. His interpretation acts as my lens when evaluating work.*

and wannabe philosopher: Arthur Koestler. He was a brilliant writer: *Darkness at Noon* (1940) is one of the best-ever written arguments against totalitarianism.

In his book on creativity, *The Act of Creation* (1964), Koestler defines an idea as "a bi-sociation of two previously unconnected thought matrices". It may not be great philosophy, but it's a great definition – perhaps for the very reason that he was a creative writer himself.

Let's paraphrase it as "an unexpected combination of two previously unconnected things".

I've always found that it helps to keep in mind this definition of an idea when looking at work. Quite simply, it helps one pick the stronger ideas from the weaker.

The more original, subtle, involving and intriguing the combination is, the more likely we are to notice it: the more it is a Big Idea.

Ideas are precious things, and in the digital world it is clear that it is strong ideas alone that will defeat the noise, the fragmentation and the clutter.

But ideas have different forms.

In fact, there is something akin to a hierarchy of ideas:

1. At the top, the *strategic* idea, where an idea about how a business should be positioned, defines a platform for a company or a brand.

2. Then there is the *campaign* idea: what is it that ties together all the creative manifestations of the brand?

3. And, finally, there are *executional* ideas, smaller ideas within the campaign that provide its substance.

Strategic ideas are longer term than campaign ideas. When I presented a new idea to Allianz, I was asked by the CEO how long I thought this idea would last. I said, "at least ten years". Campaigns are shorter: IBM wanted five years for its current platform.

In powerful strategic ideas there is usually a resolution of a tension of some kind; in campaigns the unexpected combinations are housed in a sequential framework; while executional ideas often draw their unexpectedness from how they are made or where they appear – like naughty children they can sometimes stray from the core idea, and need what can only be described as shepherding.

Ideas are dependent on execution: and in the interplay between the two lies a second cause of "bigness".

Give a weak idea to Alan Parker to film (if he would take it) and it will come out well. Give a strong idea to a hack director and it will come out poorly. I have always deployed – and trained my account people in – a simple matrix for assessing ideas, on the basis that some process might be better than none. It is very simple, but can be a lethally effective career builder!

While it's subjective, I would, for instance, rate the commercials that appeared on the Super Bowl in 2016 as shown below.

It's not just poor execution that can let down an idea, but it's also inconsistency in how the idea is executed. Quite rightly, one of the most awarded executions of the digital age is the Cannes Grand Prix Volvo film *The Epic Split* (2013) made by Forsman & Bodenfors featuring Jean-Claude Van Damme (see overleaf). Here is a strong idea: unexpected combination of *stability* and *movement*. The stakes were high, as was the showmanship, and in this it pulled the same levers as the famous Krazy Glue TV commercial of the 1980s. Both defied our expectations. But what is generally forgotten is that this execution was just part of a larger campaign. The other executions – a hamster steering a truck, Volvo's CEO supported by the truck's hook – have been forgotten. They were not expressing the same idea at all, nor were these ideas. They were stunts, not surprises.

There are two new roles that advertising ideas play in the digital age, which I don't believe they have played before.

First, they have become systems of management.

Amidst the chaos, they offer a frame of reference for all a brand's activities; a principled compass against which activities can be assessed, accepted or rejected; and a visual and physical housing for how the brand interacts with its consumer. This is an editorial role.

Second, they are connectors to other ideas, in other disciplines, which are also undergoing redefinition. Brian Collins, my former colleague who ran our Brand Integration Group at Ogilvy & Mather and now heads his own successful design agency, refers to "brand" as the promise, and to "design" as the performance, evidence of a promise kept. More than developing an identity or creating an advertisement, brands are a tool to shape business – not something to build to, but something to build from.

> "Ideas are precious things, and in the digital world it is clear that it is strong ideas alone that will defeat the noise, the fragmentation and the clutter."

IDEA VS. EXECUTION

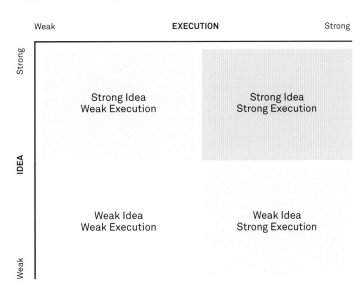

Right *Here's a simple matrix to help evaluate big ideas. Plot the strength of an idea along the x-axis against the quality of execution on the y-axis. Try it yourself with this year's Super Bowl commercials. Advertisers pay upwards of $2 million for a 30-second slot, so you would expect them all to be in the top right. You might be surprised! A slick production and a celebrity cannot make up for the absence of a good idea. Only the ads in the top right quadrant deserve to lift the trophy in my view.*

Right *Outside of the haulage industry, most people pay little attention to trucks. Yet over 85 million viewers watched Jean-Claude Van Damme perform "the most epic of splits" to demonstrate the precision and stability of Volvo's Dynamic Steering. The campaign included other executions with lesser known people showcasing innovations, such as a lead Volvo technician confident enough to risk his life to explain the ground clearance accuracy of a new Volvo truck. The other ads didn't get as much traction — not because they lacked Van Damme's celebrity, but because the core idea was less compelling.*

For Brian, brands live in four places — culture, environment, products, and the mind — and give us a blueprint to design systems that connect those spaces. The orientation is around the customer and their experience, so we put systems designers and engineers alongside the storytellers. And we use the brand to connect architecture, history, culture, product — so that when we get a brief from Hershey's to design Times Square billboard, we instead give them a chocolate factory tourist destination. (Actually, we even generate revenue as our "billboard" became the highest grossing retail space in New York City — a real return on brand value).

In surveys, clients consistently express disappointment about the degree to which their presence is fragmented. Mark Addicks, CMO of General Mills, has complained that marketers "are living in a world of chaos. They are desperate for order. They need a rulebook." Marketers, no longer able to keep track of customers across myriad touch points, find it increasingly difficult to get a single view of their customers.

The reason is that the digital world is intrinsically biased to the tactical, to ingenious small solutions, bubbling from the bottom up, but which do not really add up to anything.

The cure is simple. Find your own Big Idea. Then milk it mercilessly.

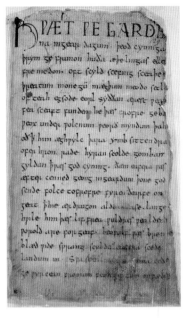

Above *Beowulf: an education in the art of storytelling.*

Telling Stories

If 30 years ago you had asked someone what Beowulf (whom I have already mentioned once) had to do with advertising you would have got a funny look and not much of an answer. Since then it seems that everyone has become a storyteller.

Just as ideas have become more important in the digital age, so, too, the power of storytelling has been re-discovered. It was always there, of course. But the internet puts the onus on the advertiser to attract users, and as advertising cannot rely solely on editorial content to bring them in, so it has become quite central.

It is stories that attract. And our stories have to be as good as, or better than, their stories.

Actually, the ingredients of a story have not changed much since Beowulf. There is a protagonist. The protagonist tries to achieve something. There is difficulty along the way. And then there is a resolution from which some lesson or meaning might be discerned. As my brilliant former client Javier Sanchez Lamelas of Coca-Cola says, "storytelling allows you to say things you cannot otherwise say".

In the digital age, our means to tell stories has expanded infinitely. Beowulf was recited; Oliver Twist was serialized in a weekly magazine. Our stories can be made available at any time, in any form, over any sequence. All they have to do is reward people.

How? Dopamine – the neurotransmitter we met in the last chapter that is released when we experience pleasure – makes us feel good. It is both a reward but it also anticipates reward, which is why we enjoy stories so much. We are just curious as to what is going to happen.

My colleague Khai has written memorably that, "Man is a storytelling ape. He understands the world through story, and this is the way to move him."

He points to the critical importance of what Coleridge called the "willing suspicion of disbelief" when we enter a story world. We accept the rules of

Right *Humans are hardwired to tell and hear stories. For more than 100,000 years we have used story structure to process the outside world.*

The original book club, circa 100,000 BC.

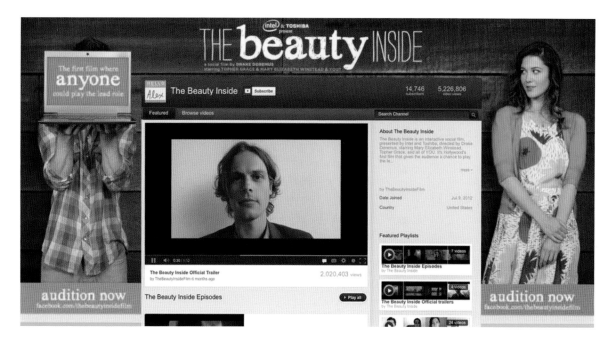

Above *"The Beauty Inside" was a pioneering social film series from Intel and Toshiba, which not only challenged the notion of identity, but also the boundaries of audience participation. Beyond commenting or voting, contributors could take on the lead role of Alex by uploading footage of themselves – becoming part of a series with over 70 million viewers. The brands? The decades old "Intel Inside" idea got a new lease of life and Toshiba's Ultrabook was a prominent feature in Alex's unusual story.*

"At its best, the art of storytelling is a foundation of advertising in the digital age."

the story, and seeing those rules play out enhances our pleasure. We expect a good story to have a beginning, a middle and an end. Great storytelling in advertising always does. We recognize similar plots – in Beowulf's case, it is the Quest. We meet similar archetypes such as the Shadow, the enemy.

One problem with storytelling in the digital age is that, at its extremes, it has become a fad. Every Tom, Dick or Harriet describes themself as a storyteller. As our friend Stefan Sagmeister pungently remarked at a festival dedicated to storytelling:

> I think all the storytellers are not storytellers. Recently, I read an interview with someone who designs roller coasters and he referred to himself as a "storyteller". "No, F***head, you are not a storyteller, you're a roller coaster designer.

Now some words of warning. It's easy for a pseudo-science to grow up around storytelling. Plots can become formulaic. I have heard market researchers trying to "guide" a story back to a formula, which there was no evidence that any consumer wanted. And archetype theory, while a helpful context for advertising, can also be dangerous. In recent years it has become popular to borrow from Joseph Campbell's model of archetypes and his seminal work, *The Hero with a Thousand Faces* (1949). Campbell spent a lifetime studying the legends, myths and folktales of societies across the world. Regardless of the culture, he identified common stories repeated time and again, and his 12 archetypes reflect these familiar characters. Whether Henry Higgins in *Pygmalion*, Gandalf in *Lord of the Rings*, or Obi-Wan Kenobi from *Star Wars*, the narrative of the Sage, who helps the hero along his journey, is all too familiar.

Brands must be storytellers, and the most engaging brand stories are often the simplest – both new and familiar at the same time – but archetypes are rarely the inspiration. By framing a brand rigidly as one archetype versus another, the practitioner narrows the scope of storytelling opportunity a brand might explore. Equally, blending elements from different archetypes – another common trick – can undermine the value of the analysis altogether. At their most useful, archetypes are a convenient starting point from which to build a more meaningful discussion about a brand's story, behaviour and role in the world. At worst, they are a passing fad concocted by brand charlatans playing the Outlaw role themselves.

However, they do appeal to clients who like rules, and who want the characters in their ads to look like archetypes. Too often I have heard clients say "but "X" is not behaving like "Y": a sure recipe for bad advertising. There may be rules in storytelling, but the more they are visible the less the story will engage.

At its best, the art of storytelling is a foundation of advertising in the digital age. And the people who tell these stories need to borrow from the ways of working of the arch-storytellers in Hollywood. A story, which is episodic, is written in a very different way to the 30-second ad.

Take for example "The Beauty Inside" (2012), a wonderful collaboration between Intel, Toshiba and the viewers who watched online over six, weekly episodes on Facebook. The story revolved around Alex, voiced by actor Topher Grace but played physically by a host of male and female actors, including some members of the audience. In a nod to Kafka, Alex wakes up every day as the same person but in a different body. He keeps a daily record of his unusual life via the video camera on his Toshiba Ultrabook, which he carries with him wherever he goes. This masterstroke meant *anyone* in the audience could upload a piece to camera (or webcam), which could then be interwoven into scenes within each episode. They are in the film.

And that, after all, was exactly how Beowulf came into being: not the work of one copywriter and one visualizer, but of many minds, hearts and tongues over time.

Sometimes the biggest ideas are found in the smallest of places. As small as an atom.

From awards alone, IBM should be recognized as one of the world's most innovative companies. Its employees have earned five Nobel Prizes, five National Medals of Technology, five Medals of Science, and a mere four Turing Awards. With a record-breaking count of 6,478 patents at the end of 2012, IBM was the highest recipient of US patents that year, maintaining 20 years of leadership in the patent space. But the public aren't interested in patents and awards.

They are, however, increasingly interested in science and technology. In 2012, there was a surge in interest in science, stimulated by news from CERN on discovering a fundamental particle supporting Higgs boson and NASA's *Seven Minutes of Terror* video showcasing the Curiosity rover's landing.

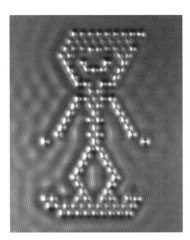

Above A Boy and his Atom *for IBM is evidence of just how innovative advertising can be. Armed with a small budget and IBM's Scanning Tunneling Electron Microscope, we used just a handful of atoms to make a unique short film. It was the first IBM video to earn a million views – literally overnight. Along with 30,000 YouTube likes, hundreds of articles, and a Cannes Lions award, it was shown at the TriBeCa film festival and features in the* Guinness Book of World Records *as the world's smallest stop-motion film. A big success!*

CNN and the *New York Times* both commented on the public's burgeoning love affair with science, and on Facebook the popularity of IFLScience blog shares indicated the emergence of science as part of mainstream culture.

IBM had a hidden gem that was ready-made for this audience: IBM can manipulate the atom. Few people know that IBM invented the Scanning Tunneling Electron Microscope, which enables the deliberate movement of single atoms, each a million times smaller than the width of human hair. Or that the company has lined up 12 atoms to create the world's smallest data storage module, a crucial future need, as big data gets even bigger and storage needs become paramount.

Rather than make another explainer video, we filmed *A Boy and his Atom*, an animated short film comprised of 242 still images and created using IBMs electron microscope and 65 carbon monoxide two-atom molecules.

So, After All, What Does Make Work Great?

A Big Idea, evidently.

An engaging story.

An appeal to the emotions as well as to reason.

And it seems to me there are other things.

In a word which I have usually resisted using, it must be "edgy". It's a word which best describes work after it's made, although it often appears in creative briefs as an aspiration. What then does it mean other than being the most general of aspirations?

Edgy to me means the opposite of average. It means being prepared to take a risk. I remember Steve Harrison, at Ogilvy & Mather Direct in

Below What do you get if you cross a polling firm with two art critics? Art that Americans want but art lovers hate. I am grateful to have been recommended Komar and Melamid's book – proof that a scientific approach to art results in banality rather than a masterpiece.

There was once, in India, an old woodcarver who was famous for carving elephants.
Other people carve elephants, too, of course, but the old man's elephants were, somehow, more galumphing
and trumpery. One day, a documentary film-crew was sent to interview him.
"What do you do," he was asked, "to make your elephants so perfect?" This was his reply:

1. "I take my little knife,"

2. "I take a block of wood,"

3. "... and I cut away everything that does not look like an elephant."

Above "How to Carve an Elephant" by Neil French and Tham Khai Meng – a quick guide to creativity that is even more relevant to the digital age than it was prior. Always strive for simplicity above all else.

London in the early 1990s, writing a brilliant brochure on it. My client at SC Johnson, Salman Amin, once showed me a book he keeps in his office to remind him of the danger of "average". It is *Painting By Numbers, Komar and Melamid's Scientific Guide to Art*.

"America's Most Wanted" painting is what happens when one follows the average way. It carries the illusion of safety, but it is in fact the most dangerous way of all. In the digital age, it simply consigns you to oblivion.

The other great requirement is simplicity. I once asked Neil French, very much a pre-digital creative, to design an in-house poster to encourage better creative ideas. It was not the easiest of briefs, but what he did is shown above: "How to Carve an Elephant".

The digital age has created complexity in a myriad of ways. I have noticed that not a few self-pronounced "digital" creatives are incurably complicated.

The best way to be noticed and listened to is to be, at the root of whatever you are doing, beautifully simple.

9 DATA: THE CURRENCY OF THE DIGITAL AGE

The first recorded reference to big data was buried in a 1997 paper, but the idea had been making the rounds at Silicon Graphics (SGI) in the mid 1990s. While big data isn't so recent as we'd like to believe, the practical use of big data has emerged only recently as a proliferation of data sources has become available.

We give off a constant stream of what my former colleague Dimitri Maex calls "digital exhaust". Consider this: I like a particular type of red socks. I buy them, and that decision generates data about my location, my preferences, my habits and my finances. Now data of that kind has been available for quite some time, but assembling it was difficult. Big data isn't, therefore, a new kind of data. Rather, it is a proliferation of data sources, both structured and unstructured, and the means to use them:

- **Structured data** – This is information stored with a high degree of organization. A database containing the inventory of a warehouse is structured data. So are the records of customers who bought a product at a certain time and by what payment means.

- **Unstructured data** – This refers to information that isn't organized in a readily machine-readable format. A blog post is unstructured data. So is your email inbox or your Facebook feed.

Since nearly every action today creates data, that data must be stored somewhere in order to be useful.

Enter "the Cloud". The Cloud is nothing more than rented storage and computing power – much as early computers used timesharing to apportion processor cycles to individual users. But while that was the rationing of a scarce resource, the Cloud fosters the efficient and cost-effective distribution of an abundant one. Cloud servers, run by companies big and small all over the world, democratize the world of big data by reducing the cost of data storage and analysis. Companies can build and host their applications in a public cloud, and add both data storage capacity and computing power with a credit card. Businesses like Netflix and Uber were built in the cloud, scaling from start-up to dominance as their data assets increased exponentially.

Abundant computing power means that algorithms can do more. A decade ago, a data scientist may have needed two days to analyze even a single stream of consumer data. He had to gather the data, clean the dataset, render it into structured data, and then run the algorithm. Confronted with such a burden, our data scientist was economical in his programing and in his choice of data. That can be done in hours – often less – today, but the principles remain: people still struggle with the fundamental questions of what data to analyze and why.

That's what's missing from those who have a vested interest in selling cloud-based products. They've romanced the Cloud to the point that it has started to seem to be an end in itself, rather than a means to something else. Cloud providers have engaged in vicious advertising wars, very much on the basis that "my cloud is better than your cloud".

But, of course, cloud technology has become a fungible commodity. Infrastructure as a Service (IaaS) and Software as a Service (SaaS) have both become commonplace. One has to look beyond to how and why they are used. For instance, the incorporation of SoftLayer into IBM in 2013 enabled it to compete with companies such as Amazon who were faster to the Cloud market. But how to differentiate the offering? That's where analytics came in. The distinguishing portions of IBM's offering are predictably rooted in the company's strengths in data analytics and business consulting.

Below *Working on the IBM Cloud makes it easier to glean more insight and boosts the industry-specific business impact of technology for IBM Cloud customers. IBM has a suite of analytics tools – many best in class – to get more out of the big data that a company might store in the cloud; a business installing the cloud will more likely find a manufacturing expert to talk to at IBM than at any competitor.*

Data is often presented as the currency of the digital age, or more aptly, as "the new oil" – a memorable phrase coined by data scientist Clive Humby back in 2006. So it is; but of course the role of data in the advertising business is hardly new. David Ogilvy loved direct response advertising for its rooting in data.

"For forty years," David wrote, "I have been a voice crying in the wilderness, trying to get my fellow advertising professionals to take direct response seriously. Direct response was my first love. And later, my secret weapon."

David's love notwithstanding, data never did give us the ability in itself to find the nirvana of perfect solutions. I remember well the advice I was given when joining Ogilvy & Mather Direct in London as its Managing Director from the data-illiterate world of traditional advertising. I was desperately nervous that a client would one day ask me what response rate I would expect from a direct mailing: "Just look them in the eye, and say, firmly, 4 per cent" was the advice I was given. (It worked, by the way.)

In the pre-internet world, the cost of data dramatically fell as a result of innovations in computing. It nonetheless remained an asset constrained by the natural limitations of its available sources, which were mainly confined to the result of one's own campaigns, even though they gave us a degree of precision we had never had before.

What the Digital Revolution has created is something radically different. Data has also become pervasive. This is what big data enthusiasts swoon over. With visibility into the entirety of the consumer journey, big data enthusiasts claim to be changing dramatically the lives of consumers. All that first party (or personal) data is going to lead us to a more customized, customer-centric world.

Actually, I don't much care for the term big data. As Dimitri says, it puts all the emphasis on the technology and not on the consumer experience. Big data has made things better for advertisers, but few consumers would say their lives have changed much as a result of it. We're focused on the data gathering and analysis instead of spending wisely on improving the consumer's life as a result of all that information.

Against the tide of (excusable if disingenuous) enthusiasm, one has to table a series of big data cautions.

The Big Data Cautions

1. There is what I call the "collection fallacy": the more data you collect, the more valuable it will be. Just keep on collecting! I see no evidence at all that this is the case. The "bigness" of big data fuels this belief. Even though brute-force algorithms can churn through vast data sets in record time, that doesn't mean the analysis they produce will make the slightest bit of difference. Just because you can collect data doesn't mean you should. Instead, as Dimitri says, "measure what you need to measure, not what you can measure. Only focus on the data that aligns with your goals." That's a decision you (and not your algorithm) will have to make.

> "Just because you can collect data doesn't mean you *should*."

VALUE SPECTRUM

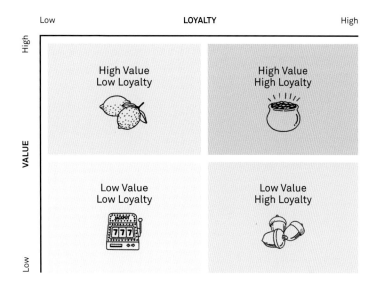

Low   **LOYALTY**   High

High

VALUE

Low

High Value
Low Loyalty

High Value
High Loyalty

Low Value
Low Loyalty

Low Value
High Loyalty

Above *A value spectrum analysis can show which kinds of customers are, as Dimitri Maex puts it, potential pots of gold to be found, jackpots to be gambled at, acorns to be nourished, or lemons to be ignored.*

2. There is a "utility deficit". The data you have is simply not used. Near-limitless cloud storage capacity means that if any part of a company produces data, there is an excellent chance that data is stored somewhere. What's holding companies back? In my humble view, it is a lack of understanding of the fundamentals of data science.

3. There is the "siloization" of big data. Silos are everywhere in business today. In agencies, the advertising team is separate from the direct marketers. The social media mavens don't talk to the PR team. Clients are the same way. One client, who shall remain nameless for obvious reasons, has one group of people decide on and assign creative work while another group is responsible for approving it! When people are siloed, they can't work together. When data is siloed, it can't work for you at all.

4. There is a "tolerance threshold". Quite simply, big data seems a very natural plaything for Big Brother. Advertisers have pledged to regulate themselves, but individuals are worried about their privacy. Big data has made credit fraud detection much more effective, and it has made significant gains in fighting global terrorism. Those advances make our world safer, but thanks to data breaches, revelations of government surveillance, and awareness of the value of personal data, we're all feeling rather more insecure as well. The more the boosters of big data talk about how unfettered data flow will make our lives better, the more we recoil from the invasiveness we must sign up to for that utopian vision to come true.

I think the time has come to think not big, but small. What is it within the enabling power of big data that is small enough to be beautiful?

Let's call it the Really Useful Data Resolution. To follow through on it, you need to combine a wide-angle lens (to see the whole business landscape) with a narrow depth of field (to see precisely what the data can practically do). But the secret is to start problem first, not data first.

DATA SETS COMPRISING A SINGLE ENTERPRISE POINT OF VIEW

• Search intent modelling: specialist firms help marketers understand keyword clusters as well as provide insight into consumer thought processes.

• Social listening: while less automated (for now) than search intent modelling, social listening can produce sentiment and semantic analysis that guides marketers. We did just that for a Las Vegas hotel. People raved about the view of a competing property's magnificent fountains. That data was fed to the creative, site development, PR, and search marketing teams, all of whom acted upon it to fill more rooms.

• Primary research: asking consumers what they think may sound hoary and old fashioned, but the Digital Revolution has made the process much less expensive and vastly more responsive.

• Results repository: it isn't a technological challenge to put all your data into one place, but it requires commitment. Performance and cost data is often stored in financial systems while marketing information is held elsewhere. By combining it, you can learn much more about what does and doesn't work – and why.

Above *A word cloud as a pipe, which David Ogilvy would appreciate! The most useful data has strong visual appeal, even to show simple stats, such as the most frequently used terms in this book.*

Right Data that works together can make instant improvements to business. Caesar's Palace sits across the street from a Las Vegas icon, the beautiful Bellagio fountains. Online reviews consistently raved about the great fountain view Caeser's Palace afforded. Rather than grumble about how much guests liked a competitor's signature feature, Caeser's Palace fed that data to the creative, site development, PR, and search marketing teams, all of whom acted upon it to fill more rooms.

Really Useful Data

Data is not necessarily useful. Here are, in my experience, the seven pre-requisites of Really Useful Data.

1. Take the single enterprise point of view

Companies have invested heavily in building "single customer view" data warehouses, storing everything the company knows about that customer. These valuable repositories of data help brands analyze the behaviour of an individual customer and target messaging to that person across multiple channels. But these days, we generate tons of relevant data that exist outside of corporate channels. My preferred supplier of red socks would be very interested indeed to learn that I've just liked a picture of green socks on my Facebook page. The solution is the single enterprise point of view which integrates company-owned data sets with consumer insight mined from platforms like Facebook, Tencent, Google, and their ilk (see opposite).

2. Defeat platform impediments

It is the tendency of platforms to present themselves as omniscient. They never are. The game used to be that you owned all the data yourself, but, because so many interactions are on platforms you do not control, marketers lose visibility into the lives of their customers. And that upsets marketers. Yes, powerful platforms can do amazing things. You can learn incredible things about consumers from Facebook; it's probably the world's largest database. Putting that insight into practice is no small task. Customers expect brands to know them when they want to be known and to be anonymous when they

> "Customers expect brands to know them when they want to be known and to be anonymous when they don't."

Right *MetLife noticed that when people searched for life insurance, a particular CNN Money article showed up at the top of their search results time and time again. So we secured sponsorship of that article page and new applications flooded in. Even with complex technologies at our fingertips, often the simplest solutions are still the most effective.*

don't. Gathering and analyzing all the internal and external data requires – at this moment at least – an intensely complicated marketing technology stack, and no one piece of software can address it all.

The problem with platforms and marketing technology is that they, and the marketers who use them, see data analysis as a technology, not creative strategy. Marketers use a small fraction of the potential of their technology because changing the organization to make use of the insights they generate is hard, even if buying some new shiny toy is easy.

3. Distinguish between measurement and effectiveness

My late colleague Tim Broadbent used to remind us of the old story of the surgeon who said the operation had been a success, but, unfortunately, the patient had died. That surgeon was a measurement culture man. He may have carried out the procedure in the approved manner, but measuring the connections of the process do not help if the end result goes wrong.

Data is dangerously prone to creating measurement cultures. But what we really need is effectiveness culture.

A measurement culture is obsessed by process; while an effectiveness culture is obsessed by results. A measurement culture focuses on ticking the right boxes; while an effectiveness culture focuses on doing the right things. Measurement cultures look to the past – "How well did we work?" Effectiveness cultures look to the future – "How can we do better next time?"

Tim gave us a real example. The client had both a problem and an opportunity. The problem was that customers who bought one of their products were unlikely to buy another one at a later date. In marketing this is called a low re-purchase rate. The opportunity, though, was huge. We calculated that if the repurchase rate went up to the average of the major competitors, our client's revenues would increase by around 30 per cent.

Consumer research showed that customers didn't repurchase because they found the product unreliable. They criticized the product's build quality. So we went to the manufacturing plant to interrogate the quality control. "How do you test the products, and what are your standards?"

We were told that product quality was improving each year. And there were demanding targets. This year's products had to be built to higher standards than last year's products, and last year's products were better than the year before, and so on. But, we asked, do you test the products against competitive products from rival companies? "Oh no," they said, "we test against our own internal benchmarks. That's the only scientifically valid comparison."

Now, the trouble with this approach is that it doesn't work in the market. When you run a race, you can beat your own personal best time but still lose if another person runs faster. Yes, the company's management received measurements from the factory every year telling them product quality had improved. But other manufacturers were building to higher standards. And it's hardly surprising that consumers, faced with a choice, chose to buy products that didn't break or let them down so often. This client had a measurement culture, not an effectiveness culture. And it really hurt the

"A measurement culture is obsessed by process; while an effectiveness culture is obsessed by results."

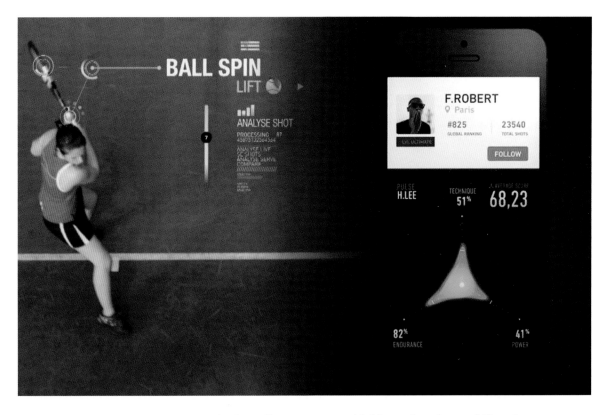

Above *Here is a useful illustration of the difference between measurement and effectiveness. What if you had a tennis racquet that could measure the power of your swing, the speed of your reactions, and the placement of your shots? We worked with Babolat to create a racquet that analyzed your swing data, and then helped you improve your swing.*

business. Revenues were a third lower than they could have been.

There is no doubt that the digital age and big data have driven a worrying reliance on short-term measures. As Binet and Field have pointed out, the language is "all about 'timely offers' delivered with zero wastage only to imminent purchases."[1] As they ask: "why bother with that slow-burn activity when sales can be switched on instantly with the latest Big Data tools?" All the IPA's data suggests that this would be injurious to profitable brand building.

4. Re-discover econometric modelling

Econometric modelling was invented in the first quarter of the twentieth century by the Nobel Prize-winning economist Ragnar Frisch. As Dimitri writes in his excellent book *Sexy Little Numbers* (2012): "Econometrics is all about developing and applying *quantitative* or *statistical* methods to prove economic principles." Those techniques can be used in marketing and sales, helping forecast consumption and demand for products and brands.

At its best, modelling really can explain what is doing well in the market place and what is not. It makes the data work for you.

Econometric modelling can do wonders. Consider this simple example: an econometric analysis of the impact of marketing on sales would help you forecast the impact a certain level of marketing spend would have on your sales. For some brands, there may be very little correlation because the most important variable is, perhaps, price, differentiation or distribution. But for another, often in the CPG (consumer packaged goods) category, the impact of marketing expenditure on sales is strong. How can you know how much you ought to spend? Econometric modelling helps find the exact level at which a brand gets the greatest possible return on its marketing investment.

It is strange that econometrics is not used more at the very point in history when the raw data it can feed upon has never been richer. We have seen that the best benchmark for studying effectiveness in the marketplace is the UK's IPA Awards. However, only in 15 per cent of case studies submitted has econometric modelling been used. What's the block?

There are three of them, in fact:

1. The necessarily advanced statistical skills are rare.

2. It is not always possible to capture the necessary data consistently.

3. Marketers don't believe in it since it is often a black box.

5. Underdose with metrics

Big data needs to justify itself with a multiplicity of metrics. It overdoses on them. I believe that we gain most by rationing the numbers of metrics we define as critical to any particular mission. The reason why this does not often happen so much is very simple: it requires the painful thinking to be done upfront. What are we really trying to achieve and why? Agreed in this way, and then adhered to, you can build "one version of the truth", rather than getting mired in multiple, unresolved debates.

For some clients we've constructed a single Report Card with as few as five metrics which sensitively capture the health of the brand and its contribution to the business. For others, we build more comprehensive dashboards.

Right *A good dashboard is used and shared. The best ones become forums for discussion about measurement. The design of the dashboard itself helps keep the marketing on target: deciding what data to show to decision-makers forces you to have a conversation about what data is important. And that leads you to align your metrics to your objectives.*

6. Insights, insights, insights

Really Useful Data gives us insight. We thirst for more and more of them. Nothing pleases me more than seeing creative teams slavering for insights from data. There are three different types of insights from data:

1. Observation: data can help show how something is doing.

2. Improvement: data can help uncover the reasons why something is working or not working.

3. Inspiration: data can spark an idea.

Creative inspiration seems like magic, and data can inspire it in many ways. For me, it all boils down to this:

Prioritization: Your data can show you whom to speak to and why.

Below *Sometimes the data itself can be the idea – at least it was for a British Airways billboard campaign. We mounted an antenna that gathered flight data from passing passenger jets, instantly cross-referenced it with the flight information from Heathrow, and checked that the location and weather conditions made the airplane visible to people in sight of the billboard. That process, which took far less than a single second, triggered our billboard to interrupt its regular content in order to show a child pointing up at the passing plane.*

"Made useful, it [big data] has the ability to take marketing and communications into whole new areas of creativity and precision."

IBM WATSON

There is no better illustration of the potential data has to transform things – things well beyond marketing – than IBM Watson. Watson is IBM's cognitive computer. Cognitive computing is the remarkable result of machine learning algorithms churning through huge volumes of structured and unstructured data. We're only at the beginning of the cognitive age, but already we're seeing where it may take us.

IBM's Watson is the world's most advanced cognitive system, built to analyze and extract knowledge from vast amounts of information with incredible speed and precision. Watson debuted to the public on the quiz show *Jeopardy* (above) in 2011, where it competed against – and handily beat – two of the best human players ever. But that was just a demonstration, a proof of concept. Soon after this victory, Watson was put to work, ploughing through reams of medical literature at a pace no human can match. It takes 160 hours a week to stay up to date on all the reading in a single medical field. This is no problem for Watson, and as a result, he's training with oncologists at Memorial Sloan-Kettering Cancer Center to help physicians anywhere make more informed decisions about patient care.

Watson also helps companies serve their customers better. Today's consumers expect them to be highly responsive to their questions, comments, and complaints. Watson enables companies to tackle even tough questions quickly and accurately. Watson is helping financial services firms make money management recommendations. Watson even helped us write the T.V. commercials! Watson analyzed, for example, all of Bob Dylan's lyrics and then worked with our copywriters and art directors to create scripts for the commercial it would star in with Dylan. Cognitive computers working with human talent – that's the real promise of big data. Big data isn't a magical panacea, but when paired with human inspiration and a commitment to creativity, it can help us go to new places.

Personalization: Your data can point you towards certain categories of people, showing you why they behave in certain ways, and how you can reach them.

Precision: Your data can help you generate the right message, delivered at the right time, to the right person, through the right medium.

7. Optimal optimization

Really Useful Data becomes optimally useful when it is designed to optimize. How do you do that? With a closed-loop system.

We keep close tabs (via a dashboard) of what is happening out in the marketplace before our marketing tactics even start to run. We make sure they're in line with our objectives, set up a testing protocol, and initiate our tracking. Once the communications are live, we assess them in four time frames: real time, daily, weekly, and quarterly. We're looking for data such as the path consumers are following, the lifetime value of a customer, and brand preference indicators. That data tells us what is and isn't connecting, and we change things on the fly to do more of the former and (hopefully) less of the latter. To keep ourselves honest, we report our results on a weekly, monthly and quarterly cycle, using that data to inform our next effort.

Big data *can* be tamed. Made useful, it has the ability to take marketing and communications into whole new areas of creativity and precision. But it will never provide the nirvana its most extreme advocates suggest. It aids and supports the human thinking process. It short circuits hard work which otherwise could not be done. Through sheer volume it sees patterns we could not otherwise see.

At the end of the day, though, data is political, however much purists may not like to admit it. It can be ignored. It can be manipulated. It can be used to score points. Its impact can be disguised.

The organizations of the digital age are no different than those which preceded them. As long as functional specializations exist, it is likely that data will reflect these political agendas as much as it reflects any great objective truth enshrined in a *sanctum sanctorum* of the temple of big data.

10 "ONLY CONNECT"

"Respondents admitted that they didn't completely understand today's marketing environment."

So was the understated conclusion of the research company Forester in 2015 when they asked clients what the shift to digital meant for them.

No wonder.

The media landscapes have shifted tectonically.

In *Ogilvy on Advertising* you can feel the old world of media. In fact, it was given scant attention. "I have never worked in the media department of an agency," David wrote, "but my observation of those who have been successful in this field leads me to think that they need an analytical mind, the ability to communicate numerical data in non-numerical formats, stability under pressure, and a taste for negotiation with the owners of media."

About 20 years ago, a structural change started which was controversial. In fact, it began on 1 November 1997, when my counterpart Alan Fairnington of JWT Asia and I agreed to pool our Asian media departments and create the first true media independent, MindShare: a decision both advantageous and dear to the holding company that owned us, WPP, and not so endearing to our immediate bosses. But it was clear that, if the agencies were to compete effectively, they needed to have both the necessary economies of scale in software development and the aggregated muscle in buying power. It was the right thing to do.

Of course, something was lost (as our immediate bosses feared), and that was the fruitful interface between creative people and media people. Who owned media planning – the creative agencies or the media agencies?

Ironically, the Digital Revolution has taken away much of the angst. We have observed the "so-and-so is dead" attitude that has accompanied it: the one claim which would be most accurate is "media is dead". That is to say the world of media in which many of us grew up. As Account Executives, there was one simple formula we learned: "80 per cent coverage at 6 OTS". That's what you'd say when a client asked you what weight of television campaign you would recommend. Reach (coverage) and frequency (Opportunities To See) were the sole media principles for managing a captive audience who had limited choices.

WPP Group plc　　　　*J. Walter Thompson*　　　　*Ogilvy*

JWT and O&M Launch MindShare Asia Pacific, The No. 1 Media Operation across Five Markets

FOR IMMEDIATE RELEASE
October 1997

Leading advertising agencies and WPP Group companies Ogilvy & Mather and J. Walter Thompson today announced the creation of MindShare Asia Pacific. The new venture, which will be launched in Hong Kong, China, Taiwan, Singapore and Thailand on 1st November 1997, will be the largest media operation across five markets with billings of over US$1 billion.

MindShare represents a new generation media operation. It offers an integrated service that not only covers traditional media, but also interactive media, sponsorship, event management, barter, programming, syndication and media modelling. Designed to operate in an environment of increasing concentration of media ownership, traditional media price inflation in most markets, media fragmentation and the emergence of new electronic media, MindShare will leverage its size to buy share of voice in the most effective way possible.

MindShare, reporting to WPP, will not only combine the media buying and planning currently undertaken by JWT and O&M, but will also seek to expand its client base, to include media only business.

Miles Young, Regional President, Ogilvy & Mather Asia Pacific, and Alan Fairnington, J. Walter Thompson Regional President, Asia Pacific, said in a joint statement; "MindShare represents a great step forward for the media business in Asia Pacific and will take conventional media wisdom into a new age. Our major investment in MindShare, to build interactive media, research, and event management capabilities, will be re-paid through its ability to provide integrated, innovative and imaginative media solutions to clients across Asia Pacific. We are very proud to be taking this initiative."

It has been announced that Dominic Proctor, formerly Chief Executive of JWT UK will become MindShare's Chief Operating Officer.

MindShare will commence operations in the UK and other European countries during 1998. In the USA, MindShare will be represented by JWT and O&M's existing media coalition called the JWT/O&M Alliance. The benefits of forming MindShare in other Asia Pacific markets is currently being studied.

From Hong Kong, Proctor said: "It is particularly stimulating to start the business in Asia Pacific. The strong regional growth, the lack of competition, the skill and reputation of the two agencies and the entrepreneurial spirit of the region makes this a perfect place to start."

Above *Minds of our own! Alan Fairnington of JWT and I went out on a limb to help create the first true media independent, MindShare. This is the press release from 1997, which made public our plan to unlock the combined media buying power of our agencies.*

What then followed was what the business technologist Steve Sammartino labelled the Great Fragmentation: the explosion of an orderly media universe into thousands upon thousands of programming options, and the parallel explosion of a homogeneous audience into one fragmented both by time and space – each fragment being, potentially, "always on".

PAID, OWNED AND EARNED

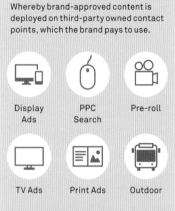

Paid

Whereby brand-approved content is deployed on third-party owned contact points, which the brand pays to use.

Display Ads

PPC Search

Pre-roll

TV Ads

Print Ads

Outdoor

Strengths
- Guaranteed scale
- Control over targeting
- Control over messaging and timing
- Easy to monitor and measure

Limitations
- Less credible
- Susceptible to being "tuned out", whether by individuals themselves or use of technology
- Requires spend of each additional impression

Best Practices
- Brands should ensure that paid media assets feature appropriate Calls-to-Action (CTA) based on the contact point's role within the consumer decision journey.

Owned

Whereby brand-approved content is deployed on brand-owned or controlled contact points.

Social Feeds

Packaging

Wireless

CRM

CES

Employee Networks

Strengths
- Control over messaging and timing
- Easy to monitor and measure
- More credible than paid

Limitations
- Difficult to scale without paid support

Best Practices
- Brands should ensure that their owned contact points are ready to receive consumers with high-quality content and feature appropriate CTA.

Earned

Whereby brand-approved content is generated and/or shared by third parties.

Blog Mentions

Ratings & Reviews

Social Mentions

Offline WCM

Influencer Mentions

PR

Strengths
- Highly credible; known to strongly influence purchase decisions
- Does not require spend for each additional impression

Limitations
- Brand has no control over scale, targeting, messaging or timing
- Balance of messaging can be positive or negative
- Difficult to monitor or measure

Best Practices
- Brands should nurture earned media through best practices in distribution (CTA, planning for moments) and creative emotional content (social motivation).

Above *Connections planning worships at the shrine of POE – paid, owned, earned. While media was previously bought and "paid" for via advertising, brands now "earn" it from PR, social mentions and partnerships, and "own" it via their digital and physical channels. The digital age didn't invent all these channels, but it did shepherd in a deeper level of sophistication in delivering campaigns.*

Paid, Owned, Earned

Media planning ceased to be central: "connections planning" emerged, in recognition that many points of connection with the digitized consumer could not just be paid for: rather, you could build and "own" your digital estate, and you could "earn" coverage. In Chapter 7 we briefly met the three unlikely letters which became the new paradigm: POE – Paid, Owned, Earned.

POE provided – and provides – a handy way of looking at the new media world, but it begs some important questions. How do you know where to connect? Or what to spend in making each connection? Or, indeed, how to connect?

There are many who place their faith blindly in full automation. But as my colleague Ben Richards, Ogilvy & Mather's Chief Strategy Officer, writes:

Pity the media operative today. Tasked into finding prospects for, say, Powerade, she checks the weather variable. She finds parts of the country where the temperature is 72° or above. She sees that morning registers higher purchase rates than afternoon. She instructs the algorithm to look for people who are searching for sports activities on mobile devices – people who are clearly out and about. She instructs the algorithm to bid at 20 percent below the going rate. Her trade successfully completes. She feels she has won – for today. However, she worries about precisely where the ads will really appear, and ultimately she worries whether she will be replaced by that same algorithm tomorrow.

Just as electronic trading has replaced the slamming phones, screaming brokers and ticker tape of the old trading floor, today's media buying appears to be hurtling towards full automation. Yet this is happening with little strategy and even less accountability. "Connections" is needed more than ever.

"It's amazing in retrospect that we simply didn't know much at all about the media behaviour of the consumers we ritually dedicated ourselves to."

From the start, intelligent CMOs started to realize that they needed to push their marketing organizations into digital media. Their spend patterns lagged their audiences' consumption patterns. So Keith Weed at Unilever, or Clive Sirkin at Kimberly Clark, started to set quotas for their markets. At one point in Unilever, the "target" for digital spend was set at 20 per cent of analogue spend. At the time, it seemed ambitiously high, and somewhat arbitrary. Now the actual level is 24 per cent. Data is pushing this trend.

The old media ecosystem delivered remarkably little data: very high-level segmentation of viewership confined to age and gender, often not ratified until 90 days later; and similarly generic circulation data for print readership audited twice a year. It's amazing in retrospect that we simply didn't know much at all about the media behaviour of the consumers we ritually dedicated ourselves to.

Now, we also have that billowing "digital exhaust" of their media consumption, their use of devices and their non-media behaviours through a platform of first, second and third party data sources. Rich and in real time, their media profiles help us connect much, much better.

Deep Integration

But something else is needed. How can we integrate everything around the consumer?

Integration has consistently emerged as the most intractable worry of the post-digital CMO in all surveys. And early practice did nothing more than to popularize what we call the "matching luggage" view of integration: if all your communication pieces in different media looked more or less the same, you're OK.

Then, there was integration in a funnel, a child of the early 2000s: organizing around tasks such as creating awareness or gaining consideration, with channels generically deployed against each.

EVOLUTION OF INTEGRATION

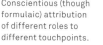

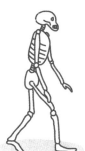
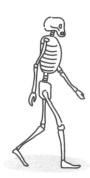
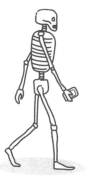

1. Graphic Integration

"Matching luggage" – marketing assets look and feel similar.

2. Funnel Integration

Conscientious (though formulaic) attribution of different roles to different touchpoints.

3. Organic Integration

Advertising, activations, one-to-one and PR tightly integrated around constituent journeys.

4. Parallel Integration

Integration across brands, sub-brands, segments, geographies and programmes.

5. Dynamic Integration

Chain reactions of every element of the business, marketing and sales mix – managed live in-market.

Above *Behold the evolution of marketing mankind! Integration has its origins in Graphic Integration, where everything has a visual coherence but little more. After several stages of development, we are reaching to the holy grail of Dynamic Integration, in which every element of the business is working in harmony and managed in market and in real-time.*

Today, best practice sees integration as something organic, to be architected around the customer's experience, and ultimately, what we are moving towards – dynamic, with communications that move around people's real lives as they live them.

David Ogilvy never believed in the disintegration that grew up in the post-war period as a symptom of disciplinary specialization – the "disciplines" of Public Relations, Direct Marketing, Sales, Promotion and so on. He also firmly rebutted the advertising-centric orthodoxies of his generation; Ogilvy & Mather brought, with his encouragement, these disciplines into our family very early on through a programme of acquisition. Still, too often, advertising strategies were developed in the advertising agency and handed over to the other disciplines for implementation. However seamlessly that was done, the integration was superficial, not deep.

When I became CEO of Ogilvy in 2008, I felt that we had both a huge advantage and huge liability. We possessed all the disciplines, which other agencies didn't, and yet we did not feel deeply integrated. I hired Ben Richards from the connections agency Naked to find a solution. Naked was the parent of Communications Planning, but their definition of communications really stopped at advertising. Concepts of influence or loyalty were remote and alien to them. What Ben did was to create an operating system, Fusion™, which was common across all the disciplines, which started with what the business problem was (rather than with the communication problem), and which, above all, was focused on the customer journey.

Until then, customer journeys had been a somewhat remote and academic construct, or something lodged exclusively in the Direct

CUSTOMER JOURNEY OF AN ADVERTISING UNDERGRADUATE

Discover
Arrive at college or university

Decide
Explore subject options

Engage
Attend lectures, study the art and science of advertising

Prepare
Consolidate learning and revise for examinations

Validate
Take examinations and submit thesis

Celebrate
Enjoy graduation ceremony

Transform
Apply for and accept job at advertising agency

"Deep integration is digitally enabled in one very particular way: now, we can understand consumers' intentions."

Above Should you wish to devote your career – or at least some of it – to advertising, you might follow a path similar to this. Customer journeys help us identify the pleasures and pitfalls of a given experience, whether buying a new car, researching an interest, or making the bold step to study for a degree and get hired. By truly understanding people's engagement at each stage, we can identify where to help rather than hinder.

Marketing discipline. But now they could become a unifying concept, through which the real barriers and the potent drivers to engaging the consumer could be mapped.

Twenty years ago, Ogilvy & Mather coined the phrase "360° Brand Stewardship", which allowed us to do holistic integration. There was no doubt that the combination of in-depth specialisms provided much better programs. But we learnt there was something more. To get deep integration you must focus only on the *10° which really matters*, and do so in a way that is not just media neutral but also discipline neutral.

Deep integration is digitally enabled in one very particular way: now, we can understand consumers' intentions. Search – in this case under its guise of Search Engine Marketing (SEM) as opposed to Search Engine Optimization (SEO) (see page 139) takes centre stage. I write "search" as we all do, as a one-word shorthand. Of course, what is meant is that we can understand *what consumers are searching for on the internet.*

It was the serial entrepreneur and journalist John Battelle who first characterized Google as the database of intent back in 2003: "The Database of Intentions is simply this: The aggregate results of every search ever entered, every result list ever tendered, and every path taken as a result," he wrote. "This information represents, in aggregate form, a place holder for the intentions of humankind – a massive database of desires, needs, wants, and likes that can be discovered, subpoenaed, archived, tracked, and exploited to all sorts of ends."[1] Battelle has gone on to add social media and check-ins to this grouping.

The root of all is the not so humble keyword. We need to think of keywords as the common denominators of the digital age.

Gerber.com/StartingSolids

Above *Here's an insight – weekly Google searches among new mothers almost double in frequency. So, we worked with baby food brand Gerber to help them learn about motherhood on their own terms, or, perhaps more accurately, their own search terms. Search intent data reveals much about a person's thoughts and intentions, and when you carefully sift it, you find a window into what they really want. For young mothers nursing a new baby, it highlights their curiosities and concerns – phrases like "when to start baby cereal" and "how to establish healthy eating habits". By understanding their knowledge gaps, we helped Gerber deliver precisely calibrated, highly-relevant videos to answer those needs in a supportive and engaging way. The idea was embraced by young mothers, and helped to get Gerber growing again.*

How Keywords Work

Google is far from being the only database of intent. Baidu, Yandex and Yahoo! dominate in China, Russia and Japan respectively. Virtually every other portal – from Twitter to YouTube to Pinterest – is, de facto, a search engine.

By constructing a keyword universe we can learn about intent, not just from within Google.com but from a much broader territory. In fact, we should think of this as the largest focus group ever: a humongous source of insight into customers – who they are, what they like or don't like, and how they journey. But, in itself, its data is no more useful than any other. The magic only happens when we relate intent to content.

We made exactly this connection in order to revive Gerber, a well-known but out-dated baby food brand in the US that had suffered five years of declining sales. The data came from looking into search behaviours among Millennials, and our observations that weekly searches nearly double in frequency once a young woman becomes a mother. We then analyzed their queries in greater depth to better understand their questions, find common themes, and produce an entire video library to help provide highly relevant answers. We published video content that mapped directly their searches – queries about childhood nutrition such as "when to start baby cereal" and "how to establish healthy eating habits" – labelled with the exact same search terms they use to ensure easy discoverability on Google. And we used playlist and tagging features on YouTube to help people find the content even without paid advertising. By first mining data to truly understand new mothers and then building the go-to source for tailored advice on motherhood, the Gerber brand is growing again.

Something that I find irritating at worst and confusing at best is the way in which "search" is treated as if it is a distinct discipline, another industry vertical. This is a great misunderstanding. Search is fundamentally horizontal. It informs and enables all the communication disciplines – Advertising, Public Relations and Direct Marketing – and, because keywords, unlike P&L owners, don't recognize the distinctions between them, it acts as a major integrator for communications in the digital age.

It's also an area which suffers almost more than any other part of the digital landscape from acronym-itis, so please see the simple glossary opposite that has managed to keep me reasonably clear-headed about it.

How to Judge a Website: The Medium You Own

The introduction that leads to the cocktail party conversation I most dread: "This is Miles, he runs an advertising agency." I can see the follow-up coming from a mile away. "I've got a website, but I'm not sure it's great. What do you think?"

My question in response is: "Well what do you want one *for*?"

There are two types of answers. One is for the sheer numbers – the *audience* – it brings me. The other is for how it explains and presents me.

A GLOSSARY OF COMMON SEARCH TERMS

Annual Search Volume Searches over a one-year period, based on the previous 12-month average. This is calculated by multiplying the Average Monthly Searches x 12.

Estimated Clicks The estimated annual clicks for a particular group of domains, domain or URL. Estimated Clicks = Annual Searches x Click-Through Rate for the Page Rank. This is then summed up for aggregate views across Categories, Topics and Subtopics.

Opportunity Clicks The estimated increase in annual clicks (by Category, Topic, Subtopic or Keyword). This involves a complex calculation that evaluates current client and competitor Page Rank as well as domains too well-entrenched to be dethroned to establish a target goal rank for each keyword. Opportunity Clicks = future clicks minus current Estimated Clicks.

Page Rank Refers to the organic ranking position on Google. Page 1 = Position 1–10; Page 2 = Position 11–20. This data is pulled from a third-party tool that captures a snapshot of ranking positions at a given date and time.

Paid Search is an auction-based media channel that places advertisements at the top and bottom of the search results page. These ads vary from search query to search query and are chosen based on a search-engine's algorithm and the results of an auction between advertisers. A search-engine's algorithm examines many data points (over 100) to find the most relevant set of ads to show in response to someone typing a query, and uses the results of the auction to determine where those ads are located on the results page. When a user clicks an ad and goes to an advertiser's website, that advertiser is assessed a cost based on the amount of the various bids placed in the auction. Many other factors can affect the results of the auction, creating a rapidly evolving, highly complex market that acquires costs and solicits website traffic in real time.

Search Trend Change in search volume based on the slope of the trend line from the Monthly Search Volume over a two-year period. Range includes Steep Drop, Drop, Flat, Growth and Steep Growth.

Search Seasonality This metric utilizes Google Trends data over a 10-year period to determine the typical fluctuation from the norm during a particular month of the year.

Share of Search The percentage of the available clicks that are likely going to a particular group of domains. This is a factor of the search volume for the Category, Topic or Sub Topic selected and the Estimated Clicks for the group of domains or domain.

Search Engine Marketing (SEM) A form of digital marketing targeting performance in the search engines. SEM is comprised of paid search and organic search (also called SEO or Search Engine Optimization, see below). SEM really begins with an understanding of what your target audience is looking for and delivering accordingly. Sometimes you have to pay for visibility and other times you earn it by creating great content.

Search Engine Optimization (SEO) Traditionally thought of as something that you do as you develop a site or after a site is developed. Success in SEO means that you have a pulse on what information/products, etc., your customers or target are looking for, what format they want that information delivered, and that you are creating relevant content that surpasses other content across multiple platforms. SEO is typically called earned media because you can't buy your way to success, you have to earn visibility.

Let's consider the numbers, first. And take, as an example, the website of a media property. Fortunately, I don't often receive direct pitches from media reps, but they go like this. There will be talk of "delivering eyeballs". It's the industry cliché for the number of visitors a website attracts, also called "uniques", which is short for unique visitors and is also known as traffic. This is the first number you want to know, and the dominant traditional measurement of a website's performance. So you ask, "What kind of traffic are you getting?"

Sales rep: "We're averaging 10 million uniques, and 60 million page views, up about 30 per cent in just the past four months."

You: "Those numbers sound rather good."

You are not wrong. Anything in the tens of millions sounds pretty good. But what the rep just told you is that 10 million individual web users, excluding return visitors, view at least one page on the website per month, and that the numbers are trending upwards. Your reaction should be one of interest but not enthusiasm, considering that online newspaper giants like the *Washington Post* and the *Guardian* register more than 78 million and 120 million monthly average users (MAU), respectively.

In any case, the next question you pose to the rep might be: "How many page views are we talking about?"

You are asking about the average number of clicks per unique, which are also calculated on a monthly basis. Each click yields a new page view. When a viewer lands on a page and immediately clicks to navigate to another site, that's known as "bouncing". A high bounce rate is bad, needless to say. Web publishers don't like to talk about their bounce rate, which means, of course, that you should ask about it. Assuming a reader doesn't bounce, she sticks around, scrolling and clicking. Generally speaking, there's a correlation between the number of page views and a reader's level of engagement. More page views translate to more time spent on a site, and a greater likelihood that an ad will be effective. Ultimately, for your client's sake, you want a visitor to click on an ad. What happens next depends on the ad's creative content, and whether the user finds it compelling. A brief video advertisement may play in a pop-up window, or a reader may be invited to fill out a form, for example, to sign up for a newsletter or a special offer from your client.

But the moment a viewer clicks on an ad, she is deemed to be engaged by way of a click-through. One meaningful metric that doesn't involve click-through is an "impression". This describes when an ad simply appears, or is served, on a webpage. The presumption is that a reader saw the ad and afforded it some level of cognition. But when a click-through occurs, it triggers brand interaction and can be measured. So, in addition to asking about page views, you will also want to enquire about the click-through rate, or CTR. The number of clicks an ad generates, counted in thousands, is used, in part, to determine its cost. CPM, for cost per mile, is the total cost of an ad placement divided by 1,000.

As your meeting progresses, you can keep it on point by asking for more numbers, such as the conversion rate. After a reader is engaged, the next incremental goal is conversion, meaning the user takes action prompted by the ad. On a retail site, a conversion is a sale. Likewise, a political or cause-related ad achieves conversion when a user makes a donation or signs up to receive yet another inbox-clogging newsletter. If an ad is shared, that's also a conversion. If an ad goes viral, that's something of a different magnitude – one conversion that can lead to millions, like toppling dominoes. Related terms include "funnels", which are the steps that a user takes on the way to a conversion. A visitor who takes these steps is called an "intended". One editor for a top-tier online publishers says that his company is "obsessed with not losing intendeds", which is another way of saying, "trying to increase the conversion rate". So, you ask the rep, "What's your conversion rate? Has an ad or any native content on your site gone viral?"

Another telling metric is the amount of time a user spends on a site after the moment she arrives. Generally speaking, the longer a user lingers, the better. On most sites, time spent on-site means more page views and an increase in ad impressions and click-throughs. But the prevailing wisdom is that session time is a less important measure than the average time spent on a page. A good website holds the viewer's attention, and the best measure of her attention is how long a single page engages her.

So far, so good. And, so many numbers. Aside from user demographics, which the rep ought to provide to you, you'll also want to know what drives traffic to the website. The vast majority of traffic is paid for. Just as advertisers pay Google AdWords for better and more frequent ad placements, websites pay to appear in the highest possible position in search results. Your question to the rep should be: "How much of your traffic is paid, and how much is organic?" Organic or incidental traffic measures the number of visitors to a site who arrive by means other than paid traffic. The relative worth of paid versus organic traffic is debatable, but on its face, the latter seems more valuable. A website that builds traffic by word of mouth, or by its content being picked up and linked out from other sites, can be assumed to have more integrity and inherent interest than a site that pays its way to the No. 1 position in search results.

We have a sense of how to judge our media site, but it appears we're on a roll – other party guests are joining us, each with a site of their own. There are many types of website, each with unique questions to ask and different metrics to measure. We might divide them into four groups.

- Media, directory and brochure sites (for example, the *Guardian*, or a brand, say, Dove).

- Blogs and personal websites (for example, a Tumblr page or milesyoung.com).

- Ecommerce and marketplace sites (for example, Amazon and Airbnb).

- Social networks and sharing platforms (for example, Facebook and YouTube).

"A website that builds traffic by word of mouth, or by its content being picked up and linked out from other sites, can be assumed to have more integrity and inherent interest than a site that pays its way to the No. 1 position in search results."

Blogs and information sites would focus on page views and time on site, while ecommerce is more concerned with converting visits to sales. Social networks and sharing platforms, which tend to make their revenue from advertising, need their audiences to convert so they prioritize click-through rates. Business model is the real driver here; for example, platforms that rely on advertising, like YouTube, need highly engaged MAUs (Monthly Active Users), while subscription services, think Spotify, grow by converting eyeballs (or rather, earlobes) into paying customers. Fortunately our analytics software is set up to capture the right metrics based on the goals we've set.

We can move on to website optimization, the process of refining the site by A/B testing alternative CTAs (Call To Actions), changing copy and imagery, editing contents or even completely overhauling the UI (Use Interface) to improve our funnel metrics. And, of course, my inquisitor will ask about benchmarks – everyone always does. It is important to find and beat the norms to ensure we're getting the most out of our site. It's worth noting that category is still very important – low involvement categories offline are still low involvement online, although we can now try to engage people more often by measuring their browsing behaviour and re-targeting to bring them back.

So much of it is numbers: how many impressions our site gets, the number of unique visitors, what proportion of them click through an ad or piece of content, how long is their average time on site and how many pages they view, what are the conversion rates at every level of the funnel, and so on. And then we look at these metrics through different lenses: segments, cohorts, time periods, devices, and so on.

But have you had enough of the numbers? I'm pretty sure I have. They are important, and should neither be ignored nor blithely accepted. But what's just as compelling is the second question: how does a website explain or represent me? And by "me", I mean anything that can be considered a brand, from an individual like you, to an automotive marque, to a digital retailer. The answer here is largely qualitative. It takes into account traditional design elements – font selection, legibility, colour palette, use of graphics, animation and video, density and placement of text, and so on. Most importantly how logical is the *architecture* of the site? How is information organised and structured so the most interesting information surfaces the most easily? Ask for a web designer and then look for an architect!

At the end of the day, though, a website is only an advertisement. And, like any advertisement, it needs to have an idea within it. If you're lucky enough to have a brand idea already, it needs to be there not as "matching luggage", but in a way that brings all the elements to life. There is nothing more depressing than looking at a website that looks, feels and behaves as if it has come from a parallel universe – as if it is an idea-free zone.

Finally, there is three-tiered chess game of interactive design. The best interactive design starts by facilitating intuitive navigation within the site itself. The less a visitor has to think about her next click, and the one after

"A good website doesn't draw attention to itself but rather serves as a hub, delivering the user to all of the components of your brand's digital ecosystem."

that, the better. The goal is a seamless experience that's enjoyable – you want a visitor to think well of your brand and return often to the site. That much is a given. But the design ideally should also steer the user to a conversion, and – here's the really difficult part – act more like a tool than a showpiece.

A good website doesn't draw attention to itself but rather serves as a hub, delivering the user to all of the components of your brand's digital ecosystem. So the final question should be, "What other digital channels are you using?" The number of uniques and page views a site generates, which are provided by web analytics companies such as comScore or Nielsen Online, are only part of the calculus of a brand's digital audience. Social channels are of ever-increasing importance, as the balance of web access shifts away from laptops and desktops to mobile devices. A brand with a good digital strategy may use its website as a hub, but it must also deliberately build its presence and following via social channels. A dedicated YouTube channel, Facebook page, Twitter and Instagram feeds – all of these mechanisms grow awareness and reach. The sum of a brand's digital parts, including its website, should be greater than the whole.

Intimacy at Scale

When E.M. Forster, in his novel *Howards End*, coined the quotable phrase "only connect", it was part of a longer sentence: "Only connect the prose and the passion, and both will be exalted, and human love will be seen at its height."

Enter the keymost of all keywords, I believe, for any vision of media in the digital world that really wants to connect intent and content, marketers and consumers, prose and passion: intimacy.

It's also probably the most difficult thing of all to strive for, because, like Ben Richards' threatened media operative, it seems as if at the end of the day everything might be replaced by a program: programmatic media trading automizes the negotiation of a price for rendering an exposure across different media. Programmatic advertising already accounts for some 20 per cent of all online advertising revenue, and it is still growing by upwards of 70 per cent per year. But as my famed colleague Rory Sutherland of OgilvyOne reminds us: "Business completely fetishizes certainty. It takes big, complex problems, strips out all of the stuff that makes them complex, and solves them as if they're optimization problems." That's a good description of what programmatic advertising can do, optimizing itself into what Rory calls, "very rapid Darwinian advertising".

Of course, there is much "bad" programmatic advertising. Rote buying results in BMW ads following you around the internet for six months after you bought a new Infiniti. Or it puts an un-skippable pre-roll ad for professional power tools in front of a middle-schoolgirl oriented school supply DIY video. And we also know that around 15 per cent of programmatic is just plain fake. But "good" programmatic allows us to buy audiences not just in context but by data; and more often than not in real time. We know that when an ad is delivered in real time to a person, they are twice as likely to interact with it.

PROGRAMMATIC BUYING ECOSYSTEMS

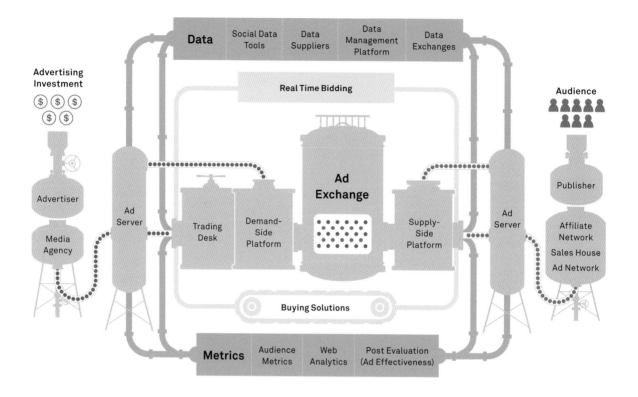

Above *Programmatic advertising is like a virtual factory. Money goes in at one end; and a delivered audience at a cost comes out at the other. The best programmatic advertising takes all of this technology and envelops the consumer in the most intimate of marketing experiences. The worst uses the same technology to undermine its own intent. Use it wisely.*

If there is one secret to getting programmatic right, I believe it is a very obvious one, and that is to remember that technology is only the enabler. You start with as granular and as comprehensive a view as you can conceivably assemble of the individual (from any available source). Then you form a view of what creative messages will best engage him or her. Then you scale up. Shortcuts to scale will never be intimate.

Search has entered the picture again, not as a clarifier of intent, but more as a channel. Or, even better, your battlefield – the "digital shelf" your product sits on, with two zones, the "organic" zone, which is owned and earned, and the "paid" zone. The organic zone refers to your brand's appearance in search results due to search-engine optimization and the independent action of the search algorithms, or those results that appear as a result of the action of others – media placements, blog mentions, etc. The paid zone refers to those search results you have spent media money to generate.

So how do you win this battle?

- Your brand must be always-on with maximum visibility across desktop and mobile, all synchronized with your TV buy

THE GOOGLE QUALITY SCORE

Google measures the quality of your website by the following measures:

1. Click-through rate
2. Landing page
3. Historical performance
4. Various relevancy factors
5. Ad relevancy
6. Keyword relevancy

Below *For Weight Watchers, we cut manual optimization out of our diet and replaced it with technology that could crunch data in real time. Suddenly we could optimize ad creative in the moment – changing messaging, images and colour combinations on the fly – and immediately optimizing our results.*

- You must have a relentless focus on your Google Quality Score (QS)

- You must use insights from keyword modelling

- You must be present in Google Shopping, while taking care to manage the tension between your brand and the retailers that sell it.

"Good" programmatic requires a reassertion of a fundamental principle of effective advertising: that you cannot separate the creative and the media processes. It can often seem that technology forces you to, but that way madness lies. Better, it can build them together, but only if intimacy is the starting point and scale the dividend – not the other way round.

Digital Video

There's one piece of connective tissue which the digital world has seemed peculiarly slow to embrace, and that is digital video. Pre-rolls and interstitials have been disappointing to consumers. Porting over a TV commercial as an unskippable pre-roll add-on digital video doesn't do much for the brand and often frustrates the consumer, especially when the context of the ad and the video are wildly out of synch, such as a pickup truck commercial running before a teen-focused make-up tutorial. But how come "good" video is still such a relatively small percentage of online advertising spend – less than 20 per cent?

I think it's down to two contradictory things: not joining the community and not collaborating with creators.

There is a failure to understand that in digital video you seek fans, you don't buy audiences. "Fandom" is moved by authentic passion; it isn't there

DYNAMIC CREATIVE

Goal: Increase Weight Watchers' user acquisition (subscription volume).

Approach: Implement "Dynamic creative" with real-time, multivariate testing.

Results: "Dynamic creative" impacts key metrics to drive subscription conversations.

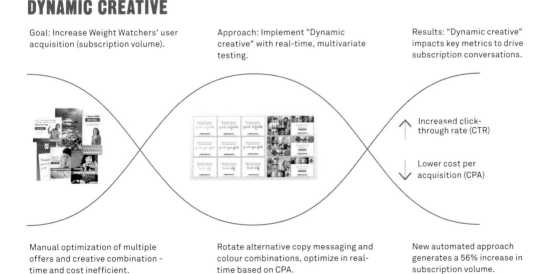

Increased click-through rate (CTR)

Lower cost per acquisition (CPA)

Manual optimization of multiple offers and creative combination - time and cost inefficient.

Rotate alternative copy messaging and colour combinations, optimize in real-time based on CPA.

New automated approach generates a 56% increase in subscription volume.

Above *Qualcomm took a brave step in shifting its annual ad budget from media spend into the production of a Hollywood-style half-hour thriller released online. The short film,* Lifeline, *resulted in advertising that people truly wanted to see. Directed by Academy Award-winner Armando Bo and starring Olivia Munn, Leehom Wang and Joan Chen,* Lifeline *tells the story of a man's search for his missing girlfriend using the smartphone she has left behind. The capability of Qualcomm's Snapdragon processors were central to the story, with the hero using its enhanced security, advanced photo and video capture, superior connectivity and faster charging to find her. Set in Shanghai, with 70 per cent of the dialogue in Chinese (China is one of Qualcomm's main markets) the film has been viewed 20 million times, with another 100 million more including trailers and the behind-the-scenes video.*

"There is a failure to understand that in digital video you seek fans, you don't buy audiences."

to be "hit", but it's there to be conspired and collaborated with. If you want to enter into the mindset, then The Young Turks (TYT), an opinionated, youth-oriented online news network provides a good example. Fans prefer it to other news outlets and mob the presenters at conferences as if they were rock stars.

I have been in many boardrooms in my career, and over the years they have not fundamentally changed. Nor have their marketing departments and their advertising agencies quite liberated themselves to be TYT. But there is something they all should recognize. It was something that Wendy Clark of Coca-Cola brilliantly encouraged: a 70%: 20%: 10% division of media investment. Seventy per cent is "low risk, bread and butter"; 20 per cent is "innovative"; but 10 per cent is spent on "high-risk new ideas". Unfortunately, it has not spread or stuck very much as a way of actually doing business. But if ever there was a case for the 10 per cent, it is digital video.

It would afford, for instance, experimental collaborations with creators. Our agency in New York actually identified the top 30 of them. They're not Boardroom material, but they have more consumer intimacy in the digital world than most influencers. Ryan Higa's launch of the Lenovo Yoga tablet was a seamless part of his ongoing fan interactions. As a result, his fans accepted, even looked forward to, a programme that was an obvious advertisement with the same sort of anticipation they displayed for his other videos.

And it would sensitize you to the "super fans": a group that influences disproportionately: the 20 per cent of enthusiasts who drive 80 per cent of the engagement and conversation. Superfans help moderate comment streams and provide community leadership for the digital creator's audience. It is they who help shape the entertainment flow, and you reach them by becoming a part of it. Rhett and Link, for example, integrated Geico advertising into their video programming, but were it not for the brand name, you'd never know it was any different from their other videos. The brand reached Rhett and Link's superfans by the simple expedient of letting Rhett and Link be Rhett and Link. Something easier said than done for most brands.

Doing these two things would allow you to have a much better chance of building a sustained audience as opposed to mere viewership. After all, audience is just the advertising world's way of describing community.

But there's also an alternative way of looking at digital video, not so much as a community-based audience but by learning from Hollywood. It requires client courage: the courage to commit, once in a while, to one big production. It means creating stories so compelling that they command attention. But then that attention, unlike the attention of a cinema audience, is scaled by a digitally informed distribution strategy.

Intimacy in Depth

How intimate can you be? How deep can you go?

Over the years the most thankless and frustrating presentations I have made were those to persuade clients to buy CRM (Customer Relationship Marketing) programs. I can now understand why.

At the very beginning of the digital era, Ogilvy & Mather perceived the value of creating not just one-off sales but long-term loyalty. We conducted tests which showed that those who received personalized communications did, indeed, purchase more than those who did not, and that they were prepared to give us information about themselves in return for useful information about our products. And we could calculate their "lifetime value" to us, and translate our data into measurable ROI (Return on Investment).

But we were seeing through a glass darkly. The medium was direct mail; the databases were primitive; the data was single source; the process was clunky and very expensive; and worst of all, it really required the clients to do a lot of hard work, too. Even when direct mail by post became email, something was missing.

Like zealots convinced that what we believed was incontrovertibly true, we kept on making presentations to audiences who could not disagree but who did little – outside of certain easy-to-implement sectors, such as airlines where initially the relationship became as much a matter of points schemes as of deeper intimacy.

CRM became a dirty acronym: and some companies have now banned it from their lexicons altogether because it brings the deeper principles into unnecessary disrepute.

What CRM never achieved was to be really intimate – or truly engaging. Like many early adopters in the Digital Revolution, we were too obsessed with the tools and not enough with the experience the customer had. But "data

DAVE

MILES' MINUTE
MEET DAVE

Click here to view the video

Hi! I'm DAVE. They called me that because I suppose they wanted me to sound like a hip grandson of the great David. I'm not sure he'd like some of the words I stand for:

Data-inspired
Always-on
Valuable
Experience

But he'd certainly sympathize with what I stand for – creating, in the digital age, engagement that sells.

Top *Brian Fetherstonhaugh (the Chairman and CEO of OgilvyOne) and I introduce DAVE to the agency in one of my "Miles' Minutes" – my regular agency update that went out to 24,000 staff worldwide every few weeks.*

plus digital" is a powerful combination which allows us to put the *customer's* point of view at the centre of what we do, and not just the brand's.

So we invented DAVE.

I don't know what David Ogilvy would have thought of DAVE, but it has certainly catapulted us into a new position as the world's premier Customer Engagement agency. It's a way of thinking as much as anything – and as it is creative at its core DAVE prompts us to do a number of very clever things:

1. To define a customer ambition, which emerges from but is distinct from a business ambition: data gives us a very precise view of whom we are engaging, and exactly what value we want to unlock.

2. To create personas of these customer segments, to spring them into life. There's no intimacy without knowing whom you are being intimate with.

3. To map the customer journey: *all* the relevant moments – touch points (and pain points) – along the persona's journey through life. It's a very thorough discovery, and needs to be painstaking. We've seen many slipshod ones. No pain, no gain.

4. Create an engagement idea: where any other idea has to execute through unexpectedness, an engagement idea also has to provoke or invite the customer to take a role in the experience. Unlike many other ideas, it looks to the long term.

5. Develop a blueprint for engagement. How do you bring it all together?

6. Then turn that blueprint into an actual plan where the customer experience is mapped: how that idea feeds through each channel, impacts on each touch point and how intimate the experience will be.

CUSTOMER-CENTRICITY

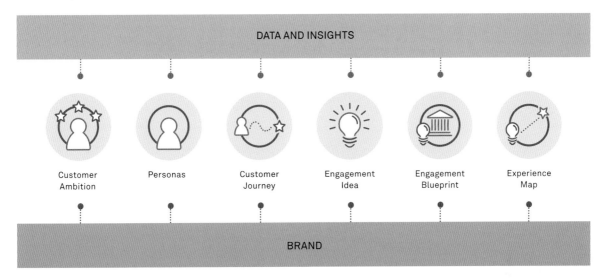

DATA AND INSIGHTS

Customer Ambition — Personas — Customer Journey — Engagement Idea — Engagement Blueprint — Experience Map

BRAND

Above *DAVE – or similar tools – finally provides a systematic path to customer centricity: the promised land of the digital age.*

The Performance Brand

DAVE (and his other companions in the industry) represents the "big" leap we had always hoped for.

But can we leap further still? Is there such a thing as the performance brand? A brand where the ability to engage, and to do that programmatically, and then change the media and creative mix dynamically based on results as they emerge, is baked in?

It's coming.

It takes us into selling digital transformation itself to our clients, especially those who are marketing online.

It starts from straightforward programmatic buying, but adds in a hefty dose of digital analytics to super-optimize the results, and does so across all the channels, paid for and non-paid for. Then DAVE takes over the steering and it moves into customer engagement. Finally, it becomes completely omni-channel, relating behaviour in-store with behaviour offline.

To make this happen we need to work with 30 different technology partners; and create a marketing cloud in which to house the data.

So finally, everything connects. As the E.M. Forster quote about only connecting continues: "Live in fragments no longer."

It does seem possible.

11 CREATIVE TECHNOLOGY: THE SWEET SPOT

There was a time in the pre-digital world when the phrase "creative technology" would have seemed like the most grotesque oxymoron. It's not necessarily a mainstream thought even now. Artists versus geeks, technophobes versus technophiles, "right" brain versus "left" brain ... the clashes run on, but with, I think, decreasing intensity. For this is one of the biggest "ands" of the Age of And: the convergence between creativity and technology makes for a transformative sweet spot.

It Starts With Code

We all use code even if we don't know our Java from our PHP, our C++ from our Ruby – even if we have never heard of Unix or Lisp.

Code is everywhere. Code, as much as electricity itself, powers the electric grid that keeps our society operating. It also runs like an underground river through every system in our lives. It is all over our homes, governing our washing machines, playing our music and refrigerating our food. It runs our economy, often through fast but ancient (in computer terms) systems built on early languages such as Cobol and Fortran. It has long been in our cars, so much so that today's mechanics are as much computer engineers as they are grease monkeys, and it is even creeping into the humble light bulb.

Simply put, code is a set of instructions for a computer, encoded in a language humans can make sense of and manipulate, that the computer can then translate into its own machine language. That language instructs the computer to configure its logic gates in such a way as to produce the result the coder desires.

You may very well come into advertising explicitly to avoid having to understand code, but just as code makes the world operate, it lies behind advertising, too.

If you really want to know how to code, find a few hours and read Paul Ford's magnificent essay, "What is Code" (2015)

It's too late for me to be a coder. But what I do appreciate is that the coder represents the foundation of advertising in the digital age. She or he assembles the foundations. There's good code and bad code, in both moral and functional terms. And there's creatively sensitive code such as the closely guarded algorithms used by high-frequency traders and search engines. In

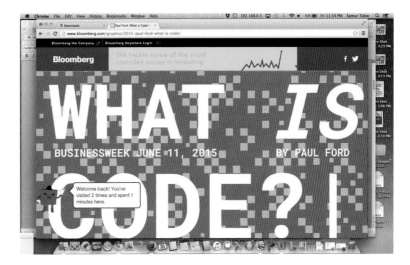

Right *Code underpins the digital age, but it need not be as mysterious as it seems. Paul Ford's "What is Code?" is primer for anyone who wants to dig in to code themselves.*

"... the coder represents the foundation of advertising in the digital age."

advertising, the programmer now defines whether you are good or bad at creative technology.

What makes a great programmer that we would want at Ogilvy & Mather? There's the obvious fluency with the main languages, technology stacks, architectures or infrastructure, but our needs go beyond that. We need an elegant coder, one who can write for mobile and desktop, for low bandwidth and high. We need one with the social skills to work with clients, data scientists, account people and creatives alike. We need one sensitive to the importance of user experience, who is as allergic to kludgy interface as he or she is to kludgy code. Alternatively, you could have the most ham-fisted service-side engineer the world has ever seen so long as he is working with product and user-experience designers who have an instinctive flair for the customer's experience. And yet, even our most tech-oriented developers must build to enhance, rather than impede, creative application. But all this needs to be coordinated, and for that, we need a new animal.

So here comes another newbie, digitally spawned. We call them digital producers. In the tech industry, these people are often project managers, because all around, there are specialists who need to be coordinated, cajoled and encouraged. But the digital producer is not just a glorified digital project manager. He is the keeper of the vision, the link to the client, and often the talent scout for the project. Digital producers sit at the hub of the project, managing everything from user journeys to market research, from design to the engineering roadmap. To put a fine point on it, the digital producer is the leader of the project.

Then there are the digital creatives: the people who dream up, write and subsequently make everything from banner ads to contextual, geo-located billboards, from company web pages to menu apps for quick-service restaurants. At one end of the scale, they handle InDesign or PhotoShop while coding a bit of HTML5 and CSS. At the other, they are artists, engineers, and architects, virtuosos of design and powerful coders. They're quick and nimble enough to get to a minimally viable product at Silicon Valley speeds while still upholding the brand's aesthetics and values.

And finally, there's a very rare bird – the inventor. The person who gets technology so strategically and in such a creative way that he brings something radically new. It is she who asks if a tennis racquet itself can double as a coach; if virtual reality can give someone the experience of being at a hotel from half a world away; if kids can be urged to exercise more by linking a favourite drink to a fitness tracker and exercise program. These are people who can see that the purpose, stated or not, of one object is in fact the solution to another problem.

These four are not a hierarchy, and treating them as such seems to me to be utterly corrosive in a creative culture. Rather, they are a virtuous circle, each incrementally improving the other.

Below *The digital producer is the lead on digital projects, though less of a pilot and more an air traffic controller. Her role is to guide; to bring the various disciplines together in a disciplined way. In the digital age it has become the best way to create innovative work, such as our aeroplane-spotting billboard for British Airways (see also page 129).*

THE CREATIVE PROCESS FOR DIGITAL

Producer
We need to manage, on time and on budget, a disparate group of specialists to deliver a never-done-before experience in the heart of London, and to ensure it fits within the total BA digital ecosystem, a larger integrated campaign in a whole range of media, all supported by a common technology and data platform.

Creative
We need an idea that inspires wonder. We want a child to follow a plane across the sky and engage onlookers in his experience. Interrupting the regular digital billboard feed will make it stand out more. No matter what, the work has to be a seamless part of the BA brand.

Programmer
We need an alogrithm that connects the ADS-B data, Heathrow feed, GPS coordinates and current weather. The code activates the billboard when the correct conditions are met.

Inventor
If we combine an ADS-B antenna with a geo-fence and data from London Heathrow, we can identify the plane, flight number, and destination. We will trigger the billboard only when the plane flies overhead in weather clear enough for it to be seen from the street.

The Front End

The front end where creativity and technology co-mingle has become known as UX – a deceptively simple acronym for User Experience. It describes what is a ferociously contested domain. As the internet developed, so did the need to make it easy to relate to. It was Don Norman who first gave us UX as a concept in 1998. As in other cases, what was originally meant morphed into something slightly different. Norman meant human-centred design. He writes, "I invented the term because I thought Human Interface and usability were too narrow: I wanted to cover all aspects of the person's experience with a system, including industrial design, graphics, the interface, the physical interaction, and the manual."[1] Now it means more like a place where information architecture meets research, strategy, content, psychology and visual design.

Ironically, for something that claims to make things simple, UX is never explained simply. It is impossible to find a chart that does so; indeed, they all look as if they have been designed by drunken locusts drawing in ink. Being as they are specialists in the user experience, UX professionals are in on the joke. I have a theory as to why that is. UX has evolved a collection of specialists who have never quite resolved their relationship with one another. Each specialism has its own view of what it is, and all have a vested interest in not defining it too clearly. And Ogilvy & Mather's charts, frankly, have not been much better. I briefed our people to design something clear and simple; and this is it:

Below This chart might not be perfect – as any UX expert knows, there is always room for improvement – but this attempt captures the UX process well.

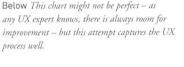

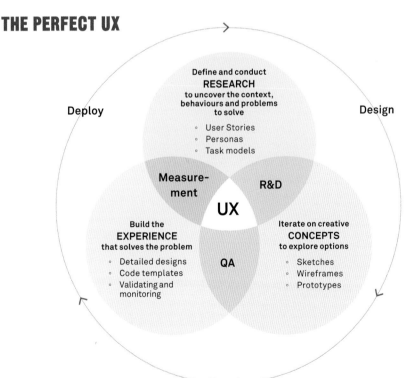

THE PERFECT UX

Deploy

Design

Define and conduct
RESEARCH
to uncover the context, behaviours and problems to solve
- User Stories
- Personas
- Task models

Measure-ment

R&D

UX

Build the
EXPERIENCE
that solves the problem
- Detailed designs
- Code templates
- Validating and monitoring

QA

Iterate on creative
CONCEPTS
to explore options
- Sketches
- Wireframes
- Prototypes

Develop

From this we can see that the UX designer sits at the intersection of customer needs, business needs, and the feasibility of meeting them on any given project. UX is as much a philosophy as it is a practice, and in many respects, it is everyone's job, particularly at an agency. That's more than just rhetoric: on some projects, the UX designer will do the work of a planner. On others, they'll be visual designers.

A true jack-of-all-digital-trades, the agency UX designer needs to move easily among the following disciplines depending on the project and platform:

- Copywriting
- Information Design
- Sound Design
- Motion Design
- Graphic Design
- Interface Design
- Interaction Design
- Code

Why the staggering breadth? Because UX is a critical part of the fabric of advertising in the digital age. User experience is often the differentiator for a brand. Uber is cited as a great example of UX, and the real magic is the whole experience beyond just the elegant app. It supplies clear delivery of the kind of information waiting travellers want most, like fare and wait time, and marries that to more effective and consumer-friendly redistribution of capital and labour in the form of cars and drivers. Put that together and you transform a poor consumer experience – the opaque taxi market – and turn it into a great one. The total experience a consumer has with Uber is so well thought out, it's almost frictionless.

And so we find a new, broader definition for the UX professional. If you book a flight through an airline's magnificent website, have a smooth check in, but then endure a terrible flight, then you've had a bad user experience. While she cannot influence air traffic control, the UX designer can address how the airline acts. In short, she is the person charged with enhancing every part of the interaction between a brand and its consumers. It is as essential as it is intangible.

The Back End

The Back End is what makes anything happen. It's also the area where companies and agencies experience the most disappointment.

But before the disappointment, there's the fear.

Consider the marketing technology business. It is skyrocketing. Taking the US alone, the number of vendors between 2014 and 2015 *doubled*.

chiefmartec.com Marketing Technology Landscape

March 2016

Above Scott Brinker continually updates his famous chart as marketing technology solutions are invented at an astonishing rate. And yes, it's almost unreadable! A warning: technology is only useful with the skills and structures in place to make it sing. And never forget the big idea.

And, of course, each vendor has a sales pitch. It is very interesting to consider the techniques technology vendors tend to use to demonstrate their products. They show simple "flash" demos to entice you, built to run smoothly in controlled conditions, on simple platforms. It all looks so easy. But it's not.

And there's what Peter de Luca calls "the 20% problem". He should know: he's head of our marketing technology practice, and spends his whole life trying to remedy it. Peter says that you just need to ask a company "what percentage of the marketing functionality of this marketing technology are you using?" So very often the answer is 20 per cent, or something close to it.

The reason is primarily structural. There was no structure in place to support the licence when it was bought, or there are organizational gaps between the work groups or departments that should be benefiting from it. Incredibly, without really understanding this, disappointed clients often switch software vendors looking for the functionality they do not believe they have (even when they often do). They will still be disappointed.

The point is not about technology; it's about internal alignment.

If you think of the primary teams or departments in your client's organization that should be aligned, they are likely to be:

- Marketing Team: These are the planners and strategists, the people who think up and design the campaigns against specific business objectives.

- Operations Team: or the campaign execution team. These are the people that are actually working with the marketing technologies, or managing the vendors that do the heavy lifting.

Right *Peter de Luca's take on making marketing automation work.*

HOW NOT TO MAKE MARKETING AUTOMATION WORK FOR YOU

• The **Marketing Team** starts off by submitting a simple ad-hoc campaign request lacking any real targeting criteria, test plan or cross-channel engagement strategy. This may be due to a lack of knowledge about the data that are available, past campaign successes, or the available functionality of the technology platform.

• Then, with this simple request in hand, the **Operations Team** needs to use only the basic functionality of the platform to create an audience, build a simple email template, and launch the campaign.

• The simplicity of this ad hoc campaign naturally leads to a lack of data to analyze, with limited insights and basic reports coming in from the **Analytics Team**.

A simple request leads to a simple execution, which leads to limited insights. And that loop continues, leading to limited use of technology – only 20% of what's available.

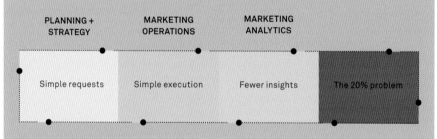

PLANNING + STRATEGY	MARKETING OPERATIONS	MARKETING ANALYTICS	
Simple requests	Simple execution	Fewer insights	The 20% problem

HOW TO MAKE MARKETING AUTOMATION WORK FOR YOU

• The **Marketing Team** is thinking strategically. They're being innovative in terms of channel engagement. They know what data exists. They're defining more complex campaigns to drive more personalization. They know what they can get out of their technology. In essence, they're pushing the Operations Team to do more interesting things.

• In turn, when the **Operations Team** is being pushed with more strategic and innovative engagement strategies, they naturally become savvier with the technology platform. They're being pushed to use more of it. They're coordinating multiple channels in their journey, applying more complex business rules to drive more personalized experiences.

• In turn, the **Analytics Team** has more data to analyze and more tests to evaluate. They're able to find more insights on what's worked and what hasn't worked. They're providing meaningful reports and dashboards to the Marketing Team in order to inspire them further.

The result is a positive loop that continues and continues.

Above *Jägermeister teamed up with Shazam to become part of the entertainment experience for Millennials in a multi-pronged, automated campaign called "Shazam the Stag". Knowing that their audience craved moments that create social capital, the brand provided a digital ticket behind the scenes of the EDM (electronic dance music) scene – and it did so in the shopping aisle itself, turning every bottle, every sign, every shelf wobbler into a portal to a world of custom cocktails, bespoke playlists, and backstage access. Shoppers need only snap a picture of the Jägermeister stag. Shazam and the back-end technology did the rest.*

• Analytics Team: people that manipulate data, find insights, and create reports for the campaigns.

So what happens when all is aligned perfectly, and the back end is on its best behaviour? For one thing, the brand's marketing technology investments are aligned to the sort of relationship it wants to have with customers. And for another, you can accomplish great things.

A Frontier How Far?

Of the waves of hype that have washed through the Digital Revolution, the most vigorous at the time of writing are those that promise the new frontier of Virtual Reality (VR) and Augmented Reality (AR); but a frontier how far away? And, indeed, how attainable?

As VR and AR are often used interchangeably and incorrectly, it behoves me to describe them clearly. In each case, technology is predicated around creating an enhanced experience.

• In VR, the experience takes place in any environment that is virtual – a movie, for instance, so that there is a simulation of physical presence.

• In AR, the experience takes place in a live, physical environment as a supplement added by digital assets.

In between there is a grey zone – mixed reality.

Above right *Since children are rarely
enthusiastic about cleaning their teeth,
Toothbrush Games uses augmented reality
to encourage better dental hygiene habits. A
two-minute game, featuring a live video of
the user brushing their teeth alongside some
fun characters, turns a chore into a challenge.
The stroke of genius? It only works when the
smartphone's microphone picks up the sound of
brushing.*

Popular attention in each case is focused on the method of delivery: how
you experience. But the innovation that has driven the experiences so far
has been much more to do with the back end of the technology, where
significant advances in individual fields have been assembled into a chain.

The first set of links is to do with capture: it's what enables us to see
things in the round.

The second set of links is about process.

So far so good. And you would need a heart of pure flint not to be moved
by some of the experience highs, which this incredible cocktail of innovation
can produce.

But then, how do you view it? And it is in the area of display that the
technology lags – and may do so for some time.

At each end of the spectrum you can view, on the one hand, with a
self-assembly cardboard kit linked to your mobile phone or, on the other,
with a clunky headset linked to a gaming PC. One is cheap; the other is
very expensive. Let's also be honest: one is flimsy and primitive; the other
is heavy and uncomfortable. There's a lot of work to be done before the
chips can be miniaturized, de-thermalized, de-powered and then put into
something resembling a hip pair of spectacles, which delivers enough speed
and pixelation to equate to reality. And that's not even recognizing the
biggest promise of all: the haptic promise.

Haptics perception is created by the impact of sensory touch. Technologists
have adopted this term to mean a touch-based interaction with a computer.
Haptic controllers add touch to the mix, enabling you to manipulate digital
objects in a virtual world. It requires a bi-directional interface between your
brain and an interface that connects you to the world: at one level "teaching"
you that you can feel virtual objects. While it's surprisingly convincing when

Above *Jim Beam makes a prized bourbon, The Devil's Cut, but you can't see what makes this spirit different from the outside. You have to know how it's made, and to illustrate that, Jim Beam worked with Bottle Rocket to create an immersive VR experience to dramatize the journey bourbon takes to become The Devil's Cut. Only in VR could you get right inside the bottle!*

done well – I've seen people flinch when they've dropped a purely virtual hammer on their imaginary hand! – any idea of mass-commercializing a hap-app in the reasonable future is haptic pie-in-the-sky. The front end has not caught up with the back end – and it could be rather a long time before it does.

There is, of course, an assumption made by all who seek to boost these technologies, which is that their effects are inevitably benign. But when the physical world becomes really indistinguishable from the digital, do we gain? Do we communicate better – or less? Do we take more out of life – or less? To be honest, at this stage – who knows? But a rational scepticism at least puts these questions on the table. The case for the "metaverse" sweeping all ahead of it is not yet proven.

It may seem that I'm "down" on VR/AR. Not at all. It is very exciting and it will move out from its hard core of gamesters into the world of advertising. Here's what it offers:

- **Perspective:** we can hyper-immerse as we tour through reality. Where we seek to simulate a product, we will be able to do so with an intensity never before managed. Imagine, for instance, wristwatch advertising. For years, designers have tried to make us believe we could see inside the workings in 2D. Now we'll be able to travel inside and around the mechanism of every last finely crafted Rolex or Piaget.

- **Context:** providing extra meaning through explanation and references. Imagine opening and deploying a new food processor for the first time. You're led not just through the basics of how to

CAMERAS, HEADSETS AND HAPTICS

Capturing the video needed for 360-degree video used to require a custom-built camera array. Now, the technology has matured to the point where prosumer 360-degree cameras are readily available. Animated VR, like standard computer animation, gets built in a virtual environment.

Headsets provide much of the VR experience my immersing the viewers eyes and ears into an entirely virtual environment. Sensors detect head and body movement, giving the sense of movement through the created environment. More sophisticated setups use external positioning sensors to create a virtual room so that the viewer can move around to roam through the environment. Headsets range from expensive, high-tech models to cardboard units in which you slide a phone to act as the screen. VR headsets are becoming more sophisticated at a remarkable clip. While most are still tethered by wires, the next generation will be wireless, increasing the sense of reality. Future systems, much smaller and less obtrusive, will likely focus on mixed reality, enabling the real world to be a part of your chosen virtual environment.

Haptics provide the feedback that make simulations feel more real. Anyone who has played a modern video game will be familiar with the "buzz" a controller can make to indicate an action. In VR, the experience is more sophisticated, but the idea is the same, but with a twist. The haptic controllers don't just give physical feedback; they give the user the means to interact with objects in the virtual environment, with physical feedback cues to fool the mind. That's now. Future devices will read hand and finger positions in space and give more nuanced feedback, leading to a much greater feeling of reality. The potential is there for much more than just entertainment, both good and bad. Take a real-life look at the book Ready Player One to get a feel for what a dystopian world based on virtual reality and haptics could be like.

assemble and operate it – but into making perfect mayonnaise, which does not curdle as each drop of oil melds into the emulsion, speeding up and slowing down with all the mentoring you might expect from Martha Stewart if she was standing beside you.

- **Intensity:** take any piece of emotive creativity, and it can be intensified a hundred-fold – at a cost, of course. Advertising has always appropriated the term "anthem" to describe its big set-pieces. "Anthemic" reality will make some corporate advertising seem very pallid. If you attach yourself to the values of the rainforest, how much more valuable is a hyper-immersive experience compared to a merely second-hand evocation of it.

But I do expect the practical uses of VR/AR will be more educational than anything else. Walking around the Alamo with context delivered to you seems a no-brainer. Having your drive to work continuously informed by extraneous context might be rather trying.

And this will also apply to advertising. So while the natural tendency is to see it developing in terms of glamorous consumer applications, it's ability to supercharge demonstrability may make it as much a B2B technique, especially in high-value categories – choosing a new fleet, or selecting an architect, for instance.

And in consumer goods, anything that lends itself to demonstration will be self-selecting: from the craftsmanship of luxury goods to the efficacy of personal-care products, to the performance of a new SUV to the hip design of a Mediterranean resort.

Pokémon Go seems to be shepherding in an era of augmented reality, beginning with thousands of Pokémon fanatics running around the city searching for computer-rendered creatures, but one that will logically expand to experiences beyond entertainment into fields such as travel, education and medicine. I confess; I am unlikely to ever go Pokémon hunting. But I would love to take a historical tour of London or Beijing using an augmented reality travel app. As digital continues to augment reality, it creates all sorts of connections – to the past, present, future, and alternative versions of all three.

VR and AR are the technologies of the moment, but as the Internet of Things (IoT) grows more ubiquitous, they may begin to merge with a growing orbit of connected devices. Trackers and smartwatches have already extended the functionality of our mobile devices and opened an extended channel for brands. But the same technologies that power front ends and back ends, and realities virtual and augmented, inspire different sorts of invention as well, further blurring the lines marking off advertising, product development, and marketing.

And, here, of course, one must sound the familiar bugle call of warning. At the end of the day these are just techniques. They will only be as interesting, engaging and long lasting as the ideas that animate them – and the brands which pay for them.

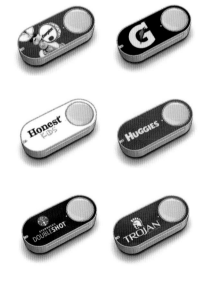

Above *Amazon's Dash Button is a simple, single-function wireless node that connects to a WiFi network. It serves one purpose: once configured through your mobile, a push of the Dash Button will place an order for a specified product from Amazon. Out of dishwasher detergent? Press Dash to have a new supply shipped to your door. The innovative device does more than connect the "Internet of Things", it connects the internet with brands. Imagine what else such wirelessly connected switches could do!*

WHERE DID ALL THE POKÉMON GO?

In the summer of 2016, a phenomenon was unleashed that captivated the world – for a while, at least.

When little-known Niantic developed a side project – a game requiring players to hunt around their cities for monsters and hurl digital balls on their smartphone to catch them – it turned augmented reality mainstream. It launched on 6 July 2016, and the world went Pokémon crazy.

Why the sudden hype? Firstly, an already powerful franchise in Pokémon, which had been popular since the late 1990s. Secondly, an inherently viral platform where players became real-world, monster-chasing adverts –sparking immediate interest from confused bystanders. And thirdly, the app store effect quickly kicked in. Pokémon Go

Left *Pokémon Go started life as an experiment, in partnership with Google's Maps and Earth divisions.*

was the most downloaded app ever in its first week of launch, achieving 7.2 million downloads compared to a paltry 2.2 million for Angry Birds 2. And it stuck at the top of the charts, passing 500 million downloads in little over a year. Free to download with in-app purchases, it drove a record-breaking month for Apple's App Store revenue. Pokémon Go was making real money from AR monsters.

By mid-July, Pokémon mania was in full swing. When a rare Pokémon was discovered in New York's Central Park, thousands of players swarmed the area for a chance to collect points and climb the league table. Few of them spotted singer Justin Bieber

$600 million	5.4 billion miles	43 minutes
revenue in 90 days.	walked by Pokémon Go players.	spent on the app every day.
2.5x faster than Candy Crush Saga.	Almost the distance around Pluto.	Vs. Whatsapp's 30 minutes.
Source: AppAnnie	*Source: GameSpot, February 27th, 2017.*	*Source: SimilarWeb, July 8th, 2016, US Android App Data.*

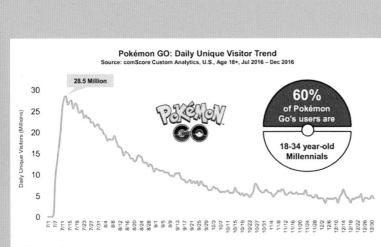

Left *A familiar pattern. A dramatic hype-driven rise in unique visitors, followed by a period of decline until the natural level of truly interested users is found. Mobile games – like Candy Crush Saga and Clash of Clans – seem particularly prone to this "faddish" adoption.*

Left *Outdoor advertising – fitting for a game played in the real world, but surprisingly un-augmented – has been spotted in London, promoting new Pokémon features. Even the most digital of platforms resorts to traditional methods of attracting attention and shoring up user numbers.*

among the crowd – all sights trained on the monsters on their screens, not real-life celebrities in their midst! Players were reportedly so distracted by the game that they were endangering themselves – one falling off a cliff, others from being mugged while roaming unknown streets looking for monsters. The app hit its peak of 28.5 million unique users within weeks.

But then reality started to bite. By the end of summer player interest began to quickly drop off, settling at around 5 million unique visitors per month. This pattern – a burst of mass interest that quickly wanes – is the fad phenomenon writ large for the Internet age. Popular mobile games like Candy Crush Saga and viral sensations like the ALS Ice Bucket challenge (pages 168–169) have followed a similar trajectory.

But falling user numbers hardly means a reversal of fortune for Pokémon Go. A highly active user base of 5 million has netted an astonishing $1.7 billion in revenue since the game launched. And it's likely a preview of what's in store – AR experiences commanding extraordinary engagement levels and creating immense value from imagined worlds superimposed onto this one. As digital continues to augment reality, our senses will surely be expanded to encompass 5,000 years of civilization – finding ourselves seemingly able to slip through space and time, to move between worlds, and to catch a few monsters along the way.

12 THE THREE BATTLEGROUNDS: Social Media, Mobility, Continuous Commerce

As the digital age starts to "settle" there are three big battlegrounds where debate still persists and, in general, the future is not yet won.
The first of these is social.

PUTTING THE SOCIAL BACK INTO SOCIAL MEDIA

If ever there was a digital Eden, it was the early days of social media – days of innocence and hope, where friendship could be "graphed", and expanded in seemingly endless, experimental ways.

Looking back, those early views of social media – the attention given to the social graph of an individual and then to the collective spread of word of mouth – still seem prescient, but not now sufficient. In the absence of any more precise and subtle measures, the more fans (or followers) you had was quite simply, the better. "Sharing" or "following" suddenly

Right Facebook is the standout social medium in the United States. Almost every 18–34-year-old in the US engages with the monolithic platform for over 1,000 minutes – nearly 17 hours – every month according to comScore. But watch out for Instagram! It is becoming the platform of choice for younger Millennials.

AGE 18–34 DIGITAL AUDIENCE PENETRATION VS ENGAGEMENT OF LEADING SOCIAL NETWORKS

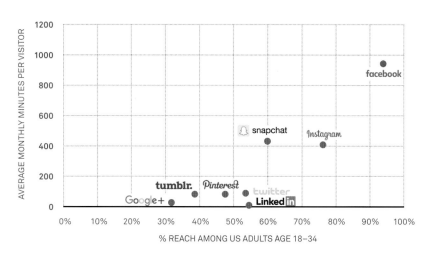

become acceptable measures of brand advocacy. However, the sheer volume of connections started to become overwhelming. By 2015, the average American was spending 3.7 hours per day on a smartphone; the average Latin American whiled away 6.1 hours per day on social media.

Marketing abhors a vacuum, and so brands rushed in. The distribution of social content by brands increased exponentially.

But something had gone wrong. The users themselves were not happy. In our research, we started to discover that almost 80 per cent of social media users felt the quality of online advertising was average to poor. Other research showed that 80 per cent of B2C (Business-to-Customer) content produced goes unnoticed by consumers.

What had happened?

In the race for fans, fans had become audiences, and brands had started to hurt themselves by delivering messaging at the fans, the classic paradigm of analogue "marketing".

The content was often superficial. When Audi represented the idea of #PaidMyDues through a series of "artistic" images, they incited an onslaught of criticism. The fans insisted that the Instagram feed go back to images of cars. That was why they had followed Audi in the first place.

Below *Authenticity matters on social platforms. When Audi started to over engineer its Instagram feed with #PaidMyDues, the audience demanded the brand get back to what it does best – cars.*

audi   FOLLOW

14.7k likes   79w

tshyde_esquire Okay, more of this non car idiocy and I unfollow.

lenoxbm @audi Didn't I just say no more crap! Do you not read your comments? People only want cars. Your social media team needs to be fired.

cyclejim There is a great Audi site called fourtitude that actually shows pics of cool Audis

blzzrd_ Where are the cars.....

dgiurk This is awesome

midonyk Audi haven't posted a picture if a car in over a week. What else is new?

midonyk @audi

kylemcgill747 @drankin23 trust fund baby ?

misiu_pysiu 👏 👏 👏 👏 👏

jsch3ll This marketing campaign literally makes me like my S4 less

♡ Add a comment...   ○ ○ ○

Above right *Hashtags can be dangerous. The NYPD found itself in a spot of bother when the #MyNYPD was turned against it. It became the hashtag of choice to criticize the department's approach to fighting crime.*

And aimless connectivity can rebound horribly, as the New York Police Department discovered when they wandered up an irrelevant alley through the #MyNYPD hashtag.

No wonder the audience fought back: it had to.

For self-preservation people contracted their social graphs, retreating into smaller private networks, looking for walls with which to surround their gardens. The burgeoning growth of "walled gardens" – the more closed and intimate social platforms such as WhatsApp, WeChat or Facebook Messenger – has been the response. Meanwhile, the social platforms themselves started to tighten their filtering algorithms.

By 2014, we started to notice a drop in engagement levels on our clients' pages and launched a global analysis of more than 100 social programs. What we discovered was the decline of organic reach, in advance of this being recognized or admitted by vendors such as Facebook.

Simply put, this data demonstrated that the era of using social media as a free medium, which could be depended upon to inspire by word of mouth

Right *As the opportunity for organic reach has declined on Facebook, brands have become increasingly willing to pay to reach the platform's audience instead.*

FACEBOOK ZERO

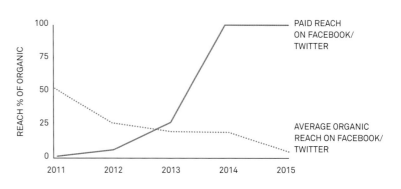

organically, was over, forever. The Earned in the triangle of Paid-Owned-Earned was about to undergo a major desertion of social media usage to the Paid.

At the same time, our understanding of what actually constituted a fan improved. There had been a strong streak of wish fulfilment in the industry: brand owners want to believe that because people are saying positive things about your brand they are brand advocates. This is not necessarily the case.

Certainly there is no shortage of liking or of followers. Eighty-four per cent of people across 11 markets said, when we asked, that they had "liked" or followed a brand, product or service. More than half had actually interacted with a brand – although in a salutary finding which punctures a lot of the rhetoric about social marketing, 79 per cent never received a response back. Around 6 out of 10 people seem to be "sharers": they share their experiences of brands – both positive and negative – with others.

Followers are not the real prize. That lies in finding the true promoters of a brand. Only 2 in 10 merit this description. They are more active; they seek direct interaction with brands; they like associating with brands; and their networks of friends also talk about brands much more. They want news. They need feedback. And they are relentlessly discriminating. They are almost as willing as sharers to discuss terrible brand experiences online. The old direct-marketing adage of "member get member" very easily translates into member-lose-member.

Alongside these sobering realities, much social marketing remains random, unmeasured and unused.

The future lies in what we call "deep social". Social has, in a way, grown up. It is moving from a marketing and broadcast mindset to a publishing

Right Social moves from basic, through strategic, to transformative, when tactics give way to deep insight and engaging stories at every step of the customer journey.

FROM SOCIAL TO DEEP SOCIAL

BASIC	STRATEGIC	TRANSFORMATIVE
Campaign and tactical	Ad hoc integration with business	Builds brands, business and reputation
Platform presence, not strategy	A communication channel, not tied to business outcomes	Social impact beyond platforms
Uncoordinated community management	Social considered in some parts of the customer journey	Social considered at every step
Creative emphasis is on channels with smaller, tactical ideas	Social is still an afterthought for creative	Creative ideas reign supreme; channels are in service of ideas

THE ALS ICE BUCKET CHALLENGE

If you go to the Smithsonian's Museum of American History in Washington DC you'll find a very ordinary bucket. Why on earth is a bucket there? Well, it set off one of the most powerful viral marketing campaigns of the digital age.

In August 2014, celebrities, business moguls and millions of others voluntarily dumped a bucket of freezing cold water over their heads, donating to the little-known Amyotrophic Lateral Sclerosis (ALS) cause for the privilege. (Or, like US President Barack Obama and UK Prime Minister David Cameron, they had stumped up a larger amount to avoid their icy fate). The challenge's sudden popularity caught the ALS Association unaware;

Above *The bucket that started a movement, which Jeanette Senerchia previously used to mop her floors, now proudly stands in the Smithsonian's "Giving for America" exhibition.*

nobody internally had initiated the idea and the first sign of something unusual was at first a trickle, then a waterfall of new donations.

So what was happening? Well, to find the source we need to visit a place called Pelham. It's a small town nestled in New York City's Westchester suburbs, only half an hour's train ride from Grand Central Station but a world away from bustling Manhattan. Pelham is a tight-knit community of fewer than 7,000 people, many of whom know each other well, or know someone who knows them. It is precisely this friendly, community atmosphere that created the conditions

for the ALS Ice Bucket Challenge to flourish.

One of the town's residents is Jeanette Senerchia, a lovely, unassuming woman whose husband, Anthony, both suffer from ALS. It's a relatively unknown neurological disorder – also known as Lou Gehrig's Disease – for which there is currently no cure. The life expectancy of someone diagnosed with the disease is often a matter of years, as motor neurons controlling their muscle function deteriorate rapidly. Professor Stephen Hawking has famously lived with ALS for half a century, but he is more fortunate than most sufferers. ALS is a terminal illness.

Jeanette had, as she puts it, a "very small" foundation generating a little money for awareness of ALS, used for families who are affected. Her cousin-in-law, a pro golfer in Sarasota with whom she has a fun relationship, one day texted her and said, "Look at your Facebook page". On it was the original Ice Bucket Challenge. He'd come across the idea in his circles, but it had never really taken off or been associated with a specific cause. Then he thought of her and her "very small" foundation. Jeanette told me she texted back, "You must be joking," but eventually she did it. Then she nominated her close friends in Pelham. They nominated their friends, who did the same. And so on – a ripple effect from a few local townspeople, to the whole community, to neighbouring towns, and finally, a tidal wave on Facebook.

The giant of social networks isn't a nebulous universe of strangers, but a web of communities where compelling content and ideas can quickly become a pandemic. Within weeks, Facebook's CEO, Mark Zuckerberg, had taken the ALS Ice Bucket Challenge (nominated by New Jersey Governor Chris Christie), alongside other celebrities such as Justin Timberlake, David Beckham and Justin Bieber, whose video gained over one million likes alone.

Likes turned into donations. In just one month, the ALS Association in the US received almost $100 million, dwarfing the $2.7m donated over the same period the year before. Awareness soared as over 2 million videos and 4.5 million Twitter mentions saturated social and traditional media. Searches for information about ALS

Above *CEO, Mark Zuckerberg taking the ALS Ice Bucket Challenge. Nominated by New Jersey Governor, Chris Christie, in return he challenged Microsoft founder Bill Gates, Facebook COO Sheryl Sandberg and Netflix CEO Reed Hastings.*

increased dramatically; the ALS Wikipedia page received 2.7 million views that August, compared to only 1.6 million in the preceding 12 months.

Yet some critics labelled the phenomenon "slacktivism", a nexus of entertainment and empathy, but ultimately a get-out from more serious involvement. While Jeanette had created a reason for the challenge, the charity risked being a footnote in the YouTube comments – more focus on the bucket than the cause, the LOLs rather than ALS. Others were concerned about a sudden redirection of donations to ALS that would otherwise go to a broader set of causes. Unsurprisingly, those involved with the disease defended the campaign, happy to finally be recipients of such large-scale awareness and unbridled support.

The critics are likely wrong.

Researchers recently identified a new gene associated with the disease that will help uncover the triggers of ALS and lead to new treatments. The breakthrough was funded directly from the ALS Ice Bucket Challenge. Of $115 million raised over the eight weeks the campaign went viral, $77m was dedicated to research and $1 million – a drop in the bucket – went to the clever scientists at the University of Massachusetts Medical School who made the discovery.

There are few things more bracing than a bucket of ice dumped over one's head. A bigger shock, perhaps, is an unplanned campaign that traded fun, peer pressure and a dash of online narcissism for a scientific breakthrough, and all of it down to the intersection between small town familiarity and social media fame.

and tailored mindset. Shallow content gives way to more sophisticated insights, more interesting stories – and much more of the "conversational" promise that the early pioneers of social media craved.

Where do the insights come from?

First, from understanding that social is something that has to be seen across the whole customer journey. Taking a category at random – say, telephone providers in the UK – we can see that not one company is getting the basics of social presence right across an even abbreviated journey from awareness to loyalty.

COMPARISON OF UK TELEPHONE PROVIDERS ACROSS THE CUSTOMER JOURNEY

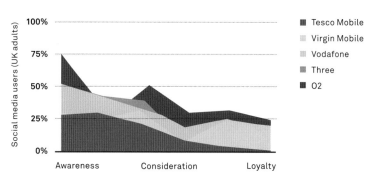

Above right *When it comes to social engagement, telephone providers in the UK have relative strengths. O2 is at least getting some things right, achieving broad awareness among UK social media users and converting reasonably well to consideration. But none get even the basics right across the whole customer journey.*

Second, from understanding that while "conversation" is an easy word to use, it's a complex thing to understand. A conversation dissected and mapped will tell you what the key content interests, influential platforms and social behaviour of your fellow conversationalists are (see chart opposite).

Third, from understanding that some social conversationalists are more important than others. Journalists are, perhaps, an obvious example. Just consider the figures below.

INFLUENCERS ARE IMPORTANT

Right *Social media has extra clout when it influences the influencers. Journalists use social media to research, investigate, verify publish stories.*

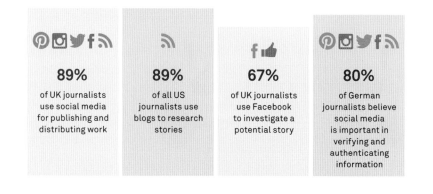

89%
of UK journalists use social media for publishing and distributing work

89%
of all US journalists use blogs to research stories

67%
of UK journalists use Facebook to investigate a potential story

80%
of German journalists believe social media is important in verifying and authenticating information

HOW THE MEANING OF MANSCAPING HAS CHANGED OVER TIME

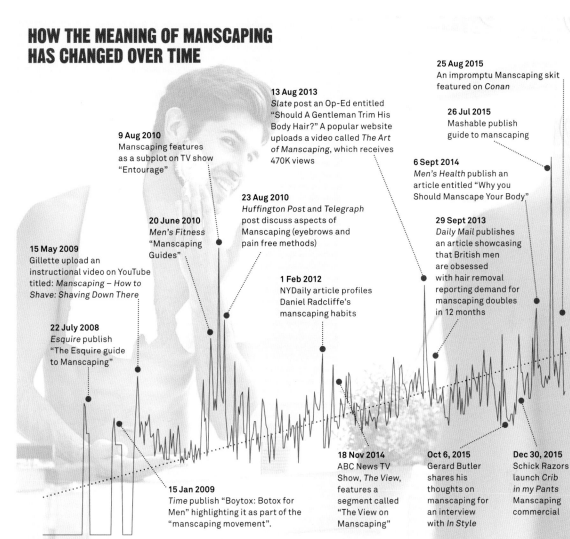

25 Aug 2015
An impromptu Manscaping skit featured on *Conan*

26 Jul 2015
Mashable publish guide to manscaping

13 Aug 2013
Slate post an Op-Ed entitled "Should A Gentleman Trim His Body Hair?" A popular website uploads a video called *The Art of Manscaping*, which receives 470K views

9 Aug 2010
Manscaping features as a subplot on TV show "Entourage"

6 Sept 2014
Men's Health publish an article entitled "Why you Should Manscape Your Body"

23 Aug 2010
Huffington Post and *Telegraph* post discuss aspects of Manscaping (eyebrows and pain free methods)

20 June 2010
Men's Fitness "Manscaping Guides"

29 Sept 2013
Daily Mail publishes an article showcasing that British men are obsessed with hair removal reporting demand for manscaping doubles in 12 months

15 May 2009
Gillette upload an instructional video on YouTube titled: *Manscaping – How to Shave: Shaving Down There*

1 Feb 2012
NYDaily article profiles Daniel Radcliffe's manscaping habits

22 July 2008
Esquire publish "The Esquire guide to Manscaping"

15 Jan 2009
Time publish "Boytox: Botox for Men" highlighting it as part of the "manscaping movement".

18 Nov 2014
ABC News TV Show, *The View*, features a segment called "The View on Manscaping"

Oct 6, 2015
Gerard Butler shares his thoughts on manscaping for an interview with *In Style*

Dec 30, 2015
Schick Razors launch *Crib in my Pants* Manscaping commercial

Above *Conversation is an easy word to say, more difficult to describe. Mapping ideas against search over time shows how the social dialogue evolves.*

But anyone – not just journalists – can become influential, and they often do not identify as topic enthusiasts. It's no longer journalists who are influential. Again, analytics allows us to identify and rank the influencers that matter to you (see diagram on page 170).

It follows that none of this can be undertaken lightly. The "community manager" has changed beyond recognition, and the premium on his/her skills is considerable. This is not a role to economize on! Their hi-touch is needed, not just to manage the original idea of a community as a group of people you somehow own, but to join in day by day, hour by hour, minute by minute, stimulating and facilitating them (see diagram on page 173).

But, more than that, they also have to have a pro-active publisher mind-set paired with the energy needed to help create a consistent brand experience.

At the end of the day, it is ideas that create conversations, and the stronger they are, the livelier the conversation and the more animated the community.

Social CRM

But it is the relatively new phenomenon of "Social CRM" that is most exciting for the future, particularly if you have ever worked in direct marketing.

A few years ago, Ogilvy & Mather acquired a small company in Belgium. Social Lab is now one of the biggest assets we've got globally. They are pioneers in targeting consumers in social media, at the right time, with the things they are interested in. It's a no-brainer. Our targeted social content out-performs non-targeted content by a factor of 2.5.

They use "lookalike" modelling to target "twins" of people who know you already, and then leverage all the known interactions there are with

Above Here's a social CRM campaign for Philips Norelco shavers. First we identified precisely the right prospects on Facebook. Then we built awareness with engaging video ads of New York celebrity hairstylist Mark Bustos giving a confidence boost to homeless men by offering free haircuts. Lastly, we drove customers down the funnel with more product-focused content to boost sales.

THE EVOLUTION OF THE COMMUNITY MANAGER

Definition of Community: not a fixed group of people you own and manage but flickering moments of opportunity based on shared passion

2009	2010	2011	2012
"Looking for a second career? Consider being a Community Manager."	"Hottest job in marketing might just be the Community Manager."	"The concept of community management has become a hot topic in the last year, driven by more mainstream interest."	"Community management...has become increasingly important in the rise of social media."
AdAge	**AdAge**	THE COMMUNITY ROUNDTABLE	**Mashable**

2013	2014	2015
"Community managers are the most powerful group online"	"There are more and more platforms where the community can respond to an organization now." #cmgrchat	"...fewer pieces of higher quality content for millions see, rather than encouraging a community manager to push out hourly updates for a handful of fans. " *The Guardian*
web-strategist.com	#cmgrchat	

Above *The role of community manager – equal parts publisher, customer support agent, brand guardian and social media maven – has changed considerably over the years.*

them, engage and re-engage with them, test and re-test, never ignoring an action, tracking and re-targeting all the way, through from the initial prospecting to the final sale.

People often ask me, how do you measure the effects of social media?

In the past it was difficult to answer, as the "intermediate" measures (e.g. likes, shares, impressions) were just that – intermediate. Of course, one gold-plated ideal would be net promoter score – quantifying the value of an individual's recommendations to someone else to try a brand. AT&T developed some interesting work in this area; most notably for their "At Summer Break" program some years back. But systems like these rely on very heavy-duty econometric models, in this case created by management consultants. Unfortunately, they are just not affordable day to day; and as a result have not had wide-scale adoption.

But, social CRM does provide an answer. As long as there is a URL, and a tracking and attribution system to follow people around the internet, it is now possible to measure customers advancing along (or not) their Customer Journey.

For Facebook in particular, this might seem a long way from that idyllic Eden of their foundation myth. But it seems it might do a lot more like El Dorado as the cash registers ring with hard sales results.

THE JOY OF MOBILITY

The heading is very carefully chosen. What's interesting is discussing what mobile enables, not what mobile is. But first, let's find out what mobile is not.

In September of 2000, I was asked to speak at the WAP Enhanced Services and GPRS Conference in London. I argued that the mobile phone would be a *sales promotion* medium. This was a controversial point of view because "advertising" was busily claiming the phone as a new ad medium. Advertising would of course claim the Taj Mahal if impact (easy!) and scale (less easy!) could be demonstrated.

I wasn't wholly right, but I was partly right. Mobile, because it gets one so close to the point of decision, is indeed especially useful in directing you to offers and deals in a specific location.

It is not an advertising medium of any significance, although the desire to think of it as such and use it as such is persistent. It is something much more than a device or a channel or, indeed, a medium.

The joy of mobile technology is that it offers mobility. It's about engagement with a whole new lifestyle, and it will be the premier platform of the digital age by far.

Everything is now driven by an explosion of mobile connectivity. As my former colleague Martin Lange wrote in an internal note:

> Telecommunications providers have essentially become utility companies, providing access to something that people need … access to mobile devices worldwide is growing much faster than access to many of life's bare essentials.

By this, he means improved water, electricity and sanitation.

As more users connect, more connection and data points develop and the demand for more services increases. The only limitations are infrastructure, reach and bandwidth; and regulations.

What is developing is fundamentally new: an engagement ecosystem. Mobility, born as it was out of ubiquitous connectivity, becomes a resource through which communications can be created – but only as a part of a larger view of what contributes service to the customer (see box on page 176).

This ecosystem in the West has been enabled largely by Apple, and in China by WeChat. Phones themselves are developing into a box of sensors which gather and deploy data.

But the software, the distribution model, the billing (including the connections to foreign exchange), and the link to the store all combine to make mobility seamless.

Calvin Carter, Ogilvy & Mather's global guru in mobility, who runs our subsidiary called Bottle Rocket in Dallas, tells the story of how he founded the company the day after Steve Jobs opened the iPhone platform. Apple

Above *Any parent knows that it is hard to get kids to drink water. Sugary, colourful drinks hold a powerful appeal, but kids need water to grow up healthy. Nestlé wanted to provide a fun way to encourage kids to drink more water. And what better way than to use another means that children are drawn to – the smartphone. Nestlé produced a children's book that lead families to an app where kids can meet their very own Tummyfish using a smartphone's camera. Managed by parents, the app uses daily data to make Tummyfish's behavior mirror children's drinking choices – water makes her happy and playful and sugary drinks keeping her sad and inactive. Over time kids watch Tummyfish grow and unlock rewards for making healthy drinking choices, while parents can monitor their child's drinking habits and track behavior change through daily reminders and statistics.*

Above *Burger King's most common ad unit is the 15 second commercial, but that's hardly enough time to tell consumers what makes their Whopper different from their competitors. But what, ask the creative team at Ogilvy's partner agency David, if a commercial could somehow trigger a digital experience? Voice activated phones and devices provided the perfect vehicle. Many people keep their home devices or mobile phones near the TV or within audio range of their computers. Android phones and Google Home operate by continuously monitoring what is happening around them, listening for the triggering command, "Okay Google." Burger King took advantage of that with a commercial that intentionally activated the Google Home and Android voice recognition, with a spot that ended with the question: "Ok Google, what is in the Whopper Burger?" The question triggered thousands of devices to start reading all the list of ingredients from The Whopper's Wikipedia page.*

only charged 30 per cent commission for hosting an app on the website, and Calvin instantly saw an opportunity. He went home that night, sketched out five apps, and set about building them with some likeminded innovators. Four of the apps tanked. One, the app for National Public Radio in the US (see image on page 178), was a runaway success, and it launched Bottle Rocket.

An app can only ever be a "bite-sized" brand experience. Now there are millions of apps, and an extreme version of natural selection winnows out the non-performers. Why? Because inviting a brand onto your phone may be a small commitment, but it is also a significant one. And if it doesn't work, or feel right, then it is a particularly negative brand experience. Bite-sized can bite back.

Done right, mobility can be transformative – indeed, disruptive. It is driving a change in bricks and mortar retail – or as Calvin calls it, "Bricks and Mobile". Your device is constantly with you. One study showed consumers pick up their phones 150–200 times a day. It's the first thing you touch in the morning and last thing you set down at night. (And nearly two-thirds of Americans, at least, keep their phone close by overnight, too, or so says Gallup.)

The graph opposite shows how it impacts on the competing strategies of footwear retailers in the US, for instance.

And it's giving brands opportunities to engage in various ways. Mobile services from retailers focus on more than just mobile commerce or tactics that drive consumers to their physical locations (such as coupons). They also use mobile to get people to the store, motivate them once they're there, satisfy them after the purchase, and keep them happy with customer service.

To make mobility happen, the mantra is "mobile first".

OLD MOBILE

Mobile is a new, shiny toy with little measureable impact and thus given little priority.

Mobile is regarded as just another communications channel added to the media mix.

Traditional metrics are applied from standard digital-marketing tactics.

Every company needs an app, regardless of value to the customer or the brand.

Mobile-specific contextual information is not exploited.

NEW MOBILE

Advanced companies create engagement platforms that are mobile-first, if not mobile only.

Mobile is regarded as a service touch-point that can deliver competitive advantage through customer-centric utility or entertainment content.

There are mobile specific metrics as standards that can be integrated into measurement frameworks.

Investment is more focused, aligning the brand's value proposition with the customer need.

Self-learning systems such as Google Now analyze different kinds of external data to provide contextual value.

Mobile is a very tough medium to compete on. By its nature, people spend less time on a given page, are often multi-tasking and switch between applications more often than on the web. It's not easy to get consumers to watch a video, read an article or browse choices. Production on mobile is harder than web, which causes strains on the technology teams. So it is important to understand that it is always more difficult to go mobile first than just adapting non-mobile content to fit.

But when building a complete content strategy, it is a minimal requirement to have content optimized for mobile. Many people think that optimizing for mobile is simply a question of reformatting the content so it is visually optimized (scrolling down as opposed to having to move the screen horizontally and vertically). But this is only a small component of what mobile optimization really means. Most apps rely on data hosted somewhere beyond the mobile device itself. So what happens when the phone's connection drops? Developers call this the "airplane mode" problem. An app needs to function with an intermittent data stream. It also needs to bring in data from multiple sources, many of which are processor and bandwidth hogs. Surfacing data from legacy systems into mobile phone apps in a way that is bandwidth conservative and fast is no simple trick.

THE RETAIL MOBILE LANDSCAPE AT A GLANCE

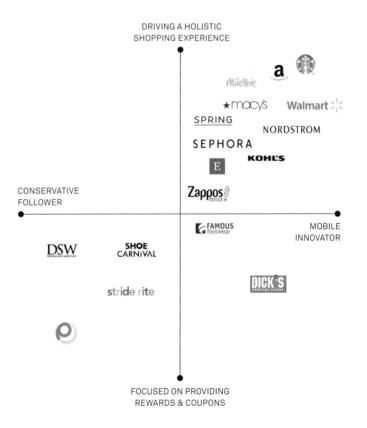

Right Mobile innovation opens doors, especially in combination with an immersive shopping experience. The more successful footwear retail brands know this, comparing themselves to the best in the business – like Starbucks and Amazon – who use mobile not just to drive sales, but to nurture relationships.

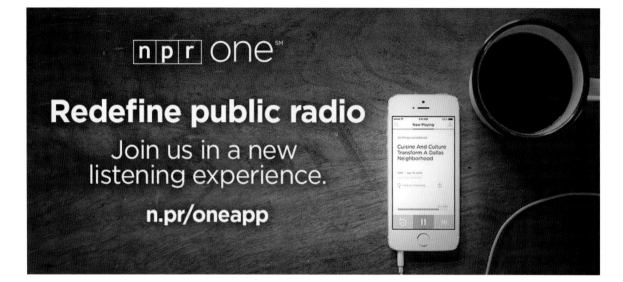

Above *NPR is the well-respected public radio service in the US, and many in the States depend on it for in-depth reporting, analysis, and entertainment. However, it's not always easy to tune in to. NPR stations are local operations of varying power, and they choose which of the network's offerings to broadcast and at what time. This makes tuning into a favorite show a potential challenge. Bottle Rocket's NPR One app solves that by providing on-demand listening for all the great NPR broadcasts no matter where you are.*

There are challenges on the consumer side as well. Google and Nielsen did a study to find similarities and differences between mobile-content consumption and web-content consumption. They found that 40 per cent of all mobile searches were performed with local intent. And this is increasing.

Mobile localization has more profound impacts in the developing world. A mobile service called Tone provides connectivity to underserved regions. In Indonesia, Tone gives local fishermen a kit with a phone, educational material and carrier access with subsidized data. Eventually the service will pay for itself for carriers and users alike as fishermen learn more as a result of services like GPS, weather and fish maps.

Mobile first should always try to localize the content and make the content useful based on a variety of available data points. Think of space and time before simply reformatting any old available content. And align content with local context to increase its relevance.

Calvin is a techie who likes pencils. His advice is always to start with a pencil, and a brutally clear understanding of what the small screen allows you to do. He calls it Lo-Fi techniques to achieve Hi-Fi solutions. Here's why:

1. If you use computer design tools, the tool starts to impact what you do. But if it's your hand, some lead, some paper and you, then there are no rules.

2. You're never going to get it right on the first try. So lo-fidelity tools like pencils and whiteboards enable you to easily let go of ideas that aren't good enough.

3. You can work in public. Everyone from Bottle Rocket does their sketching on the walls now so that they can collaborate easily and with better interpersonal dynamics.

That done, scale becomes the Holy Grail. I have to tell you: the graveyard of small-scale apps is over-subscribed.

We have found there are four passports to scale in designing programs with mobility at their heart.

The first is to provide frictionless convenience. Mobile apps that make things more automatic, more seamless, and faster, help people get the things they need – without an intrusive upsell.

The second is to promise substantive gratification. Mobile can extend a product beyond its physical dimensions by integrating a real world and mobile experience.

The third is to hyper-personalize the program. Mobile devices are intimate companions, and like all such companions, we are willing to tell them a lot about ourselves.

And the fourth is to give the customer an ultra-contextual experience. Phones know what time it is, where we are, what the weather is, and plenty of other contextual information. But, with a few exceptions like Google Now, brands tend to be parsimonious in using this data.

And what of the future?

Well, there are another billion people coming online by 2020, and they'll connect through mobile. Add to them some 25 to 50 billion new connected Internet of Things devices such as wearables, sensors, connected house applications, cars, infrastructure, and manufacturing equipment.

The current mobile infrastructure can't support the coming needs for data bandwidth. The services we're adding – such as video, virtual reality, connected homes and cars – require a massive increase in data.

Technology marches on, and 5G mobile promises to be the solution to these coming challenges, but 5G at global scale is still far in the future, and a hugely expensive proposition. You may faint at the size of your smartphone bill already, and that's without the investment in 5G infrastructure. For the foreseeable future, new services, content and applications will have to be

Right *Here's a tip: start with a pencil and let the technology follow. Lo-fi first, hi-fi later.*

bottle rocket

created for current networks in order to scale them. And we need to find ways to make this affordable to everyone.

Google and Facebook are already running initiatives to connect underserved communities, and while this serves their company-value propositions to connect people, don't forget that they are building commercially exploitable consumer segments to monetize.

If we're to do this right – and I hope we are – we'll need to find collaboration models among carriers, brand platforms and consumers that distribute the benefits of connectivity instead of making just another cheap way to put out more interruptive advertising.

CONTINUOUS COMMERCE

The ecommerce leviathans created by the big players are predicated on a very clear business model. As Jeff Bezos of Amazon put it pithily:

> There are two types of companies: those that work hard to charge customers more, and those that work hard to charge customers less. Both approaches can work. We are firmly in the second camp.[1]

Of course, the first camp works because many consumers are prepared to pay more for more – which includes intangible things. Perhaps this choice

Right *Chick-fil-A® is famous for its chicken sandwiches ... and its queues. To allow customers to bypass the line, the chain built an app to let people order and pay for food instantly. Walk in, pick up, even sit down in the restaurant and eat – all without a hitch.*

Above *Lego, a brand once strictly limited to analogue play, has greatly expanded its reach in recent years. Even before the Lego Movie delighted audiences worldwide, the Lego style of imaginative build-it-yourself fun had made its mark in console gaming. But integrating actual Lego play with the digital environment is another matter, one solved by Lego Mindstorms EV3. With them, a child can use a mobile device as a canvas to imagine what to build. The app translates that vision into a design which, when built, can be piloted via the mobile device as a remote-control robot.*

FIVE MOBILE USER EXPERIENCE MISTAKES BRANDS MAKE

1. Brands often mistake mobile to be another digital channel when in reality it is fundamentally different.

2. Brands are not geared for the speed of change associated with mobile – not just the technology but how users interact with it.

3. Brands do not take full advantage of the analytics and insights that mobile can provide to build personal relationships with consumers.

4. Brands do not recognize the personal nature of mobile and the level of relevance the right mobile tools can give users.

5. Brands have not realized how much more decentralization is coming from mobile. Mobile experiences will evolve to consist of more micro interactions that will better serve the moment and context of the user.

Above right *Starwood Hotels took a different path, aggregating contextual data to improve travel. SPG Keyless is a mobile app that automatically checks you in and out of your hotel room, based on your booking time and geographical proximity. Bluetooth connectivity gives easy access to your room, as well as to elevators, pools and saunas. With push notifications to keep you up-to-date, guests can bypass check-in, check-out, and the front-desk entirely! Most important of all, the app only works if customers sign-up to the SPG loyalty programme, meaning a host of data is being collected to personalize the experience further.*

is also not so binary. There's a time for shopping at Amazon; and there's a time for shopping somewhere else. And brands that sell through Amazon understand that there isn't a point where they stop and Amazon starts, they know that Amazon is not a commercial silo completely apart, and that there is still a continuity of marketing, right along the distribution path.

Amazon is more than just a retail juggernaut. It's becoming the shopper's main source for information. In fact, Amazon – not Google – is the leading tool mobile consumers use to compare prices, especially when they are "showrooming" (viewing a product in store while looking for a better deal online). A showrooming study has found shoppers opting for Amazon twice as often as Google. Marketers and sellers need to grapple with the implications of that.

Why ecommerce, anyway?

Digitally enabled sales now account for about 8 per cent of all US retail sales, more than 14 per cent of UK sales, and about 12 per cent of Chinese sales. Those numbers are expected to grow in all three markets, as fast as nearly 20 per cent year-over-year in China. It has become simply unarguable that most retailers must do business in both the physical and digital worlds. Giving consumers different experiences in each is hardly to be recommended. They want a seamless experience. In fact, some 80 per cent of shoppers have said they are more likely to become loyal customers of a seamless cross-channel experience.

So the question is: if the digital and physical worlds are merged (which they are) and the consumer will reward a seamless union between them

"...commerce is where you are at any given moment when you decide to search, shop, compare or buy."

(which she will), why are we dividing up the world into ecommerce, mcommerce and traditional retail?

It does not make sense.

I'm a strong advocate of kicking the "e" in ecommerce into the dustbin of lost labels.

Commerce is no longer sharply delineated in time or space – you're not in one mode while you are at home and another while getting to work, and in yet a third when you finally walk into a store, flip on your computer or turn on your phone (as if it's ever off anyway).

No, commerce is where you are at any given moment when you decide

Right *Amazon might be the giant of ecommerce, but it's a very nimble one. The company continuously innovates on its technology, media and logistics offerings to complement – and often supplement – its retail platform. It also outperforms Google as the authority for comparison shopping online.*

to search, shop, compare, or buy. Commerce is everywhere, all the time. It is continuous.

So many ecommerce solutions don't answer consumers' needs. They only solve part of the problem. Some involve robust technological solutions but offer poor customer and brand experiences. Some offer beautiful imagery and storytelling but fail to deliver a reliable and scaleable technology infrastructure. Many commerce solutions are uni-channel, when, in fact, over 80 per cent of consumers' purchase journeys involve at least two channels.

Even brands that have managed the transition from bricks and mortar to online well still get things wrong. Slow website load times, an absence of mobile optimization, indeed, anything other than a seamless integration of devices, has a big impact. Researchers at Aberdeen Group suggest that companies with a strong omni-channel presence retain 89 per cent of customers, compared to 33 per cent retention for those retailers with a weak omni-channel presence.

Many fail because they begin and end at the transaction, embracing only

Right *Showrooming – where people try in-store but buy online – is very convenient for the customer but potentially challenging for bricks and mortar retailers.*

HOW TO MAKE THE MOST OF AMAZON

The basics: Ensure that your product is represented on the site with accurate content and imagery that's optimized for Amazon's search engine, and that your inventory and distribution are set up to handle the channel's demands.

Mind your reviews: Amazon's product reviews indicate consumer intent, user experience, and propensity to recommend. Compare comments on your products with those about your competitors. Check geographic and demographic data to inform segmentation strategies.

Pricing tips: Amazon is the top source of information when a consumer is showrooming because of price and convenience. Amazon 1-Click turns a search into a sale with a screen tap. When you sell your product on Amazon, your competitors are both on- and offline; factor in this new consumer behaviour and exposure when pricing your product.

Understand the shopper: Why does she use Amazon? What's important to her? How can you take advantage of Amazon's tools to meet her needs?

Drive traffic: Learn your options, both on and off Amazon, for getting likely shoppers to your Amazon store. How can you fill your funnel with shoppers who are primed for the Amazon experience?

Check your numbers: Challenge the data Amazon provides, and build your own set of KPIs. Distill both data sets into an easy-to-act-on dashboard.

Spend wisely: Measure and adjust your tactics for driving traffic and conversion, and fine tune your marketing spend. Compare and contrast with your competitors' on-site initiatives.

Optimize your offer: Now that you have some data, ask which of your products are doing well? How can you optimize products and packaging for the channel to do even better?

Use all available tools: Use joint CRM programs and Amazon Vine to identify shoppers likely to favourably review your product, and incentivize them to do so.

part of the full commercial relationship with the customer – a relationship that begins well before the sale and continues well after the first transaction. In most relationships, the first transaction is not profitable; all the money is in the lifetime customer relationship.

My colleague Rory Sutherland reminds me of a speech David Ogilvy made to the Life Assurance Agency Management Association in 1965. David said:

> I myself have life assurance policies with three companies. Not one of them has even written me a letter suggesting that I buy more insurance from them. All they ever send me is premium notices. Bloody fools.

What David was doing was proposing direct mail as part of an omni-channel tactic to meet a perennial opportunity – namely, that it is easier to cross-sell or upsell than it is to cold-sell. This is "direct marketing", and in many ways it anticipates the world of continuous commerce in its principles, though some of the disciplines that went into it, most notably testing, have tended to take an unfortunate leave of absence. As Rory puts it so well:

> This form of advertising, though historically less celebrated, still holds great lessons for the digital age. It is based on continuous, responsive interactions, and incremental improvements rather than on fire-and-forget campaigns. It is stochastic rather than deterministic in its approach. And, at its best, it tries to operate according to the timescale of the consumer rather than at the behest of the advertiser. It is as much about target moments as target markets. And it aims as far as possible not to generalize but to disaggregate.

There are three pillars on which continuous commerce can be built:

Omni-channel

What does it mean? Very simply: continuity for the brand and the consumer across multiple channels, devices and locations to enable sales any time, anywhere. There are innumerable consumer entry points to commerce (social, web, mobile, kiosks, and more), and it is proven that the more opportunities you give a consumer to buy, the more she or he will. It could be argued that *all* marketing communications elements should carry an opportunity to buy, be it a web banner, a kiosk, even a billboard.

Here's how to do it – and do it very well indeed.

Adidas is on the front foot with omni-channel, seamlessly integrating offline and online in both directions. Moving customers offline to online, the brand's "endless aisle" concept allows customers to browse additional stock online where not available in store. Meanwhile mobile app users get custom alerts on the launch of a new sneaker model, allowing them to check out different variations, before reserving online and collecting in store. Importantly this isn't an adhoc approach, the company is integrating stores globally into its bullish – "impossible is nothing" – omni-channel model.

Increasingly, it is the phone which is the hub for continuous commerce, the place where all the channels converge.

It follows that social media (supporting commerce, but not, please, "social commerce") offers a particularly acute portal to satisfying the psychology of shopping. As consumer psychologist Paul Marsden has pointed out, it can harness our human capacity for social learning. Social psychology teaches us that shoppers indulge in "thin-slicing" – screening out most information, and retaining thin slices of important information kindled by cues, along with a set of pre-programmed rules. These latter are the heuristics.

For instance, one heuristic concerns the benefit of following what others do. *They* can't be wrong. This is all about social proof. Our Brazilian client – Magazine Luiza – is at the leading edge. Frederico, the CEO, knows the power of proof. He has launched social buying sites which perfectly match the Brazilian passion for social networking to the high penetration rate of direct sales. The concept was Magazine Voce (Your Store). It allows Facebook users to select up to 50 of their favourite items. If a friend makes a purchase based on one of these recommendations – showing proof – Magazine Luiza fulfills the order and pays the referring friend a commission.

For brands, continuous commerce says that a brand should not behave differently in a marketing mode to how it behaves in a sales mode. That often has not been the case, as different owners in the organization had responsibility for each. Those days of extreme silos must be numbered, though, in my experience they linger still to a surprising degree.

A brand where they've been collapsed – and one where it is mission critical that this should be so – is Huggies. Do you know how many diapers in the US are sold through online retail? In 2017, it is estimated to be 22.4 per cent of all sales, according to Tabs Analytics. They found that ecommerce diaper sales grew even amidst a contraction in the whole category.

Relationship

There's a word that's missing from hardcore ecommerce, and that's emotion – and for good reasons. After all, it's all about operating as an efficient mart. But I believe that emotion is an ingredient of continuous commerce.

If you think that's a trifle soft for this hard-nosed business, then consider this.

We have a partner – Motista – who has taken a big data approach to emotion. They've spent seven years looking at over a billion emotional data points for a sample of 1.2 million US customers from over hundreds of retailers. What they show, conclusively, is that emotional connection is the glue that holds omni-channel together. As Scott Magids, Motista's CEO, points out: "we want to shop at retailers where we feel we belong with other people."

The "what" of commerce is easy to define, but it's the "why" that gets emotional: that sense of belonging but also sometimes of escape, or of indulgence, or as Magids says, reinforcement of the family.

Above *The "endless aisle", a seamless journey where online and offline blend to offer customers an integrated retail experience, is omni-channel done correctly by Adidas.*

Motista's big data on emotion can shed illumination. To assess the financial impact of emotional connection and convergence, we segmented the landscape of retail customers into three groups:

1. Satisfied customers who shop and buy in-store alone.

2. Satisfied customers who shop and buy across the converged experience.

3. Emotionally connected customers who shop and buy across omni-channel experiences.

We used these segments to answer two questions:

1. What is the ROI of moving a satisfied in-store customer into omni-channel?

2. What is the ROI of delivering emotional connection through the omni-channel experience?

The answer is "a lot".

For luxury retail, the annual spend for satisfied in-store customers goes from $637 per capita to $1,157 for satisfied omni-channel customers. That near-doubling of spend puts paid to the idea of ignoring omni-channel.

Going the extra mile to create emotional connection is even more attractive. Emotionally connected omni-channel luxury retail customers spend $1,640 per capita. The benefit of omni-channel emotional connection is a staggering 257 per cent increase in sales per customer.

Above *Patagonia is a brand so committed to sustainability that it gives people reasons not to buy its own products! What might be damaging for others has become a competitive advantage – consumers make more informed choices, which influences product marketing decisions for the company and engenders a strong following among customers.*

Luxury retail is not an outlier. This pattern repeats itself in discount retail, the part of the retail segment that has the lowest rates of emotional connection so far.

Sometimes, it can be quite small things which trigger the emotion.

Take Patagonia. "Patagoniacs" have a very personal relationship with the brand. They can smell phoniness, and are quick to call it out. On patagonia.com, the brand displays this authenticity from the moment customers hit the homepage, with stunning photography of athletes experiencing the natural world using Patagonia outdoor gear. Since people who live these adventures capture the vast majority of the photos, they are always accompanied with credits. But it is the wildly popular "Notes from the Field" essays within every print catalogue which pay the biggest natural dividend. While this may seem a relatively insignificant addition, it adds hugely to the authenticity of the brand, and demonstrates an attention to detail and transparency that is woven into the entire experience.

These authentic moments are not limited to great photography or writing. The digital channel continues brand storytelling in a consistent way. The Tin Shed e-zine, for example, is a dynamic microsite inspired by the tiny outbuilding in which rock climber and founder Yvon Chouinard started his piton company in the late 1960s. The shed's interior is photographed as it looks today, out behind corporate headquarters in Ventura, California. The multimedia interface places visitors in the middle of the room, and 360-degree technology allows them to turn and face each wall. Interactive objects and preview panels hint at the dozens

Above *Yvon Chouinard is the archetypal leader – a true outdoorsman who guides his company, employees and loyal customers with his moral compass. The values of Patagonia, like those of Chouinard, place environmental sustainability above all else.*

Right *Patagonia's commitment doesn't waver even out in the wild. It's advertising simply restates the company's firmly held beliefs and weaves together passion for the outdoors, demand for high-performance gear, and concern for the environment – resulting in a sustainable and highly profitable loop.*

of videos, images and articles from the latest dispatches sent by Patagonia ambassadors around the globe. While the primary goal is to engage and inspire visitors without distraction, they also can find links to share and can visit the product catalogue at any point.

Patagonia has long been an industry leader when it comes to social and environmental responsibility. Corporate transparency is a significant part of that commitment, which leads to self-examination and improvement. In addition to supporting dozens of ongoing CSR initiatives, the company encourages employees to spend a month of every year volunteering for causes they believe in, and gives 1 per cent of sales to support environmental organizations around the world. So when designing the user experience for patagonia.com, we knew not to bury this content in some corner of the About Us page. It had to live front and centre, in the primary navigation.

And when an important issue or piece of news needed to be broadcast, the brand was prepared to release the landing page entirely. In the Footprint Chronicles, visitors are invited to take an unprecedented tour of the environmental and social impacts inevitably involved in the garment-manufacturing process. And as a brand that seeks to do "the least harm", Patagonia launched the Common Threads Initiative with eBay, encouraging consumers to buy second-hand gear or sell gear they no longer use – thus extending a product's lifecycle as long as possible.

Experience

The experience of continuous commerce must delight at every touch point. Put bluntly, if I buy something online but want to wear it tonight, I expect to be able to pick it up at the store. If they don't have my size at the store, I expect it to be shipped by the sales clerk at no cost.

Of course, I could expect more. I could expect advice before I chose. Hyper-personalized customer service can do that.

Hyper-personalized customer service is a pillar of Continuous Commerce. Based on my engagement loyalty, brand interaction and purchasing history, the offer can be personalized to me (versus a simple tiered set of criteria) and provided in a spectrum of ways.

The generality, however, is that digital channels have often lagged traditional ones in shopping experience. What research we have undertaken does show considerable dissatisfaction: some 23 per cent frustrated with websites (most of the time) and 25 per cent with mobile apps (most of the time).

Often it is systemic issues which are at fault. For instance, as our partner Salman Amin from SC Johnson always reminds us, lots of the systems and processes underpinning an "always-on" commerce experience aren't actually

Below *On the high end of the continuous commerce spectrum is Kindle's Mayday button, which launches a video chat right in the app. A customer support person is immediately available to "pilot" a user through an experience by manipulating images on screen. Suddenly barriers between intent and action are removed. Imagine the possibilities! A clothing brand, for example, could provide you with an instant fashion consultant as you consider the sartorial requirements of your evening engagement.*

always on, in the sense that they don't operate 24/7/365.

This won't do.

Brands need to face up to changing working practices and business processes, finding suppliers and services that can support uninterrupted service and creating workarounds for restrictions imposed by the IT system.

There are, however, some highly stimulating role models for beautifully delivered experience.

The more effective online shopping experiences (in terms of sales conversions) use multimedia in addition to static content. Video has become commonplace to showcase products. Tools that enable users to zoom in on details, change colours and further customize items are also frequently used. Live chat boxes pop up automatically, giving users the option to ask questions of a real person – not just to read bot boilerplate – to get a better feel for what they may buy. Luxury fashion brands such as Versace take the user experience to a new level, offering scheduled live feeds of runway shows with embedded digital mechanisms to purchase the products the user is viewing (or similar ones).

Studies have shown all of these tactics drive up sales. Video is particularly effective. Research by EyeViewDigital.com has shown that 80 per cent of users click on video with fashion content, and that those who view the footage are 1.6 times more likely to make a purchase.

For the moment, it appears that "too much of a good thing" is impossible when it comes to multimedia online shopping experiences that are designed and executed well. With augmented and virtual reality moving into ecommerce, consumers are really in for a show, and online sales sites are bound to transform, and perhaps, find the tipping point that turns multiple digital devices into effective sales tools.

13 DIGITAL TRANSFORMATIONS

The Digital Revolution has upended almost every aspect of human experience: it influences how we relate to the governments who rule us and how we choose them; it influences how we spend our leisure time and where we choose to go; it influences our appreciation of social issues – and how they might be solved.

Ogilvy on Advertising gave the classic recipes for advertising tourism, politics, and good causes. Many of these have not changed much. But digital has transformed our ability to do all this in rather dramatic ways.

DIGITAL POLITICS

David Ogilvy had a rule of no political advertising. Now and then – but not often – Ogilvy & Mather has broken this rule, only ever in an associated agency, and only on the basis that staff members are personally vested in

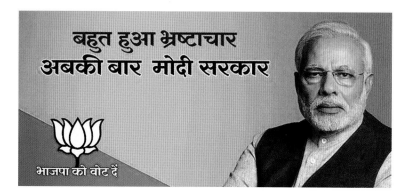

Right *Simple posters like this which rail against corruption were supported by a novel variety of techniques, from holograms to animation.*

Below *India's Narendra Modi was an early social media user, and a first of his kind in politics. Dubbed "King of social media", his titles ultimately included Prime Minister. Despite the clamour surrounding President Donald Trump, Modi has 20 million more followers on Twitter.*

it. We did so in the Indian General Election of 2014, through a subsidiary shop, and gave Piyush Pandey, Executive Chairman and Creative Director for Ogilvy & Mather India and South Asia, the space in which to create the work. In doing so, he gave creativity to a client who personally wanted it, Narendra Modi; but, more than that, it signalled how the whole genre, is being influenced by the Digital Revolution.

Political advertising has always been "parent–child": the politician telling you what is good for you. Now the "child" can speak. The initial obstacle was to persuade the Bharatiya Janata party that the campaign should be centred around the individual. But once that was cleared, the way was

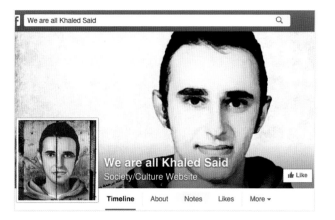

Right This anonymous Facebook page which commemorated the death of an activist was credited with starting the Egyptian Revolution of 2011. Today, two revolutions later, Facebook hosts views for and against both of them.

opened for a Modi moment which was couched in the vernacular: using the language the voters used, and not the official, formal-sounding language of national television.

Modi himself had been an early social media convert, so the mood did not have to be invented. Piyush puts it this way: "A man who's not supposed to be educated in the traditional, technological fashion adopted technology and digital. And that impacted the biggest movement that happened in our nation in many years." While Piyush and the associated agency did all of Modi's campaign advertising, when asked about digital, Piyush demures: "Yes, I worked with him and his campaign, but the digital side he did on his own. And that's where I salute him." The Modi moment became a series of simple phrases for everyone, which then spread in social media, for those who had it, and later to those who did not have it – the icing on a very traditional media cake.

Can social media be that cake? That was very much the view at the time of the Arab Spring. As one protester said: "We use Facebook to schedule the protests, Twitter to coordinate, and YouTube to tell the world." That is a pretty good characterization of the role of social media. But it was not the "social media revolution" as much as a revolution where, at one (early) stage, social media galvanized action. In the later stages of these revolutions, social media has tended to fragment the majority, as each emerging faction quarrels with another. It is a tool: it serves multiple masters. The medium is not the agenda.

Right In 2012 our agency in Tunis created an event which was designed to be shared on social media, aimed at combatting apathy and dampening any desire to revert to dictatorships of the past. In this case, a large poster of the deposed dictator, Ben Ali, suddenly reappeared, disclosing a warning message when it was torn down.

A very remarkable misunderstanding of the real power of digital social media is endemic to the standard treatments of Barack Obama's two presidential campaigns, which are often presented as the coming-of-age of new media and the displacing of traditional media. The real story is rather more complex.

It began in 2004 with the campaign for the Democratic nomination of Howard Dean, when the tail end of the anti-war protest converged with the

Right *The enthusiasm generated by the Obama campaign in 2008 is neatly symbolised by this barn in Ohio. An online activist requested through the website the correct Pantone colours and logo design, erected the necessary scaffolding and painted the whole barn in the Obama decal.*

Below *Like all great direct marketing, the Obama campaigns made much use of tried-and-tested techniques, such as member-get-member programmes, contests and A/B testing. The famous "I will be outspent" letter underwent 17 versions in tests before it was sent to the broad list. And it raised $2.4 million in one day.*

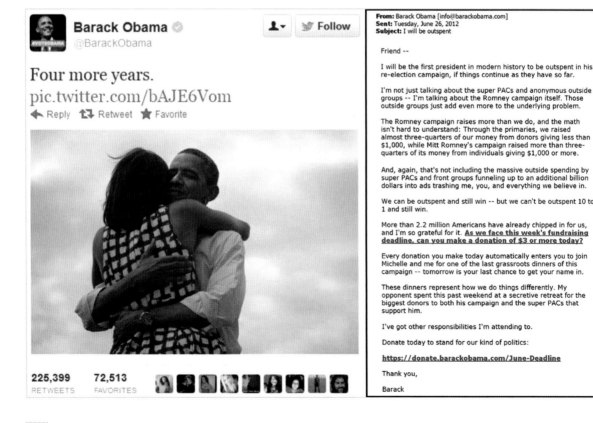

Barack Obama ✔
@BarackObama

👤▾ 🐦 Follow

Four more years.
pic.twitter.com/bAJE6Vom

↩ Reply ⇄ Retweet ★ Favorite

225,399
RETWEETS

72,513
FAVORITES

From: Barack Obama [info@barackobama.com]
Sent: Tuesday, June 26, 2012
Subject: I will be outspent

Friend --

I will be the first president in modern history to be outspent in his re-election campaign, if things continue as they have so far.

I'm not just talking about the super PACs and anonymous outside groups -- I'm talking about the Romney campaign itself. Those outside groups just add even more to the underlying problem.

The Romney campaign raises more than we do, and the math isn't hard to understand: Through the primaries, we raised almost three-quarters of our money from donors giving less than $1,000, while Mitt Romney's campaign raised more than three-quarters of its money from individuals giving $1,000 or more.

And, again, that's not including the massive outside spending by super PACs and front groups funneling up to an additional billion dollars into ads trashing me, you, and everything we believe in.

We can be outspent and still win -- but we can't be outspent 10 to 1 and still win.

More than 2.2 million Americans have already chipped in for us, and I'm so grateful for it. **As we face this week's fundraising deadline, can you make a donation of $3 or more today?**

Every donation you make today automatically enters you to join Michelle and me for one of the last grassroots dinners of this campaign -- tomorrow is your last chance to get your name in.

These dinners represent how we do things differently. My opponent spent this past weekend at a secretive retreat for the biggest donors to both his campaign and the super PACs that support him.

I've got other responsibilities I'm attending to.

Donate today to stand for our kind of politics:

https://donate.barackobama.com/June-Deadline

Thank you,

Barack

Donald J. Trump
Sponsored

America is losing. On everything. Our vets have been abandoned. We lose billions of dollars to China. Our military has been decimated. We've forgotten how to win. It's awful -- we MUST win again!

JOIN OUR MOVEMENT
★
Make America Great Again!

Donate Now

Donate today for a greater America, tomorrow.

SECURE.DONALDJTRUMP.COM
Not affiliated with Facebook

Donate Now

hangover of the dot.com bust. One of the young survivors of the latter was a charismatic whiplash of energy, Thomas Gensemer, who, along with Joe Rospars and other founders of the firm that became known as Blue State Digital, played around with email marketing and database management to help cohere an anti-war coalition which spanned young and old. The money flowed in to the Democratic campaign: and that, as Thomas says, "sort of changed the way that we all saw the economics of campaigning".

They applied a similar strategy to Obama 2008, and insisted to David Plouffe, the campaign manager, that their role was central to the whole ecosystem of the campaign: the fundraising, the marketing and, most important of all, the field organization. He agreed. They started at the beginning of the campaign cycle, with an inspirational candidate, and harnessed the energy of Facebook and Twitter. But the hard work – the important work – was traditional database management: merging the donor database with the field-activist database with the voter database. As Thomas says, "At that point you suddenly begin to look at people in multi-dimensions, whereas before they were handled incredibly transactionally."

The money flowed in again: $500 million online in 2008, $690 million in 2012. Where was it spent? On traditional TV, giving a huge share of voice advantage. This is a particularly poignant part as in the 2016 election the insurgent Donald Trump relied on a huge earned media advantage: "authenticity" fed out via Twitter.

But, more importantly, millions of people got vested in the campaign. The manager of a local field office in Cuyahoga, Ohio, could see that voter X who had given a few hundred dollars and knocked on some doors was a remarkably valuable target to create a whole experience around, with one aim – getting his or her labour. So the money financed the biggest field operation ever – tens of thousands of paid staffers, millions of volunteers, all singing from the same playbook – and socially enabled. (One technical note for non-American readers: the US "Voter File" and the long campaign cycles do make this recipe difficult to export in full – although it has been much demanded from all shades of the political spectrum in many countries.)

Right The Trump campaign unearthed a video of a 1996 speech by then First LAdy Hillary Clinton. In the closing days of the campaign, this video was the centrepiece of a Facebook-first voter suppression campaign designed to suppress African American turnout.

Below The Clinton campaign spent time and effort on "creative" programmes which talked to the young, and neglected the blue collar voters she needed to win over.

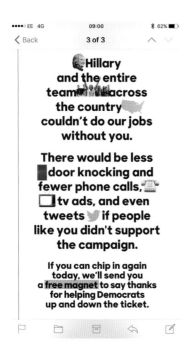

The full story of the digital US Presidential campaign in 2016 is still emerging but by now some of the ingredients are clear:

• Hillary Clinton had a massive fundraising advantage: over $1 billion compared to Trump's $650 million.

• Donald Trump's recipe of tweets and rallies huge earned media advantage.

• Clinton's digital team focused on stylish and sophisticated Facebook videos aimed at young voters.

• Trump's digital director, Brad Parscale, ran a more traditional data-driven campaign, with considerable fundraising impact, and deploying sophisticated analytics, learning all the time through testing.

• This was accompanied by some highly targeted attempts at voter suppression of key Clinton supporters, African Americans for instance.

• Clinton eschewed traditional advertising at the end of the campaign and upweighted her Facebook presence. Investment in traditional media in critical swing states such as Pennsylvania and Wisconsin was discussed within her campaign, but never implemented.

DIGITAL GOVERNMENT

E-government started off with the simple "technologizing of government", but it took time for officials to understand that there then was a bigger game: redesigning governance – to put the user, the citizen, first.

The poster children for this are two small countries: Singapore and Estonia. In the case of Singapore, the intelligent island drove a "digital transformation" of its relationship with Singaporeans in a top-down, public service plan. By contrast, Estonia's was a decentralized program, with government as the catalyst and strong investment from the private, especially banking, sector. One ID and password for a citizen grants access. Both countries have easy-to-use interfaces, and high levels of user satisfaction. Estonia pushes the frontier a bit more: in just 20 minutes, you can register an EU-based company, for instance.

But small is easy; big is hard. And there has been no more poignant example of just how hard than the Healthcare.gov fiasco, when the US government set up a digital hub for Obamacare insurance "marketplaces". As someone remarked, it was the first time in history that a president had to stand in the Rose Garden and apologize for a broken website. Subsequent official enquiries revealed a series of reasons for the failure, all of which should give any of us the chills:

- A team convinced that they had to design the perfect solution, but who didn't leave enough time to implement it.

- Rigid procurement policies leading to the selection of the wrong type of contractor.

- Poor oversight as a result of divided leadership.

- Resistance to bad news and excessive "path dependency": we must land the plane or else.

There but for the grace of God…

In the aftermath, the US turned for help – surprisingly perhaps – to the UK's GDS (Government Digital Service), a nation that was a relative latecomer to e-government. This had been created as a result of a recommendation from Martha Lane Fox to create one body in the Cabinet Office (where Richard H. Thaler's "Nudge Unit" of behavioural scientists also sat – see Chapter 15), with the teeth to "challenge any policy and practice that undermines good service design".

My former colleague Russell Davies became its first Director of Strategy and describes it as "what you'd get if you'd take a small government department and added a web development shop and a small creative agency."

Its basic premise was that by making things more human, you make them more efficient. It's probably become the best example of how best to put user experience at the heart of government service, and it totally changed the basic process for something as simple as registering your vehicle or as complex as getting power of attorney. For 20 years, governments have basically put paper-based service online. But why not redesign the service?

Right *If you go to the e-Estonia showroom, you'll get a vision of the future as interesting as any Apple Store. In fact for 100 Euros, you can become an e-Estonian; and enjoy the digital ID card just like a real Estonian.*

Border Queue Management

Drastically reduces waiting times for drivers passing through border checkpoints

DigiDoc

DigiDoc is a system that's widely-used in Estonia for storing, sharing and digitally signing documents.

Digital Signature

Digital signature enables secure, legally-binding, electronic document signing

DreamApply

International student admission and marketing management system to automatize and optimize student recruitment processes at higher education institutions

e-Business Register

Enables entrepreneurs to register their new business online in minutes

e-Cabinet

A powerful tool used by the Estonian government to streamline its decision-making process

e-Court

Enables electronic court procedures administration including: submission of claims online; electronic process management and participation in proceedings over the web.

e-Law

Allows public access to every piece of draft law that has been submitted since February 2003

e-Police

Revolutionizes police communication and coordination, maximizing effective policing.

e-Prescription

A centralized, paperless system for issuing and handling medical prescriptions

e-Residency

Estonian e-Residency is a digital identity that allows everyone in the world to do business online with ease.

e-School

Allow students, teachers and parents to collaborate in the learning process

At the centre is the website of GOV.UK, bare, clear and simple, removing everything that gets in the way of fast and easy access to information. Russell stopped a project that would have designed it with "bells and whistles", clever icons and gimmicks. The goal is not to be digital: it is to find the simplicity that digital can enable. A mantra became: "the product is the service is the marketing", and Russell, a former planner, became a kind of anti-planner, an un-marketer.

Of course, this may be too purist a utopia. And governments do use all the devices of both analogue and digital communication in pursuit of their policy aims. But the impulse for better and better user experience – impelled by the "Uberization" and "Amazonification" of commercial transactions – is only going to grow.

Right top *In the UK, the GOV.UK website was labelled "boring.com" by a popular newspaper, but swept the award shows, including a D&AD Black Pencil. Russell Davies, Director of Strategy at the UK's Government Digital Service, had radically streamlined the website for GOV.UK to eliminate everything that got in the way of easy access to information. Its stripped-down simplicity echoes classic government information campaigns of the past – as does its use of one consistent, restrained font.*

Rght bottom *Meanwhile in the US, the Healthcare.gov website that launched in October 2013 got 20 million visits but could only effect 500,000 complete transactions, causing huge embarrassment. President Obama took the blame: "Like any law, like any big product launch, there are going to be some glitches as this thing unfolds. That happens whenever you roll out a new program." In the aftermath of the Healthcare.g ov debacle, the US turned to the UK's Government Digital Service for help. Less is more it seems.*

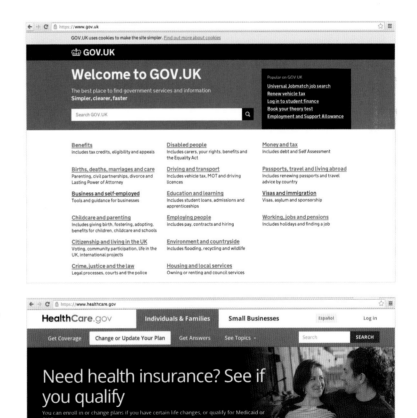

DIGITAL TOURISM

David Ogilvy devoted an entire chapter of *Ogilvy on Advertising* to foreign travel. After all, he was known, as he put it, as "the Grand Panjandrum of travel advertising". The broadening and democratization of international travel took place in his lifetime: from just 25 million in 1950 to 435 million in 1990. Since then it has risen to over 1 billion per year.

The Digital Revolution since 1990 has facilitated the whole process of researching, buying and celebrating a holiday. The particular impact of communications is to enhance the whole experience – to bring the actual experience forward in the buying cycle, making it come as close to testing it as actually possible.

Above *Incredible !ndia created a distinctive identity for the nation; depicted familiar sites in an unfamiliar way; highlighted the scenic breadth of the nation; and linked people from all over the world to the welcoming embrace of India. As befits a nation both high-tech and rich in heritage, Incredible !ndia has always mixed traditional and digital media in its quest to boost India into the first rank of tourist destinations.*

Above *The State of Madhya Pradesh is huge, full of attractions, but was never a first-choice destination. Ogilvy used "ombromanie", the traditional art of creating images by hand shadows, to show that you can evoke sites and places without having to use photography. This hugely successful "non-tourism" campaign was backed by a rustic jingle sung by MP local actor, Raghubir Yadav.*

One of the most successful tourism campaigns of the digital era has been "Incredible India". Faced with a bundle of hostile perceptions – sweaty, dirty, nasty – this campaign turned them on their head. Through beautiful photography, it evoked an overwhelming experience: different, yes, but stimulating the senses not discomfiting them. In his autobiography, *Pandeymonium*, Piyush Pandey writes that his mother used to tell him she liked to travel, to which he replied, *"Muijhe ghumaane ka bahut shauk hai"* (I like to make people travel). The programme was always digital as well as analogue: creating buzz, distributing offers and offering a digital home for the individual programs of Indian states. Piyush advertised two of these as well.

Social media now provides us with the ability to pre-experience a destination. Who doesn't relate to the conflicting feelings of envy and joy by association that accompany a feed from a friend's Facebook holiday? You want to feel like you're there with them. We helped the city of Cape Town harness those sensations explicitly by inviting people (through extensive digital advertising) to send their Facebook profiles on a five-day trip to the Mother City in exchange for some positive feedback from friends and a chance to win the trip for real. Cape Town got increased awareness for its beauty and hidden gems as well as the benefit of an implicit peer recommendation.

It was surprisingly simple. Since Cape Town tourism didn't have buckets of money to spend on splashy TV commercials, they chose to hijack the place where everybody already goes to share their holidays: Facebook. Sign up, and you'd be able to virtually explore Cape Town in a five-day holiday. Users would get personalized content in their timelines that showed them all the different things they could see and do in one of Africa's most beautiful cities. Creating all the that content meant the Cape Town Tourism shot 150 POV videos, took 10,000 snapshots, and wrote 400 status updates. As a result, people got to visit Cape Town through the eyes of their Facebook profile … and all their friends did too.

A country is the collective of its citizens. What if they were all asked to talk about their own country? That's what our amusing Random Swede campaign did for Sweden, a country where tourist revenues were reeling from recession. The campaign, which capitalized on Sweden's pride of place and historic commitment to freedom of expression, provided prospective tourists with direct access to 5,000 random Swedes who had signed up for the "Dial-a Swede" international telephone hotline. There is no better way to experience a country than by talking to its inhabitants, after all.

One hundred and ninety thousands calls came in from 186 different countries and 36,000 Swedes signed up as ambassadors. And what prospective tourists found out pleased them. They learned that Swedes are open and direct-talking people and are happy to answer any questions you may have about Sweden, that there is more to the country than its major cities, that Swedes love their country and would love for people to visit.

In *Ogilvy on Advertising*, David asserts that the main purpose of advertising for good causes is to raise money for them. To do that, it has to tell people something about those causes. Nothing changed, except that we can do much more digitally. We can mobilize people behind things in a way that engages them personally, and that creates a range of behaviours – from simple support to more active endorsement to committed advocacy. The traditional divisions between public relations (issues management) and advertising (information promotion) collapse; the issue potentially becomes ownable by anyone.

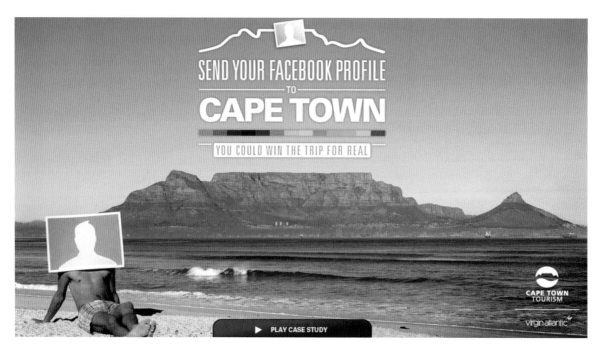

Above *Send Your Facebook Profile to Cape Town hoped to trigger consideration of the destination by potential travellers. Cape Town is far away for many people in the world, meaning that its beautiful sites remain unknown. People may have heard of the wonders of the Mother City, but nothing compares to seeing Table Mountain, the vineyards of Stellenbosch, or the V&A Waterfront for yourself. And if you can't make the journey, maybe your Facebook profile can, letting you see all the fun that could be had on a five-day excursion. The carefully constructed virtual tours did the job well. Bookings for Cape Town holidays in the year after the campaign jumped by 118 per cent.*

Right top and middle *How do you get people interested in visiting your country? Have them pick up the phone and dial a citizen directly! Your questions about Sweden, answered directly by a Swede – that's the way to find out about a place. Thirteen thousand calls were received in the first week of the campaign alone.*

Right *Another approach? Create the most appealing job posting in the world. Imagine the role of "Island Caretaker of a UNESCO world heritage site", which comes with a $100,000 salary and a job description including swimming, snorkelling, and making friends with locals. Tourism Queensland invited applicants to do just that – and over 1.4 million people from 200 countries submitted video applications online.*

DIGITAL SOCIAL RESPONSIBILITY

"Corporate" social responsibility has been transformed in the digital age from a kind of high-handed philanthropy, providing financial support to "good" causes, to a deeper engagement with issues, which involves all stakeholders – from staff to customers to the supply and distribution chains. They no longer exist in silos and do not any more rely on glossy brochures for their information, but connect and interact digitally.

Perhaps the most ambitions example of this I have been part of is the effort of Unilever to put environmental responsibility at the heart of everything it does. When Paul Polman became CEO he made the dramatic claim that he intended to double the group's revenues while halving its environmental impact. I'm not sure Paul ever did a lot of calculations before he formulated that equation, but with a gritty zeal and evangelical fervour he set out to show that it was actually possible. What it meant was an alignment behind the vision which involved everyone in the company. Some moved along faster than others, and I remember Paul saying that the challenge always lay in the middle of an organisation. But soon it became very clear in Unilever that the purpose was to be rooted in the most basic product philosophy – and then fan out with everything the company did.

Whether it was a case of buying sustainably sourced palm oil for ice cream or raising free-range chickens for eggs for mayonnaise, a demonstrable benefit could be shown, which, when accumulated over billions of consumption movements resulted in real, scaled impact.

When Keith Weed briefed us on the communications eco-system which was to support the Unilever sustainable living plan, he was very clear that it should break precedents, signal a bright future, and create a specifically digital mobilisation of all who touched the process – from the producers and growers to the end consumer. The result was an eco-system of content,

Below

Farewell to the Forest: *an ancient tree speaks – "Never in my 117 years did I imagine I'd come to this. Ironic as it may sound, it might be safer for me in the city than in the rainforest. You are the only living being that can help, and seeing your faces I know that you will."*
Unilever communicates that it is committed to making products sustainably without harming our forests.

HELPING 5 MILLION
PEOPLE ACCESS TOILETS

Above *Unilever's many brands took significant, steps to create the bright future articulated by Paul Polman and Keith Weed. By 2016, the impact of those actions could be seen and measured. The sustained momentum of Unilever's sustainability initiative led the brand to prophesize that at last the end of the old world was upon us and showing how the CPG giant's brands were ushering in a brighter dawn.*

DIGITAL SOCIAL RESPONSIBILITY: THREE RULES

1. Be extremely sensitive to anything which remotely smells of "green-washing" – of insincerely stealing the clothes of an issue.

2. Be prepared to shock the audience into understanding that your issue is important.

3. Have a clear ask: what you want people to do, and, if they do it, how it will improve the issue.

from issue raising videos which generated millions of views and shares to in-depth editorial material. .

Unilever started to show that doing good in business is good for business; and the goodwill it generated in society at large played a part in its own defence when it became the object of an attempted hostile take-over bid in 2017.

Saving the world is a big thing, but the same principles apply whatever the social task; you first raise the status and importance of the issue; you then identify your supporters; and then you mobilise them into action. It is the power of mobilisation which distinguishes the digital contribution to social responsibility. At it's most effective it can mobilize governments to change policy. One of David Ogilvy's favourite charities was the World Wildlife Fund, and we still work for them in different places. In Thailand, we created a programme against the ivory trade. It involved celebrities and ordinary individuals removing the letter of the alphabet which means "elephant" from their names. Very gradually, an army of 1.3million people was mobilised. The Thai Prime Minister felt impelled to call a press conference at the height of the campaign to declare his support for a crackdown on this appalling trade.

When same sex marriage was being debated in France, our Paris office teamed up with Google + and the association who "owned" the issue, Tous Unis pour l'Egalité, to hold the first same sex marriage in France, using Hangout, Google +'s video conferencing facility. French couples connected to a Mayor in Belgium (where same sex marriage is legal) who conducted the ceremony remotely. Millions were engaged: and the anomaly between the two countries poignantly highlighted.

Right *A shopper's best friend? This ingenious outdoor campaign for Battersea Dogs and Cats Home, an animal shelter in London, is one of the best examples of digital ideas in action. Unsuspecting shoppers would take a leaflet, only to be followed around the shopping centre by an unashamedly cute rescue dog in search of a new home.*

Mobilising support is the prerequisite for raising funds. In *Ogilvy on Advertising*, David Ogilvy asserts that the main purpose of advertising for good causes is to raise the money for them. At the end of the day nothing changes, and "digital giving" – enabled by an online giving platform – will take on increasingly larger share of the donations bowl. As digital communications became more sophisticated, it is clear that aggressive, unbridled fundraising can be counter-productive. Data protection legislation in some countries makes it illegal, too. Brave charities, such as the UK's Royal National Lifeboat Institution, which have moved to opt-in only communications, have not faced disaster so far. But this highlights even more acutely the need for the issue itself to have the salience which can only come from creative communications; and also to treat the donor with maximum respect. The donor experience is another, perhaps higher, form of user experience.

Right *A brand can be a catalyst for significant social change by staking out an unambiguous position on a cultural issue. But when you're Google, you can do more than just that: you can actively enable change. In 2013, same sex marriage was still illegal in France. In fact, it was the subject of intense cultural wrangling, and the outcome of the fight was still very much in doubt. Google saw a way to make it possible for same sex couples to gain social and legal recognition of their love and commitment while promoting their then brand-new Google Hangouts video conferencing service. Since same sex marriage was already legal in Belgium, French couples could stand – via Hangouts – in front of the mayor of Marchin, Belgium to exchange their vows while showing the world how technology and society can come together to change us all for the better.*

Right and above *At its very best, advertising can do more than just make people think or change behaviour on an individual basis. Sometimes, great social awareness advertising can change a society's views. When the letter for "Chor Chang" – which includes the Thai word for elephant – began to disappear from the names of celebrities, newspapers and companies, Thai citizens realized the damage being done by the ivory trade. In the wake of the campaign, Thailand changed its laws, destroying illegal ivory stockpiles, closing dealers, and wiping out the trade in elephant ivory.*

Below *The UK's Royal National Lifeboat Institution is the first charity to commit to opt-in fundraising. It's too early an experiment to read, but is evidently creating a different kind of donor base, smaller but more committed.*

NESCAFÉ

The digital case histories that tend to achieve profile in the trade press have intrinsic sex appeal. They are often small, sometimes interesting, but not always consequential. So for this last entry into the Hall of Fame I have deliberately chosen a much more complex and much less apparently sexy example of digital transformation. It's got a flavour of empire strikes back.

When Nestlé, the ultimate multinational, went about driving digital thinking into the hearts and minds of its global networks, it did so with earnestness, discipline and missionary zeal. It was not a question of letting a "hundred flowers bloom", but rather the opposite. They did bloom in the early days of the digital revolution: thousands of campaigns, in hundreds of markets, none scaled, none learning from each other, the sum of many parts in no way realized the promise of the cumulative investment.

In 2011 Nestlé set itself the goal of being the No. 1 fast-moving consumer goods player in leveraging digital and social media to build brands and delight customers. It hired Pete Blackshaw, an early word-of-mouth pioneer to be its global head of digital marketing and social media. Pete established DAT, the Digital Acceleration Team, as a centre of excellence, a catalyst for change, and, most importantly in Pete's mind, a vehicle to promote rapid scaling. An outpost in Silicon Valley provides a point of external focus; it monitors and interacts with the interesting innovators there. But the whole remit of DAT is very practical, very down-to-earth. It reflects Pete's belief in fundamentals – "fundamentals remain fundamental". Digital is seen as something which should exist at the heart of Nestlé's approach to "brand building the Nestlé way". It's not an adjunct, or a silo apart, or an execution facility: it's Mission Control.

A good example of pioneering digital transformation at a brand level is Nescafé. When Sean Murphy, the indefatigable global brand champion came to the coffee SBU, it was not in any way a cool brand, albeit a critical one in the portfolio, and one that Nestlé was determined (in the word they chose carefully) to invigorate. As Sean puts it, "the brand that had been waking up the world needed to wake itself up". So it should reach out to millennials – or they would pass it by. It must also look the part.

It all starts with a NESCAFÉ.

Three images which show the re-invention of Nescafé as a beverage with the kind of presence usually associated with soft drinks.
Above *An iconic red accent dramatises wakefulness.* **Right top** *An internet lounge in Tokyo.* **Right below** *Some of the series of simple digital conversation starters which helped bring the brand to life again.*

The design agency, cba, transformed an untidy hodgepodge of different visual identities and replaced them with a stylish red accent to the word mark and a modern red mug: icons made for the digital age. It took more courage than you might imagine to jettison the baggage: but, once done, it immediately signified that Nescafé was competing in a very different world of all beverages, including soft drinks. The Nescafé creative platform consolidated around the idea of "it all starts with a Nescafé".

We consume 6,000 cups of it a second, which means half a billion a day. But these consumption moments are very different from those of soft drinks or beer. They are often much more intimate – conversational moments in themselves.

But how to turn inspiration into consumption? That became the task of our office in Germany. They have created a flow of Facebook, Instagram and Snapchat posts, disseminated in multiple languages to Nestlé markets around the world which give the brand a voice – and which encourage conversations. At the same time, Nescafé has become the first major brand to move its online presence to Tumblr, de-emphasising traditional websites and increasing its engagement with a younger audience. From two million sleepy followers Nescafé now has forty million much more engaged fans – who are increasingly becoming online buyers.

14 FIVE GIANTS OF ADVERTISING IN THE DIGITAL AGE: Greenberg, Kagami, Nisenholtz, Jensen and Porter

In *Ogilvy on Advertising*, David chose six giants he considered to have been the most influential in modern advertising. They were Albert Lasker, Stanley Resor, Raymond Rubicam, Leo Burnett, Claude Hopkins and Bill Bernbach. I have undertaken the same exercise for this book, and gathered together this digital pantheon.

Like David, I've used what might vulgarly be described as "creative chops" as the defining credential for entry, although my five demonstrate creative flair in very different ways. After that, they each represent an important aspect of the development of digital creativity and digital advertising, and represent it so well that I hope their choice will be at least understood. In a few cases their names may not be widely known, but I think that makes for a more interesting selection. Of course, I very much welcome alternative suggestions.

BOB GREENBERG

When you sit with Bob Greenberg, you feel as if you are in the company of an Elizabethan magus. It is a matter both of appearance and aura. The appearance is extraordinary: clad always in difficult-to-define garments of black, the only contrast coming from three massive bracelets of steel, and topped by a black, brimless cap, from behind which two streams of grey hair cascade to his shoulders. This is surely some kind of digital Dr Dee of the twenty-first century, lodged incongruously in a huge cube dropped by Norman Foster into the middle of New York's Hudson Yards, occupying the whole 12th floor of a vintage Brutalist office building, the size of two football pitches. On the shelves behind him are ranged scores of carved stone Buddhas, all meticulously chosen (and scientifically vetted through scan electron microscopy before purchase) from just one – relatively obscure – dynastic period, the Northern Qi Dynasty, AD 550–577. Now he's migrating

Below *Bob Greenberg has made his name as a digital leader by embracing the same philosophy as his long-time client Nike. Whatever the digital challenge, Bob will "Just Do It", and typically before anybody else. Small wonder that his agency R/GA has played a big part in some of the most signficant digital innovations.*

to new territory, the Northern Wei, AD 386–534. The auras of collector and collected do seem to converge a bit, and when Bob speaks it is in a low, measured, gentle and serene tone which suggests (and demonstrates) superior enlightenment.

Bob's cube is a long way from middle-class Chicago in the 1940s, where he grew up as one of three highly creative children.

He still feels like a Chicagoan in New York, not least because of his addiction – this is not too strong a word – to architecture. But he's not an establishment Chicagoan. Born dyslexic, he's always regarded himself as self-taught. The dyslexia is a trait he's proud to share with a group of highly original and disruptive business people, such as Steve Jobs, Richard Branson and Charles Schwab. He recalls without rancour seeing his sister just fly through pages of reading. Instead, he noticed that he saw the world differently. It's a habit he's made a remarkable career out of.

His great contribution to the digital age is that he has seen it from the view of production. He is a producer: and he has elevated that viewpoint into a philosophy which is both coherent and inspiring, and which emphatically believes in technology and creativity as a partnership.

It all started by watching his slightly older brother Richard join the studio of Pablo Ferro. Pablo was the Cuban-born graphic designer who became the all-time great designer of titles. He added visual style to films. The Greenberg brothers entered a world that was quite dazzling – Ferro, Charles Eames and Saul Bass. They got the creative bug themselves, and decided to set up shop. They didn't tell anyone, but that shop was below where they were living in an apartment building at 130 East 38th, between Lexington and Park – a space just 20 feet wide by 70 feet deep. They built a studio, then brought in an animation camera. Before then the term graphic animation did not exist. Soon they were into new premises, and doing hundreds and hundreds of opening titles and special effects.

Bob started to develop technology: "I did it because that's one of my things that I do," he says. He did it across film, video and computer graphics. By 1982, the brothers had bought one of the very first licences of Berkeley Unix – and developed their own software. They also used a lot of silicon graphics equipment.

One day in 1993, Bob took a trip out to see Jim Clark, one of the founders of Silicon Graphics, beleaguered at the time because PCs and Macs would make his machines irrelevant. As Bob relates:

He was always using the F word, and he said, "What the f*** are you doing here?" And I said, "Well…", and I couldn't remember why we made the appointment and why I was out there. But eventually it dawned on me that I wanted to talk to him about interactive advertising. So Jim said to me, "That's very interesting. I want to show you this thing."

That thing was Mosaic, the first widely used web browser, which he had been working on with Marc Andreessen. Bob was impressed, and when he came back to New York, he determined to get out of visual effects and into the interactive boutique space.

> "His great contribution to the digital age is that he has seen it from the view of production."

Bob's company, R/GA, now in its third incarnation, became a rock star of the digital age. It was never mainstream: it always had a distinct take on advertising from the point of view of technology. It was the Cartier of websites. No one piece of work symbolizes the work Bob did more than Nike+ (see Hall of Fame case, pages 212–213).

Sometime around 2013, an unusual presentation box arrived at R/GA. It had a blazon engraved on it, comprising Bob's beret, his glasses – and a FuelBand. Inside was a specially created pair of shoes. It was one of those rare moments of unsolicited client gratitude (and rare enough in our lives for Bob to confess that at first he thought it a new product sample). Thanks for what? Well, for creating a digital platform, which engages more than 40 million customers.

It felt very different when R/GA first shoe-horned themselves into Nike's roster in a very conventional way, winning a small piece of digital business back in 2001. Since then they have always surprised. Nike never, ever, quite believed they had the ability to be the next "big thing": but they did. The FuelBand was the iconic device that created the whole idea of the connected athlete. Eventually, Nike was talked out of devices, probably by Apple as much as anyone. But an owned platform of over 60 million users remains, built on an unusual metric – Fuel – that's easy to use, that celebrates success, and that dives deep into just what that actually means for you. And with Nike, too, this digital landscape is tying itself into the physical world – the stores.

Nike+ took a brand into a new space. And Bob thinks in terms of spaces. Bauhaus founder, Walter Gropius, wrote that, "The objective of all creative effort in the visual arts is to give form to space." Bob started to like the Bauhaus at the age of 16. R/GA's previous office was a homage to Gropius. It is perhaps no surprise that Bob's holiday home is being conceived of as a homage to Mies van der Rohe's Farnsworth House. That steel-and-glass box is a perfect articulation of German modernism. Its orderly framework reconciles art and technology: a place for the human spirit to flourish in the age of mass production. This – Bob's fifth house – is being designed by Toshiko Mori, improbably perched on the rocks high above the Hudson Valley. Because it's glass, you can't hang artwork. So, more stone Buddhas.

The current Norman Foster office is much more than a space. It's a manifesto. It sets out to connect the physical space with the digital landscape. At the heart of this space is the tech stack, housed in its bunker. There are no crazy effusions of wiring here. Bob has directed them artfully into perfect order. Outside, if you feel calm, there's a reason. Bob chose techno lighting: it is fully programmable to match the circadian rhythms. If you want to configure a conference room to cerulean blue, you can. And as the days become longer the light becomes warmer. A St Bart's sunset? You can have it. And in the "waffle" ceiling the light is diverted so it does not shine down on you and tire you, while those same waffles are clad in noise-cancellation materials. There's a space reserved for gyrokinesis and gyrotonics. A calming environment like this might seem excessively cushy, but of course, it's cunning. "It's a systematic way of supporting people to get to the most important thing which is retention" – retention in a world where the digital duopoly of Google and Facebook are hiring by the thousands in New York.

With this connected technology, you can collaborate internally – or with London or Shanghai. The money goes into the screens, not the walls, which are blank – except for what Bob has collected. It's a luxury to be able to collect and have enough space to display what you collect. Not many people could place their motorcycle collection in their workspace: but here are the prized BMW's, including the pride of the pack, a recently reassembled Rizoma of 1973, together with a veritable stable of racing Ducatis. A small museum of past technologies – from the typewriter to the Mac – would do credit to any design museum. And then there's the art. Bob has one of the largest collection of L'Art Brut – outsider art, self-taught, vibrant pieces, often hung as a series, splashes of anarchism in this orderly environment. Of course, there's a curatorial system, mobile enabled.

Bob's frustration with architects is that they see technology as structure. He sees it as the foundation of a collaborative environment. He can't understand why R/GA's architect, Norman Foster, wouldn't see his famous Comcast Building in Philadelphia as a digital landscape as well; or, for that matter, why Frank Gehry doesn't see the same opportunity in his Facebook building. Bob's space is designed to make people enjoy working together. And not to feel big. He once read a famous *Harvard Business Review* article, which said that, after the size of 150 people, every creative organization loses something. Here, the space helps it fight back.

Bob's "collaboration gene" comes from his time in film production. It is intensely collaborative – much more so than traditional advertising. It might take 1,500–2,000 people to work on special effects for a big feature.

That collaborative mindset merges with the urge to innovate. He defines his business model as 60 per cent agency, 30 per cent consulting, and 10 per cent incubator, the last of these having hatched some 40 chickens already. I admire him most perhaps for his 30 per cent willingness to take on the accountancy practices and the management consultants. He's taking work away from them because they have no creative spirit. He's fearless in doing so, but it is his quietness which convinces. He's simply never seen the competition as the Weidens and Kennedys of this world: he's quite happy for them to fight for share among the traditional set. They just have not got digital.

Bob once stayed at Touffou, where he also slept in the library, thumbing through the advertising classics and reading the marginalia.

His advertising heroes are Leo Burnett, Bill Bernbach and David Ogilvy. He saw them all dealing with a very similar disruption to the disruption of the Digital Revolution. In their case, the disrupter was TV. Their responses to it, like his, were fundamentally creative: realizing ideas for the technology of the time.

Bob's reinvented himself three times so far; or, I should say, reincarnated himself – first as a production house, then as an interactive boutique and now as an agency for the connected world. He says he believes in a nine-year

NIKE AND NIKE+

In talking to R/GA's Bob Greenberg about Nike, it is understandable why he's such a champion of the famed sports brand. The swoosh logo is the most internationally recognized brand mark in the world. And "Just Do It" is one of the most well-known slogans. Rap artists have name-checked Nike in their music 687 times over the last decade, trumped only by Gucci and streets ahead of rival Adidas. To say that Nike has become a part of contemporary culture is an understatement; in the kingdom of sportswear and apparel, Nike reigns supreme.

Nike has always seemed one step ahead of the competition – from its launch of an innovative "waffle" shoe in 1974, to the release of "Air" technology in 1987, to a prescient Jordan sub-brand deal in the 1990s. The company has a knack for combining leading-edge technology with style and grace.

In the 2000s, it was the turn of the Nike+ FuelBand to lead the brand's evolution. Just as Apple's iPod was by no means the first mp3 player, Nike did not invent the fitness tracker. Nevertheless, FuelBand kicked off the billion-dollar wearables industry. Placing it on your wrist, it immediately felt different from anything else on the market, and it functioned differently too. This was far from a pedometer shoehorned into a bracelet: with its built-in micro USB and the later addition of Bluetooth, FuelBand combined smart technology with equally smart user insight to trounce its competitors. And it did so with an unusual metric, Fuel Points, a new currency for measuring not just steps – walking or running – but broader exercise workouts, such as yoga, cycling, weight lifting and cross training. Fuel Points are easy to use, celebrate success, and are uniquely meaningful data.

FuelBand set the wearables market in motion, and helped Nike amass a tribe of 40 million customers, the Nike+ community, in the process. So much more than a glorified CRM database, the Nike+ community is a sports club where location matters less than common goals. Members join to track their progress; they stay to motivate each other and engage in friendly competition. It transforms the lonely art of jogging, with runners competing in races asynchronously across different time zones. Football players find local matches in which to participate. Skaters share trends. Ecommerce is a click away, with links to the latest performance enhancing Nike products. The Nike+ community does more, perhaps, than any of the company's other product offerings to achieve the brand ambition of inspiring the athlete in all of us, while at the same time providing a powerful

NIKE	ADIDAS	UNDER ARMOUR
$37.5m	**$5.3m**	**$6.7m**
#24 most valuable brand in the world; #1 in apparel	Ranked #7 in apparel	Ranked #5 in apparel

direct-to-consumer channel for loyalists. The tech has changed over the years, from a sensor inserted in your shoe and synced with your iPod, to a Nike+ and TomTom co-branded GPS running watch, to the latest incarnation of Apple's Watch – which now comes in an exclusive Nike+ version. But Nike has shown itself to be a solid team player, shifting technology partners to build its intellectual property, developing breakthrough solutions for its customers, and most importantly, growing the Nike+ community.

The partnership with Apple suggests the company's foray into consumer electronics is over. The business

Above *What Apple did for portable music players with the iPod, Nike accomplished for wearables with the Nike+ FuelBand.*

and tech press speculate that cost, quality issues or even a gentle push from Apple CEO, Tim Cook (who happens to be on Nike's board) forced a strategy shift. I think the reason is a simpler one. The company's instinct is to conduct itself in business as an athlete does in sport – to focus. In an era of the quantified self, "body hacking" and the connected athlete, hardware is a means to an end, not an end in itself. It's the community that counts.

Nike+ isn't just valuable to users who keep track of their efforts, but also to Nike itself, which has been quietly transforming into an information-centric

company. The Nike+ database gives exact information on how and where products are being used, allowing for better business decision-making around materials, suppliers and distribution channels. When a runner voluntarily inputs the model of their current training shoe, Nike has a precise way of measuring the life-cycle of its products down to the number of miles covered and over what terrain. And by opening the Nike+ dataset to the broader industry, Nike is putting itself and the Nike+ community at the centre of the entire sports business ecosystem. That's quite an achievement.

But what of the competition? Nike may consistently be running ahead of the pack, but there are other notable challengers. Adidas and, more recently, Under Armour continue to make strides within sporting sub-categories such as football and American football respectively. They may play in a different league at the global brand level, but they have considerable fan bases. It all raises questions about a brand's potential for cultural dominance: if Nike really has won the cultural battle, how come Adidas hasn't died, and how is upstart Under Armour carving space for new entrants too? It stands to reason that sports brands, above most others, would engender tribes. Perhaps Nike needs other brands to build their own following; it relies on those who are loyal to three stripes to maintain allegiance to the swoosh.

So it is not a case of a single brand capturing the cultural high ground and the victor taking the spoils. Brands occupy different need states, they take variants of a cultural positioning – Nike is aspiration (Just Do It) while Adidas is confrontation (Impossible is Nothing), and Under Armour is self-determinism (I Will). The tribes that gather and grow around these ideas fuel competition among brands and the category as a whole. The game is far from over.

cycle of reinvention. The Buddha of Hudson Yards seems to have quite a few cycles left in him yet, despite the fact that he is ostensibly "retired".

But retirement is not really a very Buddhist concept.

AKIRA KAGAMI

A "gangling Japanese", that's what Akira Kagami is. He is 6 feet tall. But when he was a junior at Dentsu in 1971, he was quite portly as well, at 242 pounds: his long-term boss, Akira Odagiri, remembers his shirt buttons were always in danger of popping off. He was known as the "clever, talkative, chubby chap".

Clever and talkative still: and he is also a very sensitive and modest person. He rose to the top of Dentsu, to be Skikkou Yakuin ("corporate officer"), but he did it with his calm personality, and his gold-plated client equity, not with the political elbows often necessary for ascending that particular ladder.

Kagami-san is the most famous Japanese adman in the world. It's as simple as that. He has been the public representative of Dentsu at festival after festival, but, also, of Japan. Understanding him is key to understanding the Japanese response to the digital age; as unique or as tasty as the Japanese take on, say, express trains or Wiener Schnitzel.

Kagami's life seems to have been about simultaneously conforming and not conforming: something, perhaps, that can only be understood in the context of Japan, where rules – written, spoken and implicit – abound.

His father was an itinerant salesman, always moving around. Kagami, born in Yamagata, in the north, did not settle in one place till his fourth grade. Since then he has lived in Tokyo. He first broke the rules when he declined to go to the *kokuritsu* ("national" university), for which he was well qualified, in favour of Waseda, a private university. His father was furious. Kagami had to pay himself through by working on a construction site. He then discovered that translation was an easier gig: hence his excellent English skills.

At 19 he started writing; he's never stopped. After he left Waseda, he'd been freelancing for a TV station and thought he should work there. Restless and unorthodox, the station saw what they were dealing with. They thought he'd be bored, and pushed him to Dentsu. Admission was by examination: he got through and joined the Marketing Department.

But the Marketing Department thought and behaved by the rules. Odagiri-san, Dentsu's most creative leader, and his colleagues used to mock them: "What's the point of a marketing department that can't come up with a hypothesis?" It was the Creative Department that thought: and after a few years Kagami joined Odagiri and his brilliant cell of six creatives, the sole Waseda graduate in a University of Tokyo hive.

He read voraciously, sometimes four books a day. Under the mentorship of Odagiri he blossomed, and was encouraged to be courteously rebellious. The Japanese habit of mentorship is, to me, one of the most attractive traits of that society. Odagiri still mentors Kagami (and, indeed, mentors me!), although "mentor" in English carries narrower connotations than the

Above *Akira Kagami is the world's best-known Japanese ad man. Don't be fooled by his shirt and jacket, Kagami brings his brand of polite rebellion to every project. His work has spanned the whole of the digital revolution to date, championing creativity, continuous improvement, and a futurist's vision for what is on the horizon.*

Japanese word *onshi* which feels much more like a life-guide.

But Kagami did conform to one rule. He stayed with Dentsu: for over 40 years.

What was it like then for a rebellious young creative? For those in the West who are accustomed to a view of Dentsu as a bureaucratic behemoth, the answer will be very surprising: it was gloriously free. Complete freedom. Kagami just never appeared in the mornings. ("That's really tough for me, punctuality.")

It's difficult to grasp the essence of Dentsu unless you've worked in Japan. The best way of thinking about it is as a state-within-a-state. It is certainly not a conventional advertising agency in a Western sense. They manage everything related to communication, from TV programmes to national events such as the Olympics. As a result of this, the comfortable and mutually supportive relationship between the government, the mass media and businesses was established. Dentsu fully supported the start-up of a private TV broadcasting system. Through this effort, Dentsu built a relationship with the media beyond just placing ads; and with the government, too. Twenty-nine per cent of the media bought in Japan goes through Dentsu. Who runs the Japanese advertising awards? Dentsu runs its own advertisement awards. Who runs the Japanese advertising association? Dentsu. Who runs the Japanese Film Production Association? Dentsu.

Dentsu's product is power as much as it is creativity. For years, opponents, or even defectors (and there have been some) have wishfully talked of a Big Bang in Japanese advertising, which would sweep away the "pax Dentsua": they have been utterly and serially wrong.

As Ogilvy & Mather started to become successful in Japan – in media terms – it became apparent around 20 years ago that we should acknowledge Dentsu's success. My own ex-Dentsu advisor arranged for me to make a courtesy visit there. It was important to show that we respected their role, and that we were happy to co-exist peacefully with their ecosystem. Polite conversation in formal armchairs it may have been – but a lifeline nonetheless.

Since then, Dentsu has become – through an aggressive blitzkrieg of acquisitions – much more global. Kagami-san has been the creative face of that, himself working in and encouraging Dentsu's shift around the world, and especially in Asia. He does it with passion. It's not a duty he performs by rote. He marvels at the millennial, mobile mania of young Indonesia. He is fascinated – and also slightly scared – by China.

He tells the story of how he detected a typo in one of his ads in China, and panicked. Then he discovered that the Kanji (Chinese) character he had seen was different but the meaning was the same. His Chinese copywriter said, "In Chinese you can find any Chinese character you wish to use so there is no concept of a typo!" He sensed the exaggeration here, but at the same time felt both *Kyoi* (wonder) and *Kyōi* (threat) – *Kyōi* is the homonym and has a radically different meaning – in what he saw as the bigness of this Chinese perspective.

"Kagami's life seems to have been about simultaneously conforming and not conforming: something, perhaps, that can be understood in the context of Japan, where rules – written, spoken and implicit – abound."

But the heartland – and the way of doing business in Japan – remains fundamentally unchanged. And this explains Japan's unique take on the Digital Revolution. In one sense, it started here. When NTT's Docomo first launched I-mode, it seemed like it was just another teenage fad. But in less than a year, it started to be treated seriously by Japan Inc. One of the early adopters was Shiseido. In 2003, Shiseido-mode started sending out personalized messages containing advice on food and cosmetics during the critical days of a woman's menstrual cycle. It was anticipating the world of "mobile first" way before its richness could even be envisaged in the West.

Dentsu the media broker was initially anxious about the arrival of digital media. Would these minnows escape the great fishing net, and grow up to be whales?

Carefully and methodically, Dentsu closed the net: and "digital" never significantly escaped the ecosystem. So the Japanese difference is that TV has never ceded the high ground. It has absorbed the revolution, but has never been ideologically confronted by it, because in this market the special business relationship between TV as a medium and agencies as brokers has never been broken, and the commission system endures, which sustains it.

Kagami's view of digital is very much about improving the whole. It's not about creating another sect. Improvement is, after all, the Japanese way. Tonkatsu is an improved schnitzel; the Shinkansen an improved fast train. But the core idea remains a constant: it's just that it flows – naturally –

Below *A public service advertisement that reminds us of the scope of a child's imagination – and the limitations of our own. Consummate Kagami, this beautiful film depicts a child whose monotonous behaviour – constant scribbling on sheets of paper with black crayon – concerns both his parents and the doctors they call on. But the child has seen the whale first, long before the adults and onlookers, including the viewer. His "problem" is actually a source of wonder to us all. It is Japanese advertising at its best.*

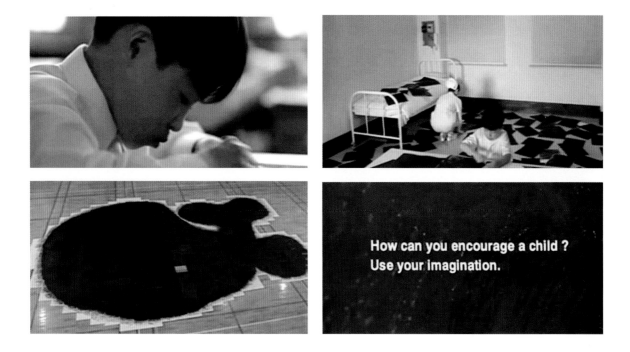

through *all* media in an integrated way. The Japanese system doesn't allow for disintegration. Integration is just assumed.

The digital work Kagami most admires outside of Dentsu is Uniqlock. Like Kagami's own work, it follows the Japanese principle of "*ichi o kiite juu o shiru,*" which means something like, "When someone says 'one', you jump to ten": you don't need to spell out all the numbers in between. So there is a very high premium on the implicit understanding in language, not the explicit.

Kagami, therefore, seems more tranquil, less engaged in the cut-and-thrust than many of his Western colleagues. He can escape into more important things – like sci-fi. When Odagiri first took Kagami to meet the client at Tokyo Fire and Marine Insurance, he was asked, "Is this *the* Akira Kagami?" Odagiri didn't know his protégé was already a well-known sci-fi writer, who had totally immersed himself in the genre since school. His current favourite writer is Greg Egan, whose works include *Permutation City* and *Zendegi*.

Sci-fi does explain Kagami a lot: why, for instance, he was the first Japanese creative to embrace video games. But also why, when some people talked pretentiously about being part of a digital generation, he ceased to be so excited. It just became the norm. In the near-future of Iran, *Zendegi* is a virtual world which turns sour: there is a message here – the advice given to but spurned by the heroine, Nasim: "If you want to make it human, make it whole."

Below *Why pay for banner advertising when you can build your free media channel? Kagami cites the work planner and creative director Koichiro Tanaka did for Uniqlock – an unusual branded widget for Uniqlo, which combines the utility of a clock with synchronized music and live dance routines – as creativity at its best. The dancers, whose audition videos alone were viewed half a million times on YouTube, showcase the latest Uniqlo styles by changing their clothing dependent on the time and season. The campaign unlocked earned media from 27,000 bloggers in 76 countries, who each embedded the widget on their sites at zero cost to Uniqlo – but maximum impact on brand awareness. Sales ticked up nicely too.*

Kagami's own famous novel, *Detective in an Uncertain World*, has never been translated into English. It once again shows him rule-breaking. Much sci-fi has the unspoken rule that if you go back into the past you cannot change it. The present is, therefore, protected. But, what if, at the moment anyone makes a decision, there are then two different worlds – the world chosen and the world not chosen?

For Kagami, the present is not protected at all. He's busy re-choosing it.

He founded the Dentsu New School in 2011. It's about educating the educated in what's important. He hates the idea of teaching. To me it seems to be much less of a school and much more of an inspiration zone, where he has assembled brilliant outsiders to engage the students. They include Hiroshi Nakamira, an award-winning architect born in 1974, who established a new lifestyle concept in Japanese architecture, and Katsura Kaisi, the comedian, who performs Rakugo, a traditional Japanese comic art. And Ryo Shimizu, born in 1976, the Japanese gaming guru, who is a pioneer in mobile gaming.

All this is done for Dentsu.

If he could travel back in time to the Dentsu figure he admires most it would be Hideo Yoshida, who was President of Dentsu from June 1947 to January 1963. He died before they had a chance to meet. But it was Yoshida who laid down the Dentsu way, and core to it was that the business we are in is both science and art. Maybe some of that "way" has been lost over time: maybe the Dentsu of now is less able to understand a creative now than previously; maybe it's just become too mature.

Kagami is optimistic about the company: the rule-breaker remains loyal.

MARTIN NISENHOLTZ

Martin Nisenholtz must find it difficult to make up his mind whether he is the accidental academic or the accidental businessman. His life has moved between the two in a remarkably fruitful way. Quietly, but with conviction, he has been a major force in the digital era of communications. But no one's erected even a virtual statue to him; and yet maybe they should.

If you ask the average employee of Ogilvy & Mather today if they know who he is, or was, I am afraid the answer would be "no". Such is the fickleness of corporate memory! More than any other individual, he laid the foundation for the company's digital transformation. But, more importantly, he brought digital into the realm of big traditional agencies, or, as the inimitable George Parker described them, big dumb agencies (BDAs).

While the debate (some would say war) between this model and the pure play model raged on for years, and while some BDAs chose not to speak the new language at all, it set the scene for many of us to change dramatically.

I have to say that it was by no means certain that Ogilvy & Mather would become digital at heart, but we did so because of the work Martin Nisenholtz did back in the 1990s.

Today he is Professor of the Practice of Digital Communication at Boston University. But if you imagine him confined to a professorial study, you'd

Below *Relatively unknown to the advertising world today, Martin Nisenholtz has done more for digital transformation than most. Part-academic, part businessman, he set up Ogilvy's first "interactive" department in the 1990s, guiding the agency onto a more digital path. Students at Boston University, where he now resides as Professor of the Practice of Digital Communication, would struggle to find a more digitally enlightened mentor.*

be very wrong. Martin is a restless man. Unlike Bob Greenberg, he doesn't really like buildings at all. He worked in an iconic one for years – the Renzo Piano designed offices of the *New York Times*. Perhaps it was just the wrong building. Shimmering and stunning on the outside because of its curtain wall, on the inside that same wall gave you a sense of looking through bars. "It felt like you were in a golden cage." Now he revels in being cage-less – and rootless. He is anywhere: and his students are as familiar with him in Starbucks as in the classroom.

He's passionate about those students. And about what he teaches. It's not a subject: he's teaching them to be ready for life – that "they're not in Kansas anymore"; or in Gansu, either (a third of his students are Chinese). He doesn't see any of the millennial stereotyping in them (although he hears them talk about their teenage siblings, who've known nothing other than a digital world, as "different"). They are thoughtful. They want substantive stuff. And that's what he gives them.

He makes them read books. Yes, books. And he requires them to write an essay each week. Because he defines the topic himself, they can't find the essay on the internet. Game up!

Like many good teachers, Martin receives a reward by drinking in their enthusiasm. There's something narcissistic at play there: he's taken back to his own student life.

In that life, enthusiasm had to be created. It didn't come on plates in the Philadelphia of the 1970s. It was the Philadelphia of ruthless Mayor Rizzo; of permanent clashes between the radical organization MOVE and the police; of gross racial discrimination. His father was a letter carrier from the underprivileged, white Western suburbs. Martin went to a public high school in Springfield – and flourished. But only one kid from that school a year would make it to Harvard, and that year it was Martin's best friend. Martin ended up with the "booby prize" – Penn, the University of Pennsylvania.

His escape from this rather brutal landscape was photography. He just went around taking photographs. At one point he became a writer on the *Philadelphia Inquirer*. So he started to migrate, at Penn, inexorably into the world of media, studying for a PhD at the Annenberg School of Communication. And his enthusiasm for the world of media grew, and grew.

At the end of 1982, he received a call from New York, from NYU, to participate in the teletext trial. Martin never looked back to Philly after that, or the PhD. It was the big escape – physically and intellectually.

It's almost impossible to re-imagine those early days of teletext. It was sparse and linear. But a grant came from the National Endowment of the Arts: how to make of teletext more than what is on the surface. The unlikely base for the project was 144 Bleecker Street, a ramshackle building where no line ran straight at all. But it was in the Village. All Martin had to do was to walk down to the bars and find someone to help loosen up the "squareness" of teletext. The person he found was the artist Keith Haring. The potential of computer graphics was shown for the first time.

Martin became Mr Teletext. The early NYU presentations seem antique, but it was these that attracted Ogilvy & Mather, looking for someone to head up a strange new project it had been given by Time Inc.: please help us make sense of our new Teletext initiative.

Soon Martin had set up an interactive department called the Interactive Marketing Group. I believe Ogilvy & Mather was too timid at that time to put its name on it! But it did make the word "interactive" famous. It was the first such department in the world.

It was really tough for Martin: he was in his own digital wilderness. The media companies' interest waned. But he attracted new clients: General Foods; then American Express; then AT&T. A lot of what they were doing in the early days was taking PCs and putting them into public locations for promotional purposes, digital kiosks. Then a client, The Equitable, with a tiny new media team of two people, appointed the fledgling unit to help its sales force. Martin gave their agents the first PC-based software. It was on a 5¼-inch floppy disc: it meant you could view interactions in real time in the customer's house. It was crude, but new and exciting and really revolutionary.

In fact, Martin has been an agent of *two* advances.

The second was in the 2000s, when he became Head of Digital at the *New York Times*. He's the person who first chose RSS (Rich Site Summary) as the home for the newspaper's stories, which would then automatically alert readers to website updates. It is a standard that has become ubiquitous. He was also the person who set about registering readers for the first time.

But I think of Martin as someone who hasn't just fought on the barricades (from different sides, too) of the Digital Revolution, but as someone who epitomizes its most anguished inner conflict.

Here he was in a storied newspaper brand, responsible for developing digital as quickly as humanly possible: the one metric – get as many digital readers as you can, to attract the advertisers in. There was a general consensus in the business that this migration was inevitable, and that it would be accompanied by some (but how much?) degradation of revenue. As Jeff Zucker famously expressed it in 2008, we must trade in our "analogue dollars for digital pennies". Then, a cataclysm: the great recession of 2010. The question finally hit home: can the model sustain giving the news – and premium news at that – away for free?

The debate was moderated in an exemplary way by *NYT*'s Arthur Sulzberger. Here was a proprietor who realized that his great-great-grandfather had created a business by charging 2 cents a paper. But he was also very sensitive to the newsroom: and those staffers enjoyed the fun of being read digitally everywhere from Ulan Bator to Uruguay. He moderated a very sane and careful debate on the topic: charge or not? It was a series of discussions over lunch, on the 15th floor executive dining room of the Renzo Piano building, where a sculpture of a huge eagle surveys the masthead.

Above *In the early days of digital interface design there were no experts to call on. Martin persuaded the artist Keith Haring to bring the blocky Teletext screen to life, which changed the face of computer graphics in an instant.*

Martin's going-in prejudice was not to charge. He was horrified at the idea of a simple paywall. It would kill off years of cultural adventure. But then the lunchers started to talk about the *FT*: they had pioneered the "metered model": 10 free articles before the wall. It was a beautiful solution, which everyone converged on. In fact, the *NYT* subscription model that subsequently emerged has been notably successful, both in absolute numbers and in relative resilience to the later challenges of the Facebook age. There was no zero-sum game here. You could win both ways, provided that you understand that journalism in the digital age is much more about creating interaction thank it ever was.

Journalism has not gone away though. Martin remains frantic and passionate about the quality of digital advertising. He swears about it. West Philadelphia breaks into the nuanced language of the Boston academic!

I can see Martin's point. There was a gale of insanity in the business. It did plaster the internet with stupid banners. David Weinberger and Doc Searls in "New Clues" posited that at one point in this revolution, direct marketing "body snatched" advertising. And so it did: the obsession with data pushed everything that Martin, or I, had learnt at Ogilvy into the trash heap – all that mattered was "how many clicks?"

The message became the medium!

The advertisers Martin confronted – from the *NYT*, as a media owner – were in rank denial. Of course, they aren't alone.

A final note. Martin had just one interaction with David Ogilvy – at the same meeting I recalled in France on page 10. Jerry Pickholz, the then Chairman of Ogilvy One, took Martin over and introduced him to David as a youngish fellow doing interesting things, and asked Martin to explain what he did. In two sentences, he did. David looked at him, confounded, and said, "This is complete bullshit", turned and walked away.

Martin, the modest academic, entirely blames himself – not David. He'd used the language of tech – all jargon and obfuscation – and it was substantially longer than two minutes. He should have said that he had found a way of making word of mouth – manna to David – into something measurable. Or that we could turn Direct Response from a long and tedious process into something where all you had to do was press a button.

Martin remains the "holist". He knows that culture in the deepest and broadest sense is what guides life, and provides the ultimate legacy of revolutions.

He has never written a book. And says he won't. But he should.

"I think of Martin as someone who hasn't just fought on the barricades of the Digital Revolution, but as someone who epitomizes its most anguished inner conflict."

Above *Matias Palm-Jensen, a jollier Swede than this picture might suggest, has been at the centre of digital since the early 1990s. His first award-winning campaign, for Swedish Post, foresaw the "on-demand" economy over a decade before Uber.*

MATIAS PALM-JENSEN

Mention the word Sweden to a multinational advertising network and it will send shivers down the corporate spine. In the past, I have felt them – full on. This is the market of doom: a global graveyard. Those of us who survive may have found an interesting niche with clients who value us – and tend to produce highly original work – but we are *not* insiders.

Yet this is no backwater. Just add the word digital to Sweden and there is a dramatic re-frame. We all admire and revere its leading role in the Digital Revolution.

It is the inventor and incubator for some of the digital world's best ideas, from Skype to Spotify. It has exported digital talent all over the world, and kept a goodly clutch on them at home, too. It's become a hotbed of digital creativity.

And, if there is to be a spokesman for this role, it would have to be Matias Palm-Jensen.

One day in 1992, he got a summons to a grand old house in the Gamla Stan, the medieval centre of Stockholm. He was a stocky, athletic, utterly self-confident young man in his early 30s, rather more saturnine than the average Swede. The room he was shown to was stately, furnished in a traditional English style. It was not unfamiliar to him and nor was his interlocutor. It was an unlikely looking room in which to foment, even a mite unwittingly, a digital revolution from, and yet that was exactly what was happening. Jan Stenbeck, for it was he who had called Matias, was a business mogul, who behaved – and looked – larger than life. A man of vast appetites, he used to go to Luxembourg to eat, and that's where his managers would fly in for meetings on a Saturday, then party with him on the Sunday. His favourite indulgence was a simple dish of mashed potatoes, egg yolk, cream and Russian caviar. This unlikely exterior belied a great visionary and innovator, and a nurturer of big ideas and big talents. Stenbeck had a simple request: "Matias, I want you to do the biggest portal in Europe for the internet." He added that it was a "meeting point that's coming on" and "we have to be the biggest".

Matias took space in the basement of Stenbeck's house. He remembered saying to himself, "this is the future", and set to work building a European portal from scratch, at that stage telephone enabled. It was called everyday.com.

Meanwhile, something was astir in Sweden. It was on its way to becoming one of the most digital countries in the world – faster than any other. Outsiders marvelled. It had much to do with government sponsorship: an early push of computers into schools. On 5 February 1994, Premier Carl Bildt sent an email to President Bill Clinton: the first email contact between two heads of government. Bildt became excited; and two days later gave a speech – a very un-Swedish rhetorical speech – and one which did not even reflect official government policy. Its themes were mankind, technology and the future. He said: "After the agricultural society and the industrial society we are facing the next big leap in human development – the information society." Bildt's moderate party and the Social Democrats ascended to power in the 1990s; the Social Democrats were later converts but by 1997 had drunk the Kool-Aid and introduced the "home PC" reforms for employees to lease a computer from the company they worked for deducted from their monthly pay. Penetration rocketed. In 1998, Carl Bildt's election manifesto contained the slogan "broadband for everyone". He lost the election but won the policy. Telia, aided by the housing cooperatives, soon created an internet with unprecedented penetration levels (92 per cent by 2010).

Matias attributes some of this Swedish exceptionalism to a national bias towards doing: "Sweden is a country of engineers." This may in part be due to a thinly spread population: the North in particular had a political impetus to be connected: the dark nights might help create legions of Nordic *otakus*[1]. The famous Swedish safety net, far from discouraging entrepreneurship, actually encouraged young entrepreneurs to take the risk, as, whatever happened, they would have a comfy landing.

Not that Matias needed that. When, in 1996, he set up his own digital agency, Spiff, it soon became predicated on taking advantage of the internet boom. "Everyone was doing home pages." They didn't. Spiff started with just four people: the other three came from a production agency, and were much younger than Matias. Spiff Industries did not create homepages. It broke the trend and made advertising in ways no other agencies imagined.

The first award they won was for the Swedish Post. For this campaign, they bought all banners on big Swedish media sites and then did daily callouts to Swedish influencers, such as Stefan Persson, CEO of H&M.

First, they sent written letters to their targets that read: "Go to the Internet today, and read the newspapers!" Then, when their targets went online and visited the websites, they were greeted with digital banners directly addressing them: "Hi, Stefan Persson, please order your lobster here!" They simply had to click on the banner and choose, "Yes, I want lobster". Thirty minutes later, they had a deliveryman at their door, with nothing other than their request, fresh lobster.

For most people, this was a totally mind-shaking experience and suddenly a lot of "important" people understood what it was all about.

Success fed success. Spiff continued to gain recognition but also grew in size. Soon they were managing 500 staff. It takes some calibre to handle that, although there's never been much self-doubt around Matias Palm-Jensen.

His mother was French, "an intellectual, stupid, strange philosophy student in Paris", who decided on a whim to go to Sweden with her best friend – "not a very Parisian thing to do". Of course she met a man. Franco-Swedish helps define Matias: Swedish he is, but with an even more exotic flavour than that might suggest. His grandparents had mixed with Miró and Dali. Pasolini came to stay – and also chose the basement.

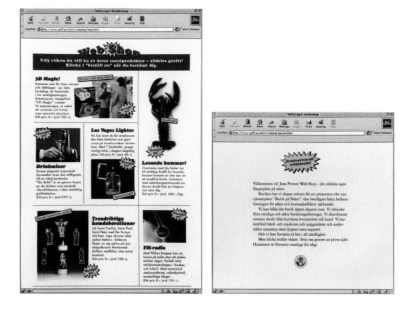

Above *Food delivery apps now seem ubiquitous, but Matias Palm-Jensen was already delivering lobster on-demand in the late 90s! His campaign for Swedish Post – which used a hack to give the appearance of personalized ads aimed at influential Swedes – was successful despite the rudimentary state of the web at the time. His agency developed campaigns that pushed at the edges of the Internet, and people noticed.*

The young Matias was very far from being the Swedish archetype, the engineer: he read and drew. Even today, if he wants to express something complex, he will draw it. But it was law and business that he studied at Uppsala University and Stockholm School of Economics, getting a degree in both. He went into government service; and became an expert in contracts before following his nose and straying off into creative consultancy.

That knowledge of contracts was to stand him in good stead. Spiff had become a hot property, and he sold it. Then there was the day when the other owners wanted to rename the agency to make it more stock-market friendly – to "Technetologies". Matias deliberated, and then gave them the name Drax, the evil business empire in *Goldfinger*. They simply thought it was a nice-sounding name, so on to the stock exchange it went. But when Matias needed people to service a client, the owners of Drax sent him untrained, unqualified heads from the North. That was it: he led his Spiff co-founders into a breakaway. All he lost was his stock; but, hell, at the end of the day, this was just a bubble.

The new name was rather warmer than Drax – as warm as you can get. What name would be the most unlikely you could find for a technology company? Something that says it is caring, and something you would look up to. Enter Farfar, the Swedish for "grandpa". And Farfar then became the hottest digital agency, housed at first, of course, underground, this time in a parking lot in Skånegatan in the southern part of Stockholm (now called SOFO). But it set out to be the best in the world – to be Swedish but global.

The work was ravishing.

First in line, was a program for Milko, which epitomized, ahead of its time, everything that digital offered. It gave people the unbelievable experience of editing for themselves.

It was viral in its market, before the word viral was stolen for digital. A Swedish dairy suddenly had a fan page in Brazil and a feature in *Wallpaper*.

The Vikings had arrived on the global advertising scene. Farfar received a Gold Lion for a campaign for Visit Sweden. This was celebrated with a big night out in Cannes. A sozzled Farfar creative buried the Lion (they are quite heavy, actually) in the sand on the beach in order to party a bit, came back to find the adjacent chairs had moved, and then after frantic digging couldn't find it. The missing lion was never recovered. This incident, however, proved to be great advertising, as Matias just turned it into a classic film.

Farfar was premised on 80 per cent work and 20 per cent innovation. Fridays were for the latter, when they did whatever they thought was fun. But the business guy, the contract man, living inside Matias became restless again, kicking the traces. Farfar was sold in 2005 – to Aegis.

It's difficult in retrospect to question the logic. Matias can still make a salesman's case. But culture is not easy to tabulate in contracts, and, not for the first time, a local agency felt the hostile embrace of a global acquirer. The media mindset of Aegis was very different. The philosopher in Matias quotes Upton Sinclair: "It is difficult to get a man to understand something when his salary depends upon his not understanding it!" Aegis did not understand Farfar. They soon bought Isobar, and Farfar now had an internal competitor.

The global Swede found that there was a jungle out there that was not so welcoming. He saw the bad side of Brazil when travelling there for an industry conference. He tweaked the whiskers of the jaguar. Following one of the giants of the Brazilian agency world onto a stage at a conference, he remembers half the audience getting up and leaving. He said to the remainder: "Guys, old media just went out of the door." The giant, "heard that, drinking his cocktail outside, and he came back, furious. He said: 'I want to ask you a question.' I declined: 'I have my speech to do.'" The organizers improvised a debate at the end of his session, but the fury did not wane.

"Even today, when he wants to express something complex, he will draw it."

Right *It may look basic by today's standards, but this early application for Milko gave users their first taste of controlling content by way of a simple editing feature.*

Above *Most people treasure their Cannes Lions award, especially their first. A Farfar creative buried theirs in the sand. The story was used in a smart piece of advertising itself.*

Below *Chuck Porter once met David Ogilvy, and resolved to model his success. Chuck's agency has been a bastion of creativity for 20 years, so he rightly sits among my list of influencers. David would approve.*

And when his local Farfar started to feel the very un-grandfatherly punches of local protectionism more directly, our Swede beat a retreat. Not just from Brazil, but from Aegis.

Nick Brien scooped him up for McCanns. A Swede on the board of McCann Worldgroup, Matias had an immediate impact. He called himself Nick's "Surprise Officer". He created a team whose role was always to make surprises. He did it deliberately because he didn't want to be an "innovation officer": he knew that they don't really make change. But you could possibly surprise someone into making change. Well, maybe you could have if Nick had stayed around, but he didn't. The game moved on. And so, again, did Matias.

Has he found a home? He deserves it. When the digital world's symbolic Swede stopped travelling and started thinking about what it meant, he was struck by – above all – the transparency which the Digital Revolution had forced. Quite simply, it's much more difficult to lie. And his new baby is The Kind Collective. It's a collective because he's grown tired of hiring people: he just brings on the very best people when he needs them. It's not about apps or tech. It's about teaching people that they can be kind, even to their customers. It's about telling stories.

The driven businessman is certainly not doing this as charity: but it's no longer a world of contracts, of hiring and firing, of global adventures. The Franco-Swede has returned home, in more ways than one.

There's time to be passionate again: music, for instance. Matias laments that there has never been anyone in our industry who is exclusively responsible for the music. And it's usually the last thing to be thought of. He was always convinced that digital music was important: "You can smell music." Right now he's working with Björn Ulvaeus of ABBA, creating an interactive party experience.

Not many digital creatives would get away with rewriting the lyrics of "Mamma Mia". But then not many would have the salesmanship to project it as a piece of change management.

CHUCK PORTER

There was a moment in the mid-1970s, when a young freelance copywriter was nervously standing in a Madison Avenue office by a wall festooned with his concepts for a British Tourism Authority campaign, when David Ogilvy swept in, with his entourage, asking, "Did you do these?" Chuck Porter – for it was he – remembers that David looked "kingly"; and also that he said to himself: "Someday I want to be like that."

The agency he built was the most striking of the new agencies that grew up in the Digital Revolution: a creative boutique that then transcended itself, and found both fame and scale.

But as Chuck says: "I'm the most un-cool guy." A thoroughly nice 70-year-old, bursting with energy, who dotes on his Labrador and likes cooking, he has lived with his wife in the same Miami house for decades while the

neighbourhood changed around them. He was, though, the "master of the fireworks" of the agency that bore his name, as it blazed through the crazy noughties, "the agency that couldn't lose."[2]

The niceness comes from Minnesota: but it's not the "bad" Minnesota nice of legend where you smile courteously at someone even if you're angry with them. Chuck does do angry when necessary: if, for instance, the writing is not up to scratch and the writer doesn't give a s**t, he'll yell at them. It's the *real* nice of someone who doesn't seem to have an enemy, and who has a very controlled and un-jealous ego.

Growing up in Minneapolis was not difficult. Everything works. It was a largely Scandinavian and friendly place. His parents owned restaurants; life was comfortable. You didn't notice the cold because you played hockey all winter. Jim Fallon (later founder of the agency bearing his name) and he were best friends at high school, and hung out all the time together. There were big brands in Minneapolis – General Mills, Pillsbury, 3M, Honeywell – and a marketing and advertising industry around them. Chuck remembers going to the house of a friend of his from Junior High, his dad was an art director at BBDO, and he would be doing layouts. It seemed a swell thing to do.

He started his first agency as an undergraduate, with some fellows from the advertising department. The father of one of them ran a company that made pre-stressed concrete panels: Chuck presented an ad for an architecture magazine featuring Mies van der Rohe and a "terrible" line about great architects. This first client asked what the heck it was. His blocks were cheap and quick, and had nothing to do with Mies van der Rohe. But they'd shot and set it already, so he ran it. Then he won a prize for a radio spot for the campus drugstore. He was hooked.

After graduating, he did the dutiful thing and headed to law school. It never held him, although, like Matias Palm-Jensen, he did like the law. He lasted till the first Christmas, when he went to visit his brother, a Delta pilot, in Miami. He fell in love with the place immediately. He'd been looking at *Advertising Age* and had read about two award-winning copywriters: he met with them, said he was a really good writer and asked them to give him a shot. They did. So he abandoned Law School, left his then-girlfriend, packed everything he had in a Chevy Camaro, and drove down. His first brief was a billboard for a bank installing cash dispensers. He wrote over 100 headlines: they thought around 99 were terrible, but alighted on one that read, "Get out of Line". It was put up by the airport, and he's never forgotten the thrill of seeing it. One of those copywriters, Rick Green, became his freelance partner for years.

As their family grew, it was Chuck's wife who suggested he get a proper job. He'd been 17 years a freelancer. One of the Miami agencies he had worked for was run by a man called Sam Crispin. Jamaica Tourist Board was a client, and one night in Montego Bay they were out drinking when Crispin handed him a legal pad and said, "Write down what you want to come over here." Chuck wrote that he wanted his name on the door, and handed the pad back. Crispin said "okay": and so began the agency Crispin Porter, in 1988.

Crispin was not an adman, but a successful businessman. After three years, he was content to sell out to the Midwesterner, who later bought his son's share. It was one of the few agencies in Miami. There was an exceptionally large freelance community – strong talent fleeing the winter in New York – but no one could afford to take them on full time. Chuck set out to build a proper agency. Crispin gave him the licence from the first day. So Chuck called the whole agency together and told them that the only thing he knew how to do was good work. He introduced one of his mantras: "Try to do something really good today, and we'll let the future take care of itself."

Clients started to come: the local clients – the Florida Marlins, the *Miami Herald*, the B2B arm of Del Monte. They won a Cannes Lion for one of the local clients, and then started attracting some out-of-state clients – from California, from Michigan.

Meanwhile, Chuck had hired Crispin Porter's sixteenth employee. The agency's work didn't *look* good. He had written some ads for a boat company to run in a boating magazine, but hated the designs. So he sent them to the owner of a design shop he had collaborated with in his freelance days and asked him to improve them. What came back was spectacular. Chuck called Bill Bogusky to say he had blown the boat out of the water. Bill said: "It wasn't me. Alex did them." So, Chuck called his son Alex over and hired him. Alex Bogusky was then 20-something years old, a motor-cross junkie; but Chuck had known him since he was 10. There was a bond to build on: and one cannot help seeing a lot of Chuck's future role as that of an indulgent, energizing and patient parent.

Bogusky was – and is – one of the most brilliant creative people of his generation. It is the particular genius of Chuck that he enabled that genius – stormy and intense as it could be – and moulded it into a compelling partnership. By 1993, Bogusky was kicking the traces, so Chuck made him Creative Director instead of himself, "because he was a better creative than me".

Iconic work started coming out. Chuck had a very simple philosophy to "research the hell out of strategies", and then to let the work take care of itself. He has a pathological dislike of putting work into focus groups. The model first came to light with an anti-smoking campaign in Florida aimed at teens. It was called "The Truth". The research showed that a conventional message – "smoking kills you" – actually made rebellious kids want to smoke more. The Truth channelled this rebelliousness towards the behaviour of the tobacco companies, with students encouraged to make crank phone calls and provocative invasions of lobbies. Some of these were filmed, and turned into low budget TVCs. From the start The Truth website was the hub for the campaign. The budgets grew; the productions became glossier. But The Truth embodied Chuck's view that "popular culture is currency". You just need to capture it. And you needed someone with Bogusky's own rebelliousness to push the envelope, sometimes dangerously close to the edge.

So began the glory years. Chuck's next mantra was "Don't feed the gorilla." He was puzzled that the default strategy for challenged brands was always to bend over backwards trying to behave like a category leader. In fact, you need to do the exact opposite. When BMW's Mini Cooper launched in the US, the default instinct was to behave as with any other car launch, and so run a large outdoor campaign. However, they put together a 22-city pre-launch tour of Minis on top of SUVs with banners that asked: "What are you doing for fun this weekend?" Not only was this a celebration of the Mini's small size, but also made the statement that fun stuff goes on top of a car, whether it's your mountain bike, surfboard or camping equipment.

Work like this did set part of the agenda for the digital age. It never started with television: Bogusky would refuse that brief. Chuck and he always thought in terms of "fame": what would this idea be if it were a press release? They did so because they had to. There wasn't enough money to do anything else.

Chuck always believed that they both benefited by not having ever worked in an advertising agency before. There was no rulebook, although when they came to write their own, its definition of advertising was: "anything that makes our clients famous".

As the business grew, Miami started to feel confining. It was difficult to attract staff there. The tipping point was when their chief recruiter got three refusals in a row from digital producers whose families did not buy

"There was no rulebook, although when they came to write their own, its definition of advertising was 'anything that makes our clients famous'."

Miami. They huddled, and decided to open a place that would be the exact opposite of Miami – and remain true to their inner challenger. They looked at Santa Fe (poor links), Portland and Boston (not different enough), and then, Boulder, Colorado. Both Chuck and Alex were skiers: they fell in love with it. And it certainly was the opposite of Miami: it's small, it's tightly integrated; everything's closed by 9.00 p.m. The only escape is nearly an hour away in Denver. And it's the "most granola place you could find in the US". At the agency's Christmas gathering, Chuck held up a big sign saying: "Here's the good news: we're getting a new office." Then another sign went up: "In Boulder, Colorado." Chuck asked anyone who wanted to make the move to come and see him, guessing that around 60–70 would vote yes. Two hundred and seventeen people came to see him that day to say they were in. And when, in 2006, Alex decided to move, a large part of the creative department followed him.

Bogusky's charisma started to flourish in an outsize way in the fresh Colorado air. Meanwhile, they had made a deal some years before with a small Canada holiday company, Multi Destinations Club (MDC), and Chuck became more involved in that. He had a very simple message for Miles Nadal, the CEO: "You don't know anything about advertising, I do. If you let an agency do its creative best, it will make you money." At a high point, Crispin Porter + Bogusky was contributing 25 per cent of MDC's profits.

Chuck drove an expansive strategy for Crispin Porter + Bogusky. His first venture was to acquire Daddy, one of the new brilliant Swedish digital shops in Gothenburg. But he soon learnt that Europe is not the US: and that a challenger city strategy here was not appealing to clients. He needed to be in London. Other offices followed. And, for MDC, he assembled a kindergarten of Crispin feel-a-likes: Kirschenbaum, for instance, then 72andSunny. I think only a copywriter with legal training could have done it. And all the time he was protecting their own agency: buying it the resources and space it needed.

Meanwhile, the Bogusky charisma continued to expand. It's interesting to reflect on how completely he captured (or maybe seduced is a better word) the trade press. Appearing on the covers of *Businessweek* and *Fast Company*, he had good looks, a whiff of danger, and overwhelming self-belief. The Agency of the Year awards flowed. The myth-making became more about Alex: the move to Boulder his own invention; the agency revelling in its image as a street shark. Clients also succumbed: Brandon Berger, my digital partner of recent years, recalls the relationship between the Boulder Managing Director, Jeff Hicks, and Alex: "It was almost like Jeff was a drug dealer: bring Alex in, get them hooked on him, then take him away, and make them beg for more."

There was something of a cult around Bogusky. He chose his followers to be loyal to him. There was the "Birthday Book" he used during hiring interviews: where he would use the subject's birthdate and astrological profile as a means of testing which ones could cope with such an unusual inquisitorial line. He was ruthlessly demanding of his people – nothing

Creative Department, Crispin & Porter Advertising, 1992

Here's to small agencies with big dreams.

Above *Crispin & Porter in 1992 – when the right team got together to create magic over the next two decades. Chuck Porter sits front left, beside a cross-legged Alex Bogusky (front centre), whose name would later appear on the agency door.*

wrong with that. But something about him could bug people, and allowed some escapees to become detractors. They created counter-myths: the sense that the Boulder office was some kind of advertising Jonestown. Of course, it wasn't. And, as someone has reminded me, "Chuck was always there." It was a long rope, but there was a rope from the calm enabler to the brilliant firebrand.

Perhaps, inevitably, a breaking point would come. Probably, Chuck was not surprised that it came. For a while, Bogusky had become disengaged from the business. Then they had both collaborated on a light-hearted book called *The 9-Inch Diet* (2008). But Bogusky was moving well beyond that, to a deeper ideological disgust with the whole of the food supply chain. The storm finally broke when Chuck was at Cannes in June 2010. He started getting calls – from Miles Nadal of MDC, and from his clients. Only later was there a mail from Bogusky attaching a violent blog he'd written, asking Chuck what he thought about it. Chuck mailed him back and told him he had to decide: take this cause up and leave the agency – or stay. At 3.00 a.m. the call came: he resigned. Chuck has never evinced anything other than the total support he always showed him. He remains calm. Not "Minnesota calm", but real calm. And who can imagine that it was an easy experience for him?

"Crispin Porter + Bogusky at its best captured the opportunity of advertising in the digital age."

Does Bogusky deserve that niche in the Hall of Fame? I like to think of it as another "and". He's somewhere there, unofficially. These two were joined at the hip, literally inseparable for years in anyone's mental landscape of the business. But it was Porter who noticed Bogusky, who chose Bogusky, who enfranchised Bogusky, who enabled Bogusky, who protected Bogusky. No Bogusky, no Porter. But, even more so: no Porter, no Bogusky.

At the end of the day, Bogusky's heart was never in advertising. I think that shows in some of the work, where deep brand sensitivity is sometimes not there. Fame without brand can be a dangerous thing. In retrospect, the "King" of his Burger King work does feel like that. He himself said: "My relationship with advertising was that I was not fond of it." It can sometimes show.

Crispin Porter + Bogusky at its best captured the opportunity of advertising in the digital age. It believed in the internet because, at the beginning, the internet was cheap. And then it started to become more serious. In Boulder, Chuck and Alex acquired Selective, a technology company. They were early understanders of the fact that if you want to protect the work you also have to understand the coding. But they attracted a different type of talent. Jeff Benjamin, for instance, had made websites at Goodby Silverstein. Chuck didn't want to do websites. As he put it: "digital was just another way to not do traditional advertising." But Benjamin made the ideas work.

When the need came to remind people that Burger King makes chicken, the idea was as simple as "what if we put a chicken" on the World Wide Web – their claim was that it would do whatever you want. So: "Can we do that"? And, the answer from everyone was: "Yes, we can give them 300 commands via the web that he can react to." And, so, enter the Subservient Chicken.

More central to a brand, perhaps, is the way the fusion between creativity and technology works for Domino's Pizza. This is a company that defines itself as a technology company that happens to make pizza. A beneficent client like this has allowed the agency to narrow the boundary between customer experience and connection. Anyone who has ordered a pizza and been glued to the countdown timer will know what I mean.

Crispin Porter + Bogusky today is no longer a challenger – and that's the joy of being a successful challenger. Seven years after the rupture of his Faustian pact with Bogusky (and I do think there was something at least mildly Faustian about it), Chuck Porter is a man at ease with himself. But he's still working hard – though now with an agency that's probably more at ease with itself and, in fact, a network more comfortable with building brands rather than just making fame. He has no hobbies, so nothing to retire to: it's the work. And he's proud as he sees that work reviving in the agency that has been his home.

He divides his time between Miami and Boulder. But when he needs to retreat close somewhere, he goes back to Minnesota. Not a pied à terre in Manhattan or Paris for him, but a retreat he designed in Greenwood, MN,

Right *They say the early bird catches the worm, well this one caught the internet's imagination in one of the earliest interactive and viral campaigns of the digital age. Type in a command and Subservient Chicken would fulfil your request from a host of pre-determined moves – cleverly reinforcing the brand's "have it your way" message. (Anything outside of his repertoire would receive a humorous shake of the head).*

Below *Domino's Anyware has almost as many platforms connected as pizza toppings. Customers can order from their smart TV, smart watch, Ford car, Twitter and by text.*

population 200. There is no nicer place for this nice man to re-fuel.

As someone who once worked with him once told me: "I have never met anyone who doesn't love Chuck Porter."

There are not too many people in advertising you can say that about.

15 MY BRAIN HURTS

The arrival of the digital age coincided with big leaps in neuroscience. In fact, MRI (Magnetic Resonance Imaging) is dependent on digitalized imaging, a technology of the 1970s – those pretty brain scans we became familiar with. Consequently, our knowledge of how the brain works is much greater than David Ogilvy's was. Without any doubt at all, it is knowledge he would have relished:

> The quality of research will improve, and this will generate a bigger corpus of knowledge as to what works and what doesn't. Creative people will learn to exploit this knowledge, thereby improving their strike rate at the cash register.[1]

From the 1990s on, breakthroughs in academic neuroscience suddenly became populist, and the chief popularizers were the husband and wife team, Antonio and Hanna Damasio. They studied the case of the patient zero of neuroscience, Phineas Gage, a Vermont railroad foreman, who, in 1848, accidently set off an explosion that drove a steel rod into his skull from under his left eye through the top of his head. Miraculously, he survived. But Gage was not the same afterwards. From contemporary accounts, he seems to have lost all his charm – his emotional intelligence, or EQ. He turned from nice to nasty.

Amazingly, the Damasios, from his surviving skull, re-built his brain with 3D software, and then were able to identify that the "neural machinery" which enables decision-making is informed by "emotional" parts of the brain as much as by "rational" parts. Those first parts had been removed by the rod, along with his charm.

This is the neural "and" underneath the "Age of And". It's the story that not every schoolchild knows, but should, because it explains that mankind is not purely a rational species.

The Damasios' academic research continued by using MRI to probe the workings of different parts of the brain: they identified very different roles for the limbic system, especially the almond-shaped amygdalae, governing emotional inputs to decisions, and for the ventromedial prefrontal cortex, contributing intellectual reason.

Face agnosia, along with the varied neuropsychological disturbances that may accompany it, can now be analyzed with experimental paradigms and correlated with neuro-anatomical loci of damage identified by neuroimaging methods.[2]

My brain hurts!

Fortunately, Antonio Damasio in his popular book, *Descartes' Error* (1994), demystifies it all. The Cartesian precept – "I think, therefore I am", was just plain wrong. "I feel, therefore I am" is more like it: or, in Damasio's

Above Descartes' Error *by Antonio Damasio, which explicates the role of feeling over thinking – that man is above all an emotional rather than rational animal.*

words: "we are not thinking machines, we are feeling machines that think."

Of course, this is rather convincing proof of what one school of advertising has always believed. Rosser Reeves, turn in your grave.

The industry has implicitly absorbed these findings, although they are still insufficiently taught and explained. (A notable exception is my colleague, Chris Graves, who has read many academic articles on the subject and used them to distill afresh a scientific basis for Public Relations, which returns it to its roots as an applied social science. His brain does not hurt).

Unfortunately, one of the besetting sins in our business has always been to grab on to the "next new thing", and treat it as a universal panacea. Thus was invented the pseudo-science of neuro-marketing.

Correlating the impact of marketing activity on the brain can be interesting – but as any statistician will tell you, correlation does not equal causation. Increased neural activity in the insula, for example, is linked to feelings of love and compassion. So if a brand triggers activity in this region this could be a positive sign. However, activity in this region is also linked to functions of memory, language, attention … and anger, disgust, and pain. We are a long way from a sophisticated enough understanding of the functioning of the brain to directly link neural activity to purchasing patterns.

As Dr Molly Crockett from the Department of Experimental Psychology at Oxford advises, we must avoid "neuro-bunk". She says: "We haven't found a 'buy' button within the brain … yet."

As such, our focus should remain on the outcome of actual behaviour, rather than the intermediate measure of neural activity.[3]

There are plenty of ways to use the foundations of neuroscience to improve marketing and advertising without building a dedicated superstructure above it. The opportunity, as my inimitable colleague and co-founder of Ogilvy Change, Rory Sutherland, who has done as much as anyone to evangelize its relevance, is to create the messages and cues which work on the "adaptive unconscious". For that we owe the ground-breaking research to the psychologists Amos Tversky and Daniel Kahneman, though it was Kahneman who, in this case, did the popularizing. He divided the brain into two parts and "branded" them "System 1" and "System 2". System 1 is the adaptive unconscious – instinctive, habitual, and often irrationally guided by biases and external circumstances. System 2 is more thought out, condensed and rational. When you are driving a car you might be in System 2; when you're in a food shop you are more likely in System 1.

At the Hay Festival in 2012, Kahneman was asked, "Is there such a thing as a System 1 business?" "Advertising," he replied.

As Rory points out:

Most good people are instinctively good psychologists. What we have lacked to date is a vocabulary and body of scientific work which

KAHNEMAN SYSTEM 1 AND SYSTEM 2

System 1	System 2
Fast	Slow
Unconscious	Conscious
Automatic	Effortful
Everyday Decisions	Complex Decisions
Error-Prone	Reliable

Above *Kahneman's System 1 and System 2 model, where System 1 is our adaptive unconscious with its unthinking emotionality, and System 2 our rational side.*

we can use to explain and justify their own often counter-intuitive recommendations.

What is now becoming apparent is that at the heart of most human decision-making lies something called the "adaptive unconscious". Far from being the rather pervy, dark part of the brain, much of what it does might be broadly characterized under "common sense". A collection of reliable heuristics and rules of thumb, which, over time, have become embedded in our inherited mental hardware.

These mental processes are the product of evolution. They operate automatically, effortlessly and to a great extent beyond our conscious awareness. They control the behaviour of people not by generating reasons but by generating feelings (approach/withdraw/trust/punish/anxiety/arousal). They do not necessarily obey the rules of conventional logic, but they do have a logic all their own. And the metalogic of the unconscious is much more influential than previously thought: in fact, much as we want to believe the opposite is true, our feelings give rise to our beliefs, not the other way around. We do not rationalize and then form feelings – we feel and then we post-rationalize (or "confabulate"). We can no more directly and consciously control the workings of our adaptive unconscious than we can directly control our heart-rate.[4]

The brain was also being re-evaluated from a very different angle. What exactly was homo economicus, and how did his or her decisions impact as behaviour on the economy in which they lived? The debate had begun in 1955, the year when David Ogilvy gave his famous speech on branding in Chicago. Herbert A. Simon had published an article, "A Behavioural Model of Rational Choice" in the *Quarterly Journal,* which for the first time questioned whether economic behaviour was only rational. By modelling the various alternatives open to close, the relationships between them which determined the "pay-offs", and the order of preference of those pay-offs, he concluded that real behaviour was largely unlikely ever to conform to the rules. How, for instance, can one ever be sure that a pay-off X will emerge from an outcome Y? What happens when alternatives are evaluated separately rather than all together before the process of choice starts?

The economist Richard H. Thaler adds:

> Following Simon's lead subsequent research has identified not only 150 or more heuristics or biases (mental shortcuts) that lead us to often make irrational (or erroneous) decisions, but also that the presentation of too many options can lead us to make no decision at all. Contrary to the received wisdom that abundant choice makes it more likely homo economicus will make the decision, the "paradox of choice" (as coined by Professor Barry Schwartz) means that biases are more likely to come to bear and we will make a decision based on much more limited criteria, or even delegate or defer the choice.[5]

The question then comes: how do we organize the messages and the cues in such a way that they might better push us into a change of behaviour? Otherwise, this will all remain fascinating but useless.

The Nudge

While Herbert Simon's approach was largely falling on deaf ears in the financial world as it was so far removed from the economic orthodoxy of the day, there were a group of economists from the Chicago School that developed his work much further. The most famous of these are Richard H. Thaler and Cass R. Sunstein.

Together they built on Simon's work by taking the irrational operator and categorizing him as a "human", as opposed to the fictional "econ" of neoclassical economics. Their work led them to look at the heuristics and

BRAIN MAP

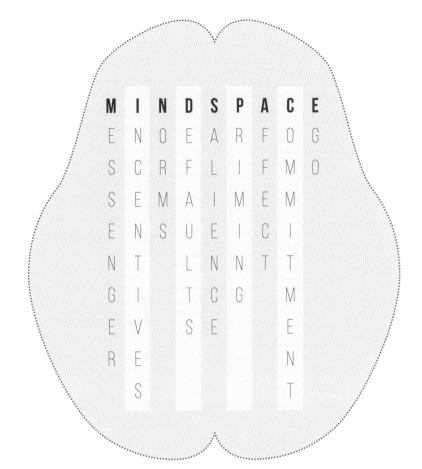

M	I	N	D	S	P	A	C	E
E	N	O	E	A	R	F	O	G
S	C	R	F	L	I	F	M	O
S	E	M	A	I	M	E	M	
E	N	S	U	E	I	C	I	
N	T		L	N	N	T	T	
G	I		T	C	G		M	
E	V		S	E			E	
R	E						N	
S							T	

Above *The MINDSPACE framework was developed by a UK government office with input from academics and behavioural scientists. Working through each letter of the mnemonic – M for messenger, I for incentives, and so on – can generate practical ideas that instigate real behavioural change. Our client, Kimberly Clark, adopted the framework and added an extra letter to create MINSPACER. The all-important 'R' – for reciprocity – asks how people might act for others, not just for themselves.*

biases that influence all manner of economic decision-making and particularly to advocate "libertarian paternalism" – encouraging governments to structure processes and systems in such a way that the most socially beneficial choices are the easiest to make.

Together, they popularized – in an eponymously titled book in 2008 – the idea of a "nudge", a behavioural intervention which pushes people in the right direction. Nudges at their best are optional; they should help people do what they want to do anyway; and they should be easy to avoid. "Choice architecture" is the system by means of which we structure nudges.

Nudging became immediately interesting to governments: how to nudge people into better behaviour – be it paying more taxes or drinking less. President Obama hired Sunstein; Prime Minister David Cameron hired Thaler. Ironically, though, the application of behavioural economics in its purer form has been far more popular in the UK than the US where it was "invented" – something to do with its simultaneous adaptation built by the Cabinet Office and by the IPA (Institute of Practitioners in Advertising), who have stimulated debate and encouraged good practices.

To be honest, not all the experiments have been useful. Some findings seem blindingly obvious. Isn't it to be expected that an organ-donor programme where you have to opt out will show better results than one where you opt in?

And it has taken time for its opportunities to manifest themselves in strategic approaches which "fit" the usual ways we do strategy. One such is the "Mindspace Framework" – a process geared towards changing behaviour rather than changing minds and attitudes. It is that rare thing: an academically validated framework that integrates the findings of cognitive psychology, social psychology and behavioural economics – around a real-world problem.

Originally developed by the Institute for Government and the Cabinet Office in the UK to influence policy, it can be applied to any behavioural challenge as a checklist for generating practical ideas. It was borne out of a collaboration between a multi-disciplinary team of academics and behavioural science practitioners in London, who conducted a meta-analysis of the hundreds of heuristics, biases and principles available, and collected them into the simple mnemonic MINDSPACE[6]. Each letter stands for a fundamental behaviour change principle: M for Messenger; I for Incentives; N for Norms; and so on. As such, it is a useful tool in the arsenal of organizations like Ogilvy Change for turning decades of research into practical application.

Neuroscience helps us persuade better; behavioural economics assists people to make choices. They emerged from different academic disciplines, but are mutually reinforcing. Of course, there are those who dislike consumerism in principle and may see them as dark perversions, preying on the unwary. But it is a great mistake to blame these methods for something much more fundamental you disagree with. Like any other tool in life – including a spade – they can be used for good or ill purposes. In the main, they have made advertising more responsible, not less. And in the era of transparency, they are easily audited. They are the bright secrets, not the dark secrets of the Digital Revolution (see following pages).

Nudges – whether they are big ones or small ones – are becoming an increasingly helpful way of making communications grounded in a business issue which might not otherwise have been clearly identified as such. For instance, you will sell more of your nappies if you frame yours as a positive opportunity for bonding time rather than simply a routine negative behaviour – and, for instance, put the hug into Huggies again.

The essence of a nudge is to change behaviour without coercion, to work with people's existing intentions. An unexpected opportunity was seen in food-processing plants around the world, whose hand-hygiene practices often fall short of agreed standards, not because workers don't want to wash or don't understand what to do, but because they simply haven't built effective habitual behaviours. For Kimberly Clark Professional, who design and create innovative hand-washing solutions, this presented an opportunity to nudge. It took a collaborative research and development project with Ogilvy Change to invent a big nudge, which would subsequently be shown to reduce instances of dirty hands on the factory floor by 63 per cent.

"The essence of a nudge is to change behaviour without coercion, to work with people's existing intentions."

Form **3305**	**Research Study Tax Return**	Keep a copy of this return for your records.
(Rev. June 2010)	For the period June 1, 2010, through August 30, 2010	OMB No. 1555-0111
Center for Decision Research		

I declare that I will carefully examine this return and that to the best of my knowledge and belief it is correct and complete.

Sign Here

► _____ ► _____
Signature   Date

Write Clearly

Name | PID | For Administrative Use Only

Address (Number, street, and room or suite number) | | T
 | | ...
City, State, and ZIP code | | FF

Part 1   Please fill out the questions below to compute your taxed payment.

1. Please enter the payment you received on the problem solving task ($1 per correct matrix you solved in the other room) .... | 1 |

2. Tax on payment: Please enter the equivalent of a 20% tax on your payment (i.e., 20 cents for every dollar earned) .... | 2 |
| | 3 |

3. Please subtract the value specified in box 2 from value specified in box 1 .... ►

Part 2   Participants will be compensated for extra expenses they have incurred in order to participate in this study. In Part 2, you are asked to estimate the costs incurred in order to participate. These costs will be deducted from your tax return.

1. Please estimate the time it took you to come to the lab. You will be compensated $0.10 per minute, up to a 2 hour maximum .... ► | 4 |

2. Please estimate the cost of your commute, if any, to come to the lab. You will be compensated up to a maximum of $12 .... | 5 |

3. Please add the value specified in box 4 and the value specified in box 5 .... ► | 6 |

Part 3   Please compute your final payment.

1. Please add the value specified in box 3 and the value specified in box 6. This is the amount of your final payment for today's session .... ► | 7 |

Above *Smart ideas can nudge people into changing behaviours. Our client, Kimberly-Clark, used a big nudge to improve factory hygiene levels by applying a washable stamp to workers' hands, which could only be removed by purposeful scrubbing. A small nudge can be equally clever, such as re-designing the language and layout of tax forms to encourage people to be more honest in what they report.*

Pages 244–246 *My "12 Bright Secrets" are a set of individuals who have each advanced an important area within neuroscience or behavioural economics – from "habit formation" to "goal dilution". Some of them are names you may have heard before, others are less well-known but influential in their own right. As you'll see, the principle developed by each has been successfully applied in advertising to effect change.*

This nudge took inspiration from a study conducted in a UK hospital and involved the creation of a washable ink hand-stamp that, when applied before the communal wash process, would put a nasty looking bacteria stamp to the backs of workers' hands. The specially formulated ink was just sticky enough to require diligent washing to remove it. This made previously invisible germs "visible", created a familiar trigger to build a washing habit and made good hand-washing practices a social norm (because after all, each individual can now see that everyone is else washing, too). This nudge was big because it changed behaviour significantly, but also because it materially enhanced the hand-washing product itself, something that a typical communications approach can rarely claim to achieve.

An example of a smaller nudge can be seen on application forms. This nudge was to simply move the signature box to the start of the form, rather than the traditional position at the end, because such a move primes honesty and acts as a commitment device for applicants. A study by a car insurance company found that when they ran a randomized controlled trial (RCT) on over 13,000 applications, there was a 10 per cent increase in the honesty of the mileage reported in the "sign at the top" forms, which equated to an average of US$97 on annual insurance premiums. Such a nudge is fascinating not just because it is low cost and scientifically validated, but because it highlights how there are "unseen opportunities" to change behaviour by designing the world for how people *really* behave, rather than how we traditionally *think* they think.[7]

12 BRIGHT SECRETS: FROM EARLY NEUROSCIENCE TO CUTTING EDGE BEHAVIOURAL ECONOMICS

HABIT FORMATION

Behaviour becomes habitual through repetition.

EDWARD THORNDIKE
(1874–1949)
Psychologist

1905 (Thorndike): The Law of Effect. Behaviours followed by pleasant consequences are more likely to be repeated than behaviours followed by unpleasant consequences.

2010 (Lally et al.): Habit formation modelled in the real world with eating, drinking and activity behaviours revealed that automaticity takes anything from 18 to 254 days to achieve.

Ogilvy Change: Stamping Out Bad Hand Hygiene

The use of hand hygiene safety stamps in food-processing factories encouraged habitual hand-washing through repetition.

SOCIAL NORMS

Behaviour is influenced by the need to be publicly compliant.

MUZAFER SHERIF
(1906–1988)
Social Psychologist

1936 (Sherif): Social norms were first illustrated by the "autokinetic effect". Frames of reference were modified in the direction of group conformity.

More recent research shows that normative messages have the power to influence behaviour in a range of decision-making environments (e.g. energy conservation) without being detected.

Ogilvy Change: Direct Debit Leaflet Optimization.

Normative messages used to encourage direct debit sign-ups for UK council tax payment.

CHUNKING

Separating long strings of information into smaller "chunks" allows for better memory retention.

GEORGE A. MILLER
(1920–2012)
Cognitive Psychologist

1956 Miller's Law: The average person can hold seven chunks (largest meaningful unit of information) +/- two in their working memory.

2001 (Cowan & Nelson): A review of capacity limits revealed four chunks to be the mental storage capacity for short-term memory.

Ogilvy Change: Medical Adherence

Separating a 21-day course of medication into three manageable chunks increased compliance by 21%.

CONFIRMATION BIAS

People favour information that confirms rather than challenges their current beliefs.

PETER WASON
(1924–2003)
Cognitive Psychologist

1960 (Wason): People focus on confirming their initial hypotheses rather than challenging them.

1979 (Lord): People discount evidence that challenges their beliefs regarding capital punishment.

MRI scans reveal that areas connected with reasoning are subordinated to those connected with emotion when beliefs are challenged.

People are Fragile: Vancouver Pedestrian Awareness campaign

Using the confirmation bias to reduce jaywalking in Vancouver.

AMBIGUITY AVERSION

People prefer known risks over unknown risks.

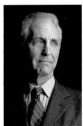

DANIEL ELLSBERG
(b. 1931)

Economist, Activist

1961 Ellsberg paradox: thought experiment showed people's overwhelming preference for gambling on known chances over unknown chances.

2010 (Alary): In the real world, ambiguity aversion leads to an increased demand for insurance because people are averse to unknown events that will affect their lives.

Transport for London (TFL): Pedestrian Countdown at Traffic Signals

The introduction of countdown timers between red and green pedestrian signals makes the "risk" of crossing the road known and increases feelings of safety.

IDENTIFIABLE VICTIM EFFECT

The extent to which the vividness created by one human example creates superior impact.

THOMAS SCHELLING
(1921–2016)

Cognitive Psychologist

1968 (Schelling): An identifiable victim will stimulate a more powerful emotional response than a statistical victim.

2013 (Genevsky et al.): fMRI revealed that effect elicited by identifiable information reliably shifts preferences for giving.

No More Abuse: Memac Ogilvy and King Khalid Foundation campaign

Utilizing the Identifiable victim effect to raise awareness of domestic violence.

CONCRETENESS EFFECT

Words which are concrete (real and tangible) are processed faster and more accurately than abstract ones

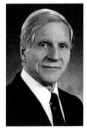

ALLAN PAIVIO
(1925–2016)

Psychologist

1971 (Paivio): The dual-coding theory. Concrete words activate both the visual and verbal systems in the brain.

1983 (Schwanenflugel & Shoben): The context availability theory. Concrete words activate broader contextual verbal support allowing for faster processing.

2000 (Jessen): fMRI suggests that both models combined explains the effect.

Nutrition Action Health Letter: Center for Science in the Public Interest

We can more easily process the unhealthiness of popcorn from concrete descriptions (equivalent foods) than abstract ones (grams).

ANCHORING

In decision making, people rely very heavily on the first piece of information received.

DANIEL KAHNEMAN
(b. 1934)

Psychologist

AMOS TVERSKY
(b. 1937-1996)

Psychologist

1974 (Kahneman and Tversky): In fast decision making 8x7x6x5x4x3x2x1 elicited four times higher estimates than 1x2x3x4x5x6x7x8 showing participants' heavy reliance on anchoring to the first few digits in the calculation.

2006 (Ariely et al.): People placed 60–120% higher bids in auctions when anchored to the last two digits of their social security number if those numbers were high compared to low.

Durex Cheaper campaign

Advertisement anchors people to the high cost of baby products putting the cost of the Durex product into context.

HYPERBOLIC DISCOUNTING

A time inconsistent model of people's greater valuation of immediate rewards over distant rewards.

GEORGE AINSLIE
(b. 1944)

Psychologist

1974 (Ainsley): An overwhelming preference for sooner, smaller rewards over later, larger rewards was demonstrated with pigeons.

More recent studies show that people choose $50 today over $100 in a year. However, when given the same choice shifted in time by five years, they prefer to wait an additional year for the greater reward.

Jason Vale Dieting campaign

Dieting campaigns famously attract people by focusing on quick fixes with more immediate rewards.

FRAMING EFFECT

People react to choices differently depending on how they are presented.

DANIEL KAHNEMAN
(b. 1934)

Psychologist

AMOS TVERSKY
(b. 1937-1996)

Psychologist

1979 (Tversky & Kahneman): "Prospect theory". People make decisions based on the potential value of losses and gains rather than the final outcome.

1997 (Rothman & Salovey): Loss-framed messages are more persuasive for risky behaviours and gain-framed messages are more persuasive for low risk behaviours.

Ogilvy Change: Grubs campaign

This campaign encouraged people to try grubs by activating people's fear of missing out: "Don't miss your chance to try".

NEURAL COUPLING

When we witness another's actions, our brain mirrors the neural response and we "feel" what we see.

GIACOMO RIZZOLATTI
(b. 1937)

Neurophysiologist

1980's (Rizzolatti): A monkey's motor neurons fire when watching and performing grasping actions. Monkey see = monkey do.

1980 (Chong et al.): Neural responses will mirror neuron properties found in humans.

2010 (Stephens et al.): Similar brain responses found when telling and hearing stories as though we are acting out the story ourselves.

Ogilvy Change and Nestlé: United for Healthier Kids in Mexico

Created the Emmy-nominated reality-TV show "Hermosa Esperanza", which followed five families adopting lifestyle changes which encourage children to be healthier.

GOAL DILUTION

The more goals there are, the less likely we believe one of them is likely to be fulfilled.

YING ZHANG
(b. unknown)

Assistant Professor of Marketing

2007 (Zhang et al): An increased number of goals (e.g. building muscles and losing weight) is perceived as more difficult to achieve than when those goals are combined into a single means (e.g. exercising).

Ogilvy Change and Public Health England: The 10 Minute Shake-Up campaign. Made exercise seem more achievable by focusing on a simple burst of activity twice a day.

It's clearly the case that choice architecture is made for the digital age. Not only do nudges help provide an integrating "glove" for digitally-led programs, but they are directly enabled by social media in particular, creating immediacy in helping a big decision, for instance, or turning otherwise private actions like voting into behaviours people can publicize, share and talk about.

Even the most traditional actions can be treated with behavioural economics. In one of the largest ever randomly controlled trials, at the 2010 US Congressional Elections the Facebook news feeds of nearly 60 million people were modified. Salient information like the location of the nearest polling station, an "I Voted" button, and pictures of six friends who'd already done so were added to the News Feed. The results were conclusive with an additional 340,000 people going to the polls. The analysis showed that not only were people more likely to vote if they just saw other people they knew were doing the same, but even their more distant friends of friends were triggered as well.[3] The seemingly inconsequential addition of a button and a picture can be enough to foster a behaviour as profound as deciding who governs the country.

David Ogilvy is popularly quoted as saying: "The trouble with market research is that people don't think what they feel, they don't say what they think and they don't do what they say."

Decoding the human brain will never definitively solve those conundrums. But it has helped a bit. We can now apply a little more rigour to our understanding of why they may feel differently to what they say; and then to nudge them a little into actually doing something.

Below *Social networks provide a boost to the polls. Peer pressure from "I voted" badges alongside pictures of Facebook friends encourages political involvement.*

Today is Election Day   What's this? • close

Find your polling place on the U.S. Politics Page **and click the "I Voted" button to tell your friends you voted.**

VOTE

I Voted

$$0\ 1\ 1\ 5\ 5\ 3\ 7\ 6$$

People on Facebook Voted

Jaime Settle, Jason Jones, and 18 other friends have voted.

16 THE NEW SHAPE OF THE WORLD

Ogilvy on Advertising contained one chapter with a provocative title: "Is America still top nation?" Its influence is still huge, but "top nation" would be difficult to defend as a claim. The world is getting a different shape.

In September 1995, I arrived in Hong Kong as the Regional Director for Asia. In 1991 Ogilvy & Mather had opened its first mainland office, in Shanghai. Doing business on the mainland required a joint-venture contract with a domestic company, so we signed with the Shanghai Advertising Group. We have always benefited from having a first-mover advantage. Our first (and continuing) Chairman there was TB Song, a kind of Chinese David Ogilvy, endlessly curious and very literary (he would, before Ogilvy became too big, buy a copy of every new book he liked for each of our staff). TB was someone who seemed to define "the Tao of advertising", but nonetheless was a vigorously single-minded driver of growth. He had formed the first agency with foreign investors in Taiwan in 1985, later to become Ogilvy & Mather Taiwan. Over on the mainland, China still had only representative offices, which was the state of affairs until TB moved to Shanghai in 1991 to establish our new joint venture. So welcome was he in China that the Government gave him "grace and favour" lodging in the Summer Palace in our early days.

As I arrived, TB had just had a request for the hire of a significant executive turned down. This man was not cheap, but was going to be the catalyst of our next stage of growth. The refusal came from on high – from Farm Street, from Mayfair, and from Martin Sorrell himself of WPP.

"The mountains are high and the emperor is far away" is a very useful Chinese proverb if you are an expatriate manager, but I never found it worked particularly well with Martin. I argued the case; Martin refused. I argued again; he refused again. And again. Finally, there was the response: "China is a black hole. On your head be it." Martin will (I hope!) forgive me for saying this, but at the time he felt much more comfortable in India than in China (well, they played and talked about cricket). That changed very quickly; and he has been the person who, more than anyone else, saw the potential of Chinese advertising, and then relentlessly drove WPP's growth there. No city has ever been too far, no client ever too remote, for him to visit.

By 2017, China (including Hong Kong and Taiwan) accounted for over

$1.6 billion of WPP's annual revenue; WPP is at least double the size of any of its competitors in the region. So much of that growth has been driven by the Digital Revolution. It has become a mature advertising market, which has enforced the Western theory of branding wholesale. I have always believed that there is something about the rich symbolism inherent in Chinese culture that has made it especially receptive to brands. It's very fertile territory. And, then, the concept of branding fitted perfectly into a government agenda committed to making state-owned enterprises modern customer-focused organizations.

Having said all that, the Chinese characters for brand 名牌 denote "Ming Pai" – *famous* brand – and give a Chinese take on the concept, which has been rather more to do with fame than with uniqueness. This is epitomized by the infamous CCTV auctions, when all that matters is whether a brand gets the slot viewed by 130+ million[1] people at once: instant fame. The Digital Revolution, however, as we'll see, changes that model.

We quickly expanded beyond the global clients into the state-owned enterprises and private Chinese companies; and from the two big coastal cities, Shanghai and Beijing, into the provinces, where we believed the differential growth would be. For me, a proud moment came in March 2004, when the first Chinese-produced advertising, Motorola's HelloMoto campaign, ran in the US.

It was symbolic of the small beginnings of an impending shift of influence in the world. Asia, so long the importer of creativity, actually could export it. A one-way world could become two-way.

And it was around this time that an iconic chart started circulating, which to me, a historian manqué, was most seductive. It showed the global share of trade represented by China over time. Between AD 1 and the middle of the nineteenth century, it held steady above 25 per cent, number one in the world. In 1820, it reached a remarkable high-water mark of 33 per cent. Then it slid drastically to a low of 4.6 per cent in 1950.

But by 2017, China's contribution to the global gross domestic product stood at 14.84 per cent, not quite the record level it enjoyed in 1820 but a significant number – second only to that of the US and growing fast. It's back to the future, in a very big way.[2]

In India, the advertising stimulus has been less digital, since, of all the markets in the world apart from Japan, it has remained addicted to the commission system. The earning of fees for digital work has therefore been artificially repressed. It has also been constrained by a complex and multi-layered wholesale and retail distribution system – the lack of a "modern trade" – which is what drives the expansion of advertising in the developing markets, as an efficient "puller" of demand. In other words, India's great advertising days are still to come. We have just seen a foretaste. It is *quantitatively* under-playing.

However, it has *qualitatively* over-performed. An efflorescence of creativity has placed India among the most lively and exciting advertising markets in the world. Piyush Pandey, our Indian Chairman, who started life

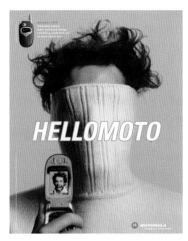

Above *We created the signature HelloMoto campaign for Motorola from China in 2004, then ran it widely in the US. It marks the beginning of a shift in seeing China as not just a huge target market, but an enormously creative one.*

as a tea taster, is recognized as the prime mover. He demonstrates that the beliefs of David Ogilvy about what makes an idea – and then what makes an idea big – can have an Indian manifestation that owes nothing to the West, culturally, but draws from the deep, deep waters of Indianness; and Indianness is a multi-faceted and brilliant thing.

As a result of the personal charismas of Piyush and his colleagues in the industry, Indian advertising has developed a status in society difficult to find elsewhere in the world – film-star status, and very well deserved, too.

It is underpinned by something very important: Piyush has never forgotten where he came from. As he says, he does not wear India on his sleeve, but he does wear it on his heart. He avers he learnt as much from the carpenters who made his family's furniture as a child as he ever did formally. He combines great humility with a larger-than-life charisma. And he is generous to the last wicket, cricket being his abiding love, and team play such a natural analogy for producing great advertising.

Piyush's advertising is culturally rooted. As a result, he has helped build definitively Indian brands – Pidilite, for instance – by telling powerful stories that resonate.

Piyush's work is so popular, it's inherently viral. It spreads. But in his words: "Let's all remember Paduyikiphed. If the story is not great or if the story is not human, no technology will save you."

He reminds us that it's not enough to be a multinational. You have to be multicultural – and multicultural even within India: to be Telugu or to be Tamil as much as to be Hindi. As Piyush once told me: "Never forget that when a Rajasthani visits Kerala, he is stunned that the same coconut oil that he uses on his hair is used in cooking the fish he is eating."

Below *India has become one of the most creative hubs in advertising, one where the industry still has a touch of Hollywood (or Bollywood) glamour to it – and it produces some of the best creative ideas in the world. This brilliant ad from Fevicol is a memorable example, where the product benefit is depicted by a common site across India – people clinging to the roof of a bus. Its inherent "Indianness" in both storytelling and tone is unlike anything elsewhere. And most importantly, the brand certainly gets stuck in your head!*

Velocity

I have no doubt whatsoever that these anecdotal characterizations of China and India do betoken a new shape of the world.

But, of course, it's broader than that.

For many years I, like many others, used in presentations, meetings, reviews and plans the concept of BRIC (Brazil, Russia, India, China), but I did so with increasing distaste. This was an acronym useful at a time in history, but also one which reflected the interests of those who coined it – in this case, Goldman Sachs. It was a financial markets' view of the world. There is nothing at all wrong with that. But it does not reflect the world of marketing and advertising, and of the masses of consumers (and businesses) who fuel it.

There is no shortage of demographic predictions about the future of the world, but it seemed to me that none of them really hone in on what makes advertising tick. So I asked a distinguished economist and demographer, Dr Surjit Bhalla, to go back to data purely from the point of view of where the consumer future lies. The results are startling.

The global middle class is on the cusp of what can only be described as an explosion. By 2025, it will have increased by 35 per cent – rising to 4.6 billion people, almost 60 per cent of the world's population.

But the surprising thing is what the new shape of the world will look like.

There are 12 countries which are growing disproportionately: India, China, Pakistan, Indonesia, Bangladesh, Nigeria, Egypt, The Philippines, Vietnam, Brazil, Mexico, and Myanmar (and, one which will – politics permitting – quickly join the list, Iran). These are the V12 or Velocity 12 countries.

If you want a genuinely futurist index for charting bottom-line impact, this is it. It is composed of two primary indicators – a country's share of middle-class consumption in the world; and the projected rate of growth (or velocity) of this consumption, adjusted for Purchasing Power Parity.

This gives another angle to the concept of inequality. The world when measured by asset distribution is not equal; and grossly unfair concentrations of wealth exist, be it in 1 per cent or 5 per cent of the population. But when measured by income distribution, the world *is* becoming more equal: the ground occupied by a middle class is becoming bigger and bigger.

At Ogilvy & Mather we like the word "velocity": it signifies more than just the economic growth of countries, which the expansion of middle-class consumers enables, but also the pace at which their daily life (increasingly digitally enabled) and their sentiments evolve.

Of course, no projection will be perfectly fulfilled, and short-term bumps in the road there will be. Governments can accelerate or decelerate the velocity. The "Lula middle-class" of some 140 million people in Brazil grew up as a result of government policy in the administration of President Lula in the 2000s; as those policies have subsequently foundered, their purchasing ability has collapsed (and their sentiment has become dangerously embittered). But the cycle will turn – be it in two, five or 10 years.

> "The global middle class is on the cusp of what can only be described as an explosion."

Following pages *Cartographers, avert your eyes! If the world map reflected middle class population growth, it would look something like this. North America and Western Europe give way to a dominant Asia and South America.*

THE NEW SHAPE OF THE WORLD:
GROWTH IN MIDDLE-CLASS CONSUMERS 2015-25

	2015	2025
MEXICO	93	106
BRAZIL	140	159
NIGERIA	33	61
EGYPT	56	81
PAKISTAN	63	122
INDIA	431	828

	2015	2025
MYANMAR	13	26
INDONESIA	139	189
VIETNAM	30	49
BANGLADESH	22	59
CHINA	758	945
PHILIPPINES	25	43

2025   ■ NET GAIN (MILLIONS)

MEXICO
+13

BRAZIL
+19

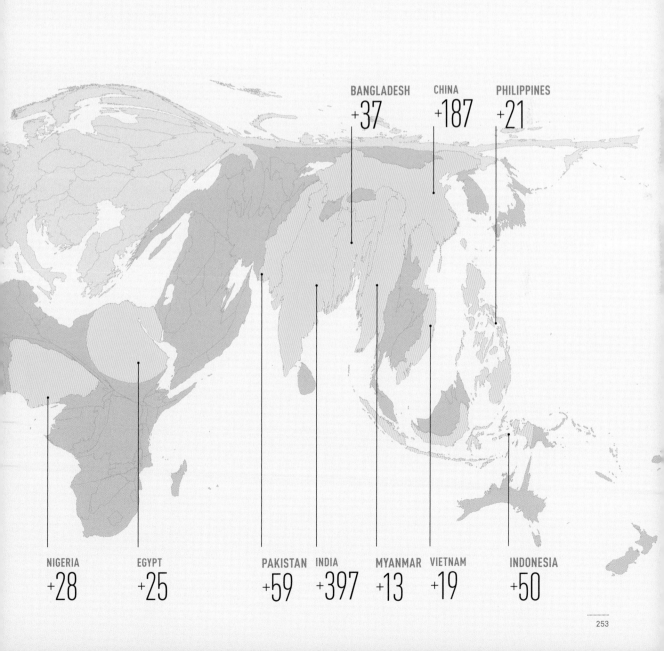

Source: Bhalla, Surjit S: Second Among Equals – The Middle Class Kingdoms of India and China; 2007; revised and data updated till 2025.

BANGLADESH
+37

CHINA
+187

PHILIPPINES
+21

NIGERIA
+28

EGYPT
+25

PAKISTAN
+59

INDIA
+397

MYANMAR
+13

VIETNAM
+19

INDONESIA
+50

There's one overwhelming thrust to this view of the world, and that's the shift to Asia; but within that a more dramatic shift to South Asia. It's not a shift that is yet viscerally recognized as something real by most multinational businesses. I set up our office in Pakistan in 2007. I can demonstrate there a strong consumer base; can show that it's much easier to grow a business to a particular fraction of an average Indian business than it would be to expand that Indian business by the same amount; can point to the exceptional local talent; can exhibit the success stories of a few multinationals who *have* taken it seriously: and I still feel that I'm preaching in a wilderness of prejudice.

The fact is that we will be moving well beyond the Rise of China. In the next two decades, Chinese velocity will abate. India, Pakistan, Bangladesh, Indonesia and Vietnam will take up the slack. In particular, the next half-century will be India's: and yet in my view, most global marketers have not yet adjusted psychologically to this fact.

What will this new world feel like?

Well, very different to the world the West thinks of now.

It will be female, Muslim and urban.

Women are entering the labour force in the millions, spurred by better education. The Muslim middle class of the V12 will rise to 583 million people by 2030. And India will add 400 million, China 300 million and Nigeria 200 million new city dwellers by the middle of the next century.

Those women, even in traditional societies, are starting to eclipse men in purchasing decisions; Muslims are looking for Halal values behind the products they buy. And the city dwellers will increasingly rely on digital connectivity as both citizens and consumers.

The digital age will have a very different global flavour. It's probably time to wake up to that fact.

> "It's the V12 markets which will lead the world into the next big leap of internet growth."

The connectivity it brings is the dividend of this digital re-shaping of the world. Most commentators to date focus on the sheer scale of the advance of the internet.

I remember visiting Facebook's Menlo Park HQ in its early days: conference rooms were named after countries representing the numbers of new users found: 75 million users – that's the Turkey room. It seemed a little overweening and, anyway, they soon ran out of rooms.

It's the V12 markets which will lead the world into the next big leap of internet growth. Of the unconnected globally, nearly half reside in China, India, Pakistan and Bangladesh. While the internet in India took more than a decade to move from 5.5 million to 100 million users, and another five years to reach 375 million users, it could reach 600 million by 2020. Six of the top 10 markets in internet growth are V12 markets. Low-tech markets like Bangladesh and Myanmar are emerging as "straight to smartphone" markets.

There are two big implications of this.

The first is that these populations want local content. Conceived in an English-speaking bubble, the mature internet now is non-English.

And the second is that velocity is the sister of connectivity. Where penetration grows, economic growth roles accelerate disproportionately.

The Internet with Chinese Characteristics

The exemplar of both is China: an internet that has gone its own way. I sometimes have difficulty in persuading my American clients that the digital ecosystem in China has become more sophisticated and more far-reaching than it is in the US. The "Great Firewall" acts as a perceptual screen, and is conflated into a general miasma of China detraction. Yet the reality is that, just as Deng Xiaoping's formula has worked for socialism, so it has worked for the internet: digitalization with Chinese characteristics.

In September of 1987, just a few subway stops to the west of Ogilvy's Beijing offices, at the Institute of High-Energy Physics, China sent its first international email. The famous subject header read: Crossing the Great Wall to Join the World (越过长 城 走向世界).

Ironically, the first 30 years of China's internet has not been characterized by "joining the world". Far from it. The prevalent theme has instead been one of a domestic internet that has, in many ways, developed in parallel to the world's internet.

Although the sender of that email was wrong about the first 30 years, he might be right about the next 30. Looking forward, I think we will see an outbound flow of internet innovation. Arguably, the non-Chinese internet will begin to look more and more like its Chinese counterpart. And as this happens – and it has already started – marketers will be looking to China to understand how to address challenges and opportunities faced years ago by their more experienced Chinese counterparts.

Every commentator has their own way of describing the scale of China's internet – a population of 688 million, at the end of 2015[3]. To drive home the enormity of this number, some will tell you that that's twice as many Chinese internet users as there are Americans. Others might note that there are more Chinese internet users than there are people in Germany, Iran, Turkey, France, Thailand, the UK, Italy, Colombia, Spain and Canada combined. Wittier China watchers might tell you there are more Chinese internet users than there are teenagers in the world, or than there are cats or dogs alive today.

What made it possible? And so quickly?

First, the government. Chinese leadership believed in the internet as the basis for a modern society. Early evidence of this includes the funding in 1988 of the country's first email system (via packet-switching), which provided a digital connection among governmental agencies and academic institutions in nine large cities, including Shanghai, Beijing and Guangzhou. In August 1993, Premier Li Peng approved a $3 million expenditure to begin building a national digital network providing access to public economic information; this was known as the Golden Bridge Project. A watershed event occurred in 1994, when China's internet was connected – over infrastructure provided by Sprint – to the global internet. Over the next several years, Chinese computer scientists and electrical engineers networked among their foreign counterparts, chiefly in the US and Japan, to accelerate the growth of China's internet. Today, only a small segment of the nation's population,

> "I sometimes have difficulty in persuading my American clients that the digital ecosystem in China has become more sophisticated and more far-reaching than it is in the US."

> "Chinese leadership believed in the internet as the basis for a modern society."

20 million rural people, have no broadband access, and efforts are underway to get them connected.

At the same time, the government protected the local platforms as they developed; their international rivals were either blocked altogether or severely constrained.

Meanwhile the traditional media, largely government-owned, had gaps that the new media have been able decisively to fill. Dull and distrusted, Chinese internet users deserted state-controlled media and turned to each other for new ideas and fresh information: social media filled the gaps. Similarly, gaps in China's fragmented and creaky offline retail environment allowed sellers quickly to build distribution online at scale.

In the West, the predominant view of the Chinese internet is that it is fatally repressed by government censorship. Far from it. The controls that exist have done little to rein in the rampant usage of netizens. The few topics the government bans are of interest only to a minority. This is not to apologize for censorship, but simply to describe the reality – even though I know it is difficult to accept if you have not actually lived or worked in China. Far from feeling like an oppressed population with no freedom of speech, the vast majority of Chinese internet users behave online exactly as they would like to. We know: we watch them hourly.

Below *It might look like an ordinary office, but it isn't. Our agency in Shanghai closely monitors real-time dashboards that provide instant metrics on activity across social platforms like WeChat, Weibo and Baidu.*

Welcome to BAT!

BAT is the tri-partite world of the Chinese internet: Baidu, the biggest domestic search platform; Alibaba, China's number one ecommerce platform; and Tencent, the owner of China's biggest instant messaging apps.

BAT is presided over by the "three kings", each one brilliant in his own way: Robin Li, the multi-billionaire founder of Baidu, the search engine with a phenomenal 80 per cent share of the Chinese market; Jack Ma, the self-made mogul who launched the ecommerce giant Alibaba in 1999; and Pony Ma, the instant-messaging pioneer who founded Tencent, which created WeChat, the largest instant messaging platform in the world.

Following a theme of Chinese history, each king is building his kingdom to be as complete as possible.

Can a winner take all? It's called the One Emperor Syndrome. So, they all now have a video site: Alibaba's TMall Box Office (TBO); Tencent's QQLive; and Baidu Video.

And increasingly, they go to a client and offer a one-stop shop: so Alibaba will seek to bundle a client's logistics with its media and with its content. That doesn't just seek to disintermediate an advertising agency; it knocks it out of the game altogether. Fortunately for us, the individual offers are not, in the end, compelling – a case of generalization finding it difficult to trump specialization.

Innovation is the driver of BAT. It started with Sina Weibo, a microblog platform, which began with a similar functionality to Twitter: 140-character text updates in reverse chronological order. Then, later on, it tended to innovate much more; Twitter has followed, with the addition of video, for instance.

But it's WeChat that is most remarkable – and most revolutionary. A messaging, social and commerce app, it has fuelled China's use of QR codes – a technology that had fallen out of use almost completely in the West. Thanks to the platform, the scanning of QR codes is now ubiquitous in China: used by friends to exchange contacts, by marketers instead of links,

Below *The three kings: Robin Li of Baidu, Jack Ma of Alibaba and Pony Ma of Tencent, who preside over China's largest search, ecommerce and messaging platforms respectively.*

Robin Li, the graduate from New York State, chose the name Baidu for its meaning: "search for one's own dream", a reference to a Song Dynasty poem. His fierce battle with Google led to the latter's retreat from the Chinese market.

Jack Ma, 5 feet (1.52m) tall, lean and charismatic, could be China's richest man, by some counts. He was famously rejected for 30 jobs before becoming an intent entrepreneur. But he's also a self-confident face and voice of China.

Pony Ma founded Tencent in 1998. More private, even secretive, than the others, he at various times worked in the lowliest roles – including a janitor – to keep the company afloat. That's no longer necessary.

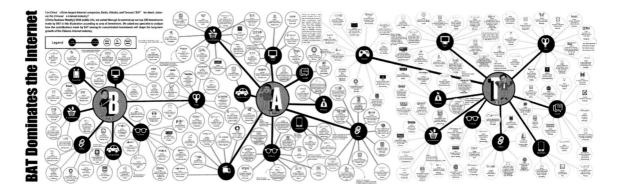

BAT Dominates the Internet

Above *This is a chart we show to our clients in China to explain the Chinese internet. BAT dominate, with each individual company having a near-monopoly on its primary business. For Baidu, that's search. It is China's answer to Google. For Alibaba, that's ecommerce. In fact, it's the world's largest ecommerce company (by number of sales, not revenue). Its pearls are Taobao and Tmall, which are the two primary ecommerce sites in China. For Tencent, that's social. The company owns both WeChat, the innovative and enormous mobile-based social app, and the QQ messenger service. Those are just the primary business lines. The BAT companies also dominate travel, e-payments, maps, games, entertainment, news, and security.*

and by merchants to facilitate payment. Ogilvy's staff in China have QR codes on their business cards.

The killer advantage is the cross functionality. Without leaving WeChat, its hundreds of millions of users split the bill with friends, buy flowers, and even book doctor appointments. Facebook, Twitter and other Western platforms, although woefully behind in this regard, will be scrambling to provide similarly rich, multi-functional experiences over the next few years.

As WeChat continues to be the most used messaging app in China (impressive, since it launched a mere six years before this book went to press), advertisers on WhatsApp are struggling to make the platform work for them. WeChat itself is clear that it is morphing from a platform into a lifestyle brand: it does not want to be defined by anything that has gone before it. The average user uses WeChat 11 times a day.

For agencies, by the way, it has changed the way we relate with our Chinese clients. We often present work on WeChat, and client feedback more often than not will come on WeChat.

There is also much less time for "over-thinking". I find that Western advertisers operating in China often bemoan what they see as a lack of strategy: clients in China rush to execution without the due diligence that might be applied in the West. Yet rather than laziness and a lack of rigour, might this be a sane response to shorter attention spans and the fragmented media – trends we're likely to see more of in the West? Time will tell whether Chinese advertisers are right to think less, do more.

The export of China's social and digital innovation is a trend certain to continue. Chinese advertisers may even have reason to be smug, as their Western counterparts rush to make sense of the changes on the way. What can we then learn from Chinese marketers already succeeding in this world?

1. Social as a mindset

Successful Chinese brands have, on the whole, skipped the setting up of separate social, or even digital, departments within their organizations. In doing so they've avoided the silo structures that often stymie success in the West.

Social in China, more than anywhere else, has the power to make and break brands. In this most connected nation in the world, 91 per cent have at least one social media account. This massive population follows an average

VISIT BRITAIN

WHAT'S IN A NAME?
QUITE A LOT AS IT TURNS OUT...

Among young Chinese wealthy enough to travel, Britain has a reputation for being unwelcoming compared to other countries.

So, our agency helped VisitBritain – the government organisation responsible for tourism to Great Britain – to get better at speaking their language. How? By letting Chinese citizens rename British landmarks!

For the first time in history, one country invited the citizens of another to come up with new names famous places. The campaign kicked off with a call from the British Ambassador to China, alongside cinema and outdoor advertising, to submit names for over 100 iconic British attractions online.

People immediately rose to the challenge. One participant suggested axing the name Sherwood Forest in favor of "The Forest of Chivalrous Thieves". Another renamed London's Shard the "Tower to Pluck the Stars", while the Lord Mayor's Gherkin was reduced to "The Little Pickled Cucumber".

So, we made the offer more enticing – come over and claim a landmark in person! Over 13,000 people did, including a die-hard Beatles fan who raced to rename Abbey Road. Each participant was rewarded by their suggested name appearing on Wikipedia, Baidu and Google Maps.

An unusual campaign, it unleashed online advocacy through a social idea and came to life in traditional channels too. Seen over 300 million times on Chinese social networks, it earned around ¥15 million in free media. But the biggest success? Brits were seen as a little less standoffish, and Chinese tourism to Great Britain increased 27% that year.

of eight brands via social, which gives these users enormous influence over the brands choices their peers make.

Yet despite its importance, social is not seen as a separate team, nor is it a separate line item, or a separate type of campaign. And never has it been.

Advertisers here know that to succeed in social – to get people talking about your brand in a positive way – you don't need to do something called "social". They know that the best social campaigns are not social campaigns. The best social campaigns, as measured by their ability to create positive word of mouth, are good TV commercials, good events, good PR campaigns and, even, good products.

To succeed in China has been to succeed in doing things outside of social, but with social in mind.

2. New interconnectivity between social and ecommerce

More ecommerce promotions and exclusive products are built specifically with campaigns in mind. Brands such as Ray-Ban and Bulgari have created products specifically for launch via Chinese apps: Nice, a photo-sharing platform like Instagram, and Meipai, a social/video platform akin to Vine.

3. Co-development, with consumers, of products using online communities

Chinese marketers have been skilled in listening to the online conversation. In some cases, entire communities are engaged online to develop new iterations of products. Consider Xiaomi. The smartphone maker, claimed by some to be one of the fastest growing tech companies ever, owes its success partly to its online communities that provide feedback and suggestions to the operating system, which is updated weekly.

4. Is radio coming back to life?

China consumes more podcasts per person than any other country. Twelve per cent of Chinese smartphone users claim to consume podcasts, compared with 5 per cent in the US and 4 per cent in the UK. Its music consumption is also growing faster. Marketers in China have been quick to respond to this, leading to a revival in the audio ad – a sleepy backwater for many years in Western advertising.

5. Bringing internet culture to the mass market

China's internet culture spills into mainstream culture faster than in Western countries, and Chinese advertisers have been quick to exploit this. FatCat pet toys, a series of colourful, inexpensive (less than $2 apiece), plush toys for cats and dog, are available on Alibaba's AliExpress ecommerce site only to those who opt in to chat about the products. In other words, social media is the key that unlocks the privilege to buy the product. The mere act of engaging with others via a social platform is viewed as an inducement to buy a product.

Mobile Africa

If China provides the first-era model of digital velocity, I think Equatorial Africa will provide the second. There's a mobile revolution at work – and one built around mobile money. The laying of cables along the coasts of East and West Africa has been accompanied by the arrival of affordable smartphones. In Kenya, they account for 50 per cent of mobile phone sales. But the innovation here has been mobile payments. Equatorial Africa has the majority of the world's mobile money accounts, linking the unbanked to a world of choice and security often lacking in cash-based operations.

How did it come about?

A consortium of researchers unearthed that consumers in Uganda, Botswana and Ghana were trading mobile phone airtime as a proxy for currency. This caught the attention of a Kenyan mobile network operator, which supported the launch of M-Pesa – a mobile system for sending money – in 2007. Since then, it has grown in size, scope, and reach. M-Pesa can now be found in many African countries, India and Eastern Europe, and it accounts for fully 25 per cent of Kenya's GDP. M-Pesa has inspired another business called M-Kopa, which lets people in rural areas pay a small monthly fee wirelessly to have solar lighting and mobile-phone charging in their homes. Other, alternative payment forms are facilitating commerce in previously unbanked communities, ranging from Bitcoin in Afghanistan, to bKash in Bangladesh and Pay TM in India.

The mobile money culture has led to some exciting developments. Nigeria had a slower start with ecommerce. There are real barriers to wider adoption of online shopping: cost of delivery, concern about getting the right product and worry about the security of online payments. But enter Jumia, which builds in fle xible, mobile-first payment structures and a pay-on-delivery model. It's now Nigeria's most trusted ecommerce brand.

Finally chamas are credit unions popular in African economies. They offer consumers the means to create "virtual stores" for bulk purchase and distribution to individual consumers. Text messages or bulletins sent through messaging apps provide the access while mobile vouchers and mobile payments help smooth the transactions.

The End of Globalization?

For marketers and communicators, "right shaping" to this new world is an existential challenge.

Of course, it all depends on whether you are primarily a local brand or an international brand.

Local brands are no longer pallid, "me-too" feel-a-likes. They represent much more than half of our business, and they utilize all the tools and techniques of their global competitors. But they have one massive asset: their superior closeness to their customers. And in large part, this is enabled by their ability to think digital-first, whereas a global brand tends to think platform-first (because it is looking for efficiencies of scale) and digital second.

Whenever I go to Manila, an irresistible craving comes over me. I yearn for a Jollibee's Peach and Mango Pie. Yes, I can recommend it as one of the most delectable desserts you could ever have, and I have over-indulged in it all over the archipelago. Jollibee leads Filipino fast food, above both McDonald's and KFC. It fills the "need space" usually occupied by McDonald's, which has been a formidable and aggressive attacker. When they created a campaign, "What's in Joy's chicken?", in which women named Joy confirmed that Chicken McDo was their chicken friend of choice; Jollibee hit back with a strong dose of Filipino pride, #ChickenJoyNation. Jollibee remains undeterred.

Above *Chicken fights in the Philippines: when McDonald's relaunched its Chicken McDo, the local brand Jollibee with its Chickenjoy quickly asserted its position and responded.*

An example of localism is Wardah, a personal care brand in Indonesia designed on Halal principles for progressive Muslims. It prospers in Indonesia's fertile social landscape through a digital engagement using hashtags such as #CantikHariDati (meaning Pretty Heart) and featuring users' Twitter and Instagram posts on its website, providing feedback for customers to see other real users and learn from them.

Meanwhile, global brands no longer automatically enjoy the privilege of preference. Our research shows that in the V12 markets the proportion of consumers preferring local brands exclusively is twice as high as those preferring international. Of course, most do continue to buy both.

But, for the international brands, this presents a complex environment to navigate through. In fact, my client Alan Jope of Unilever says that, "it takes marketing into the world of the Rubik cube".

You have a local competitor that builds a millennial franchise in new channels in secondary cities using digital media. There's no off-the-cuff defence strategy that can be created in London or New York for that. So whereas the television age enabled one-size-fits-all global advertising with translation and minimal transculturation, the digital age has pushed the game the other way. To compete, you have to go digital (20 per cent of the global budget would be a modest number). And to go digital, you have to be, to some extent, local. That's not to say that there's no such thing as a "global digital campaign". There is. And it works by a process of hierarchy: a global strategy; a global creative platform; a global playbook of digital programs – but then there comes the point where every playbook fades and the highly localized, sensitive playground takes over. It's a very finely balanced art, because communications now meets politics. Can one be digitally impactful and still responsible to the strategies and creative definitions? Or is one impelled by local control of budgets and a sense of "not invented here" to indulge in a sense of localness which may not be responsible behaviour for the brand as a global whole? This will remain a perennial debate in the digital age.

"Rubik marketing" is compounded by the multinationals' lack of stretch. It's the biggest change I have lived with over the last 10 years – the phenomenon of market drop off – where whole markets simply go "dark". Many of the dark markets are, ironically, the markets of the future.

The reasons for focus are unanswerable, but the consequences are unavoidable – it's like licensing competitive advantage in the long term. Enter the new Asian brands to fill the vacuum.

And the case of Japan is a different type of example. In the 1970s, 1980s and 1990s, its value dramatically skewed the P&L of any multinational. Now, it is as if it has bowed, and politely left the world to which international companies market.

The Rubik syndrome isn't just something that affects Western brands. Back in October 2004, I organized a conference for Chinese companies that were contemplating a move into the rest of the world. It coincided with the Chinese government's statement of an objective to build Chinese brands. We held that conference at Touffou, and Herta Ogilvy recalls that the biggest fear of these early Chinese globalists was not the complexity of global markets but the presence of thirteenth-century ghosts in their bedrooms. More than 10 years on, Chinese brands represent the soft side of the hard power of the world's second largest economy.

That is not to say that they find it easy. In fact it is very tricky for them. The traditionally hierarchical structure of a Chinese company finds the fluid management of a global matrix unfamiliar. And, there is a "manufacturing superiority complex" baked into the culture of many enterprises, not to mention a (now changing) reluctance to configure products according to the tastes of foreign consumers as opposed to domestic ones. It works here in a market of 1.3 billion, so why change it?

Right *Dabur is an Indian beauty brand with a rich local pedigree. It has a nuanced understanding of a strong cultural stream in Indian thought – Ayurveda – a system evolved over millennia relating to the continent's unique therapies and herbal compounds. This isn't just heritage positioning, it is a modern brand connecting well culturally through vivid, creative, rich stories about ingredients, responsive communications, and a utility portal to showcase beauty videos. Dabur uses these deep, local roots to protect against international competition.*

Above Huawei's campus in Shenzhen, Guangdong, houses over 30,000 of its employees. The company will be one of the defining multinationals of the future.

Of all the Chinese companies, the one that has committed the most seriously and successfully to branding in the digital age has been Huawei.

A client meeting at Huawei's headquarters in Shenzhen is unlike any other. It's not the sheer scale of the multi-building campus (housing nearly 60,000 people, most of whom look like students); nor the Babylonian feel of the building where visitors come to be wowed by the Huawei experience; nor the frisson of realizing that all this has come about in just 25 years or so. Rather it is the sheer gutsy energy of the meetings, the sense that everything is impelled by a missionary, yet at the same time, very pragmatic, zeal.

What is driving this? One of the most interesting business cultures to have emerged in the digital era, and the creation of Ren Zhengfei – who deserves a place in the global digital pantheon, which is as yet unfairly denied him in the West. He has a very clear sense of objective: amidst the deluge of data: "Google will provide the water, and we will provide the pipelines". He is driven as much by a sense of history and philosophy as by the future. (He has, for instance, encouraged Huawei's top 20 managers to study the rise and fall of the great nations from the sixteenth century, admires the British Glorious Revolution of 1688 and quotes the Duke of Wellington).

Perhaps this is what gives him a uniquely Eastern-Western perspective of the "Age of And".

Huawei culture officially lauds "greyness". The Chinese concept is *"hui"* (灰) – which represents those shades of grey which lie between black and white. It implies the ability to be flexible, to compromise, to "control the pace", without losing the sense of direction. This does not imply softness:

the wolf is the animal metaphor much used in Huawei, but also a distinctly Chinese "animal", the legendary "Bei" (狈). This wolf had long front legs and short hind legs; the Bei has short front legs and long hind legs. "The most effective organization is one that has Wolves and Bei cooperating closely", Mr Ren says. And however vulpine and Bei-like the culture, all are encouraged to be restlessly self-critical, a Chinese sense of "divine discontent": "people in ancient times even put aside a room for self reflection. Can't we learn to reflect on our failure?" Such reflections have driven remarkable success. Huawei will be the first Chinese global brand – a global brand that happens to come from China.

Huawei, Haier, Lenovo all continue their global advance. They will be joined by other "new globals", from India, Mexico and Indonesia in the first wave. And they will be part of a digital economy and a "two-way" world that was just inconceivable in 1982.

Below *Mark my words, Huawei will be the first truly global brand originating from China. Just look at* Shark Dancer, *an early experiment in content for them that beautifully emphasizes the power of touch to allow us to communicate. This is a brand on the attack.*

17 CULTURE, COURAGE, CLIENTS AND CASTANETS

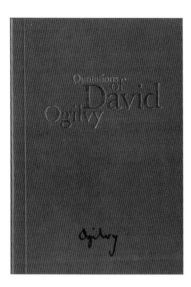

It's a sultry spring evening in Seville in the late 1980s. Fatigue and release, the end of another training programme. We're in the bar. And suddenly there is, from amidst our number, the strident sound of heels on the floor. It breaks the ennui as surely as a storm. The group opens out, and there's Jost van Nispen, no graceful Andalucian but one of the best direct marketers of his generation. A Dutchman, he moved to Spain and became besotted with it. And taught himself to dance. Nostrils flared, he looks very creditable. And then there's the sound of castanets.

Applause. And somehow that memory – the clack-clack-clack of the castanets – sticks, one of hundreds of such moments in a career, trivial, transitory, fundamentally uninteresting except to those who were there – but accumulating like sediment to create a culture.

It helps if that culture rewards such memories, and treats them as significant. David Ogilvy created a culture like that – one of the strongest in the business. It shares a system of meaning, from his many aphorisms to his blind faith in the colour red.

I'm often asked to define that culture.

My answer is that it is a humanistic culture, not a mechanistic one. It stemmed from David's interest in and liking for people (except very boring people, the "dull dogs" he advised agencies not to succor). In this he fell into the same camp as peers such as Bill Bernbach and Leo Burnett, but in a very different camp to Rosser Reeves, his one-time brother-in-law, who seems to me to have been fundamentally mechanistic in his approach to both life and business. When Ted Bates – his agency – was eventually sold (to WPP in 2003, and thus partly merged with Ogilvy & Mather), I remember some of the survivors there describing how completely void of culture it was. It was like they were walking out of a gulag and into a cathedral. Of all the founder cultures, David's has remained the most intense and vital. (Of course, I'm prejudiced.)

My predecessors and I have actively marketed it. It's powerful, because it combines a view about what good advertising is with some very basic rules of proper good behaviour and civilized etiquette.

There is no either/or here. This is a big case of both/and. The happier the agency, the better the work. Someone unkindly once said that joining Ogilvy & Mather was more like joining a cult than an agency. But, it tends to work. As other strong agency brands have found, taking the medicine which we prescribe to clients makes people want to join more and leave less.

There is no shortage of theories as to what makes an organization – collectively – courageous. Let me add mine: and it is quite possible that it is distorted by my experience in a creative services agency.

I think it is directly related to the degree to which leadership can inculcate a day-to-day sense of being dissatisfied with where you are. The courage emanates not out of grand injunctions to be brave, but out of a sense of insecurity about where you are: that it's not good enough, that others are doing better, that something's missing, that you need another leap forward, that if you don't do something big, you'll … and so on. Courage is born of discontent.

The philosopher José Ortega y Gasset captured this sense of restlessness, a knowledge of what could be, coupled with a sense that we often fall short:

> The essence of man is, discontent, divine discontent; a sort of love without a beloved, the ache we feel in a member we no longer have.[1]

He wrote that in Argentina in the 1940s; and David used the same phrase, consciously or unconsciously, when he wrote: "We have a habit of divine discontent with our performance. It is an antidote to smugness."

It's what leads you to tear up work and start again; to present something that hasn't been asked for; to break the conventions of a category; to ignore a research result if it doesn't feel right.

I was once asked to assemble my ideal advertising agency from famous figures. I chose them because of their Divine Discontent. Enter BFME, the newest kid on the block (see overleaf).

David described the skills required to run an agency in *Ogilvy on Advertising* as those of:

> … enthusiasts. They are intellectually honest. They have the guts to face tough decisions. They are resilient in adversity. Most of them are natural charmers. They are not bullies. They encourage communications upwards, and are good listeners.

They remain.

But the digital age imposes some very specific requirements for someone who aspires to run an agency. Now, we would have to add three more qualities:

1. You have to be a simplifier: because everything is so much more complex, it's not enough for managers just to preside as often they do – the law of complexity says that it, not they, will start driving outcomes. The ability to identify the simple core needs of a project or a mission does usually demand intellectual acuity. It's ironic,

BFME

The agency start up which never made the front cover of *Ad Age* or *Campaign*...

BFME

The most brilliant agency ever? Designed for Divine Discontent, recruited from history. Here's whom I chose to run it:

SARAH BERNHARDT (1844–1923)

The "divine Sarah" of Oscar Wilde, discontent ran through every vein of this actress's body. She slept in coffins to better project herself into the mood of death. When she was dying, she chose to live on a 5th floor. One of her visitors asked why, and she said, "so that when a man enters my bedroom he'll still be panting." That's the passion that attracts clients. She's the **Client Service Director**.

CHRISTOPHER MARLOWE (1564–1593)

The dramatist, the best wordsmith money could buy, and great to go drinking with. Discontent killed him, unfortunately – he died in a tavern brawl. His heroes are somehow hipper than Shakespeare's, his more famous contemporary. His words terrify, as for instance, from the mouth of the dying Tamburlaine: "Come, let us march against the powers of heaven/And set black streamers in the firmament/To signify the slaughter of the gods." More "black streamers", please. He's the **Creative Director**.

SIGMUND FREUD (1856–1939)

The Viennese provocateur, mercilessly probing the unconscious for insights. He's the **Account Planner**. In *Civilization and Its Discontents* (1930) he sees love as the way of galvanizing creative endeavour, which helps us re-find our lost selves. "The way of life which makes love the centre of everything, which looks for all satisfaction in loving and being loved." I have never seen great creativity come up out of hate. Hating consumers, hating clients: it's surprisingly common.

CHARLES EAMES (1907–1978) // RAY EAMES (1912–1988)

The husband-and-wife team gave design a cultural and social importance that energized post-war America and shaped the twentieth century. What a team from hell to manage, but what divine discontent. From a converted garage in Venice, LA, Charles's mechanical mind and Ray's avant-garde leanings transformed the abstract into beautiful yet practical design. As Charles said: "The details are not the details. They make the design." An early boss of mine used to repeat: "Remember, God is in the details." At the time, I never knew why. Charles and Ray are the **UX team.**

but dunces aren't great simplifiers. After that it requires a ruthless ability to weed out all that is not necessary – in thinking through it, in processing it and in delivering it. "Is it really necessary?" is the question the parrot on your shoulder has to ask each waking minute. Distilling that aim in the compelling language of lucid simplicity distinguishes the great simplifiers from the merely good ones.

2. You have to be a collaborator, because nothing anymore is really apart: no man, but now no business, is an island. Some managers pretend theirs is, jealously guarding work they believe to be their proprietary skillsets. That "proprietariness" is a delusion. In the inter-connected world, even if it did exist, it would be largely useless. I always identify two types: the crocodiles, who are snarkily concerned with how big is their slice of pie; and the lions, who grow the pie. If you have IP it will be enhanced and empowered by collaboration, not diminished. And if you are ambitious, you can harness the skills and assets of others. Profiting from but actually enjoying ambiguity is what makes you great. Certainty is the barbiturate of small minds.

3. You have to be curious, because, if you aren't, you just won't attract the people you need to work for you. The best of them now are driven by curiosity. They are not excited by status or by money or by conventional badges of success, but they are insatiably curious – and their curiosity will drive the restlessness, the ferment, and the inventiveness which are in themselves intrinsically rewarding. Can an organization learn? If there is a tipping point at which curiosity at least corrects the natural tendency of organizations to conform, then it can. And, when it does, it will gather to itself a kind of differentiating charisma that kills the addiction to the comfortable, which will always drag it down.

Partners and Servants

Of course, all the above, however true I believe it to be, does not mean very much unless it is put in the context of why we are here at all. "Wouldn't this be a wonderful business without clients?" is the age-old question of the agency folk, in all agencies, at all levels.

Maybe it would.

But it's probably more helpful to our survival to consider how we turn our clients into supporters rather than wishing them away.

It's easy to oscillate between contradictory views about what constitutes the ideal relationship of an agency with a client.

Clients get the advertising they deserve. I know some who are a malediction, and others who are an inspiration. Don't keep a dog and bark yourself. Any fool can write a bad advertisement, but it takes a genius to keep his hands off a good one.[2]

Since that era, the industry associations in both the UK and the US have worked hard to project the image of advertising as a profession, worthy of taking its place alongside accountancy or architecture. To some extent, they have succeeded, though such efforts have always run the risk of pushing too hard in the direction of its strategic role at the expense of its creative role, something to which the Digital Revolution has actually been a corrective.

Such efforts encourage our view that we are partners to clients. Our plea to them so often is for partnership. And it is certainly true that the best work invariably comes from relationships which are deep, long term and which have at their core the premise of partnership – a shared sense of responsibility for the results.

One danger of the partnership syndrome is that it creates blindness in agency people as to the real amount of time a client actually has to spend talking with us. We fail to see the pressures they face; the other priorities which pull them; the inconvenience which time wasted through a poor response can cause.

Thinking too much about partnership can lull us into a sense of security. We are a service business – and our partnerships are only as good as our last piece of work was liked (or, less importantly, worked). David intuitively recognized this. And is quite explicit about it.

He was quick to point out where processes were slowed down and produced bad advertising in the process. As he remarked in his book:

> One of the biggest corporations in the world allows five levels to chew up its advertising. Each level has the power to veto, but only the Chief Executive Officer has the power of final approval. Don't strain your agency's output through more than two levels.

I think the reason for this lies in the fact that while, for accountants, sets of accounts are, in the main, objectively assessed things, we have to sell, after all the strategic work is done, a product on which opinions will always contain some subjectivity. Cajoling, encouraging and assisting a client through the process of committing eventually to something subjective requires service skills with a higher-than-usual emotional component. Successful advertising people are hard-wired for that after years of experience. That is why it is challenging for clients successfully to cross over to the other side: there are few examples, and I would be hard put to name any who have been highly successful.

Quite simply, it's difficult to turn from master to servant. So however much we may get close to realizing the aspiration of partnership, it behoves us to remember that we are partners *and* servants, as I have tried to remind generations of trainees. At root, we are all waiters and waitresses really – however much we may not like to admit it.

There's one thing, though, which transforms the client-agency relationship, and that is actually liking your client. This sounds very trite, but, like many obvious things, it still deserves to be stated. The clients I have gone on to become friends with, we tend to do the best work for. They trust us and like us in return. Conversely, clients are quick to sense when we don't really like them. I've told my trainees that they have to think of a new client as being like a semi-trained and insecure dog: they sense hostility and they detect fear unconsciously.

Respect for clients has, perhaps, diminished over time. My first client meetings were formal set pieces. When a client such as Cow & Gate came up from Wiltshire to see my agency in Lintas, London in the late 1970s, it was a big day out; rehearsed presentations followed by a sumptuous lunch in a private dining room until it was time for them to catch the early evening train home. The first time I organized a lunch like this, I was surprised to be asked what ice sculpture I wanted for the table centrepiece. I chose a dolphin playing with a ball.

In the digital age, it is so normal for ideas and programmes to be presented virtually, by video conference, or even, in China, on WeChat in text-based dialogues. But I believe that this does not displace the need to have personal contact – face-to-face, work into leisure – with clients. In fact, it makes it more imperative. And explains why many digital micro-shops fail to grow. They don't have the service gene.

More than ever, we need to re-personalize the de-personalized.

So, it's time to hear the castanets again. A shared culture of fun between client and agency is the strongest bond possible – assuming that the work is good. And agencies which appear to be having fun are – in my experience – invariably more attractive than those which do not.

Now, sometimes I see the words "have fun" on a list of objectives presented by an office head. I know there is no fun to be had there. At least, I suppose, it is recognized as a need. But fun does not come organized from on high; it bubbles up from below. Like the flamenco, there is something spontaneous, zestful and uncontrollable about it.

¡Olé! Así se baila! (That's how you dance!).

18 EPILOGUE

David Ogilvy succumbed to the blandishments of the publisher of *Ogilvy on Advertising* and wrote 13 predictions. In a similar spirit, here are mine.

1. TV will continue to be the lynchpin medium, albeit transformed.
2. The Indian ad market will be the most attractive in the world.
3. The mobile handset will become as important to the whole of humanity as the bedtime pillow.
4. "Content" will cease to be a dirty word and will increasingly distinguish brands that offer a service to customers from those which don't.
5. WeChat will surpass Facebook.
6. Virtual reality will find a niche, but will not take over the world.
7. Top-notch writing skills will carry a huge premium as they decrease in supply.
8. "Pure play" agencies will wither, or become main plays.
9. Candidates for political office will continue to use dishonest advertising.
10. New Asian multinationals will create the world's most dynamic brands.
11. The debate as to whether our business is an art or a science will carry on forever, without resolution.
12. A breakaway from Cannes will form, which is more purely creative.
13. The word "digital" will ultimately disappear.

ENDNOTES

CHAPTER 3: THE SHORT MARCH

1 Orrin Edgar Klapp, *Opening and Closing*, Cambridge University Press, 1978.

2 John Lorinc, "Driven to Distraction", *The Walrus*, 12 April 2007.

3 Quoted in The Slant, Grapeshot Q&A, grapeshot.com, 28 May, 2015.

CHAPTER 4: THE DIGITAL ECOSYSTEM

1 Steve Miles, speech

2 Pete Blackshaw, quoted in *The Internationalist*, February 20, 2015.

3 Holt, Douglas, *How Brands Become Icons*, Harvard Business School Press, 2004.

4 Professor Mark Ritson in *Marketing Week*, 10 May 2012.

CHAPTER 6: THE POST-MODERN BRAND

1 Holt, Douglas, ibid

2 Arthur W. Page Society, "The Authentic Experience", An Arthur W. Page Society Report.

CHAPTER 7: CONTENT IS KING; BUT WHAT DOES IT MEAN?

1 Charlene Jennett, Anna Cox, et al, "Measuring and Defining the Experience of Immersion in Games", *International Journal of Human-Computer Studies*, 66 (9): 641-666, September 2008.

2 Jamie Madigan, "The Psychology of Immersion in Video Games", psychologyofgames.com, 27 July 2010.

3 Robin Sloan, "Stock and Flow", Snarkmarket, 18 January 2010.

CHAPTER 8: CREATIVITY IN THE DIGITAL AGE

1 Tim Broadbent, *The Ogilvy & Mather Guide to Effectiveness*, 2012.

2 Les Binet and Peter Field, "Marketing in an Era of Effectiveness", World

Advertising Research, 2007.

3 To read David's great speech, plus a lot more of David's memorable writing, dip into a copy of *The Unpublished David Ogilvy*, 1986.

4 Tham Khai Meng in an all-company memo, 2009.

CHAPTER 9: DATA: THE CURRENCY OF THE DIGITAL AGE

1 Binet and Field, ibid.

CHAPTER 10: "ONLY CONNECT"

1 John Battelle, "The Database of Intentions", John Battelle's Search Blog, 2003.

CHAPTER 11: CREATIVE TECHNOLOGY: THE SWEET SPOT

1 Peter Merholz and Don Norman, "Peter Merholz in Conversation with Don Norman about UX and Innovation", Adaptive Path, December 2007.

CHAPTER 12: THE THREE BATTLEGROUNDS

1 Jeff Bezos's opening remarks in a letter on Amazon's homepage to introduce the Kindle.

CHAPTER 14: FIVE GIANTS OF ADVERTISING IN THE DIGITAL AGE

1 *Otaku* is a peculiar Japanese term for those with obsessive interests.

2 *Advertising Age*, February 2014.

CHAPTER 15: MY BRAIN HURTS

1 David Ogilvy, *Ogilvy on Advertising*, 1985, p.217.

2 Antonio R. Damasio, D. Tranel and Hanna Damascio, "Face Agnosia and the Neural Substrates of Memory", *Annual Review of Neuroscience*, 13(1), 89-109.

3 Chris Graves, "Brain, Behavior, Story", Ogilvy Public Relations, 2014

4 Sutherland, Rory, (2014, December) This Thing For Which We Have No Name, [Edge Interview], retrieved from www.edge.org/conversation/rory_sutherland-this-thing-for-which-we-have-no-name

5 Richard H. Thaler, *Misbehaving: The Making of Behavioral Economics*, W.W. Norton & Company, 2015.

6 Dolan, P., Hallsworth, M., Halpern, D., King, D., Metcalfe, R., Vlaev, I. (2009) MINDSPACE: Influencing Behaviour Through Public Policy. London: Cabinet Office & Institute for Government.

7 Lisa Shu, Francesca Gino, Max Bazerman, et al, "When to Sign on the Dotted Line? Signing First Makes Ethics Salient and Decreases Dishonest Self-Reports", Working Paper 11-117, Harvard Business School, 2011.

CHAPTER 16: THE NEW SHAPE OF THE WORLD

1 CCTV's main evening news broadcast, Xinwen Lianbo, has a daily viewership of roughly 135 million, and is also one of the most expensive shows for ad buys, with its 2013 advertising slots selling for a record 5.4 million yen.

2 Data from the World Bank, February 2017, retrieved from
http://databank.worldbank.org/data/download/GDP.pdf
and
Robbie Gramer, "Here's How the Global GDP is Divvied Up", *Foreign Policy*, February 24, 2017

3 According to CNNIC (The China Internet Network Information Center).

CHAPTER 17: CULTURE, COURAGE, CLIENTS AND CASTANETS

1 José Ortega y Gasset (1916), from his course lecture, "Historical Reason", Buenos Aires, 1940.

2 David Ogilvy, *Ogilvy on Advertising*, 1985, p.67.

3 Bond, R.M., Fariss, C.J., Jones, J.J., Kramer, A.D., Marlow, C., Settle, J.E., and Fowler, J.H. (2012). A 61-Million-Person Experiment in Social Influence and Political Mobilization, Nature, 489 (7415), 295-298.

Additional reference material:

Jeffrey Bowman, *Reframe the Marketplace*, Wiley, 2015.

Richard Dawkins, *The Selfish Gene*, Oxford University Press, 2016 (40th Anniversary Edition).

Paul Feldwick, *The Anatomy of Humbug*, Troubador Publishing, 2015

Paul Ford, "What is Code?", *Businessweek*, 11 July 2015. (Bloomberg.com/graphics/2015-paul-ford-what-is-code/).

"Timeline of Computer History", The Computer History Museum

Shelina Janmohamed, *Generation M*, I.B. Tauris, 2016.

Arthur Koestler, *The Act of Creation*, Last Century Media, 2014.

Rick Levine, et al, *The Cluetrain Manifesto*, Basic Books, 2000.

Dimitri Maex, *Sexy Little Numbers*, Crown Business, 2012.

Nicholas Negroponte, *Being Digital*, Vintage, 1996.

David Ogilvy, *Confessions of an Advertising Man*, Southbank Publishing, 2012

David Ogilvy, *Ogilvy on Advertising*, Prion Books, 1983.

David Ogilvy, *The Unpublished David Ogilvy*, Profile Books, 2014.

Piyush Pandey, *Pandeymonium*, Penguin Books, India, 2015.

Rosser Reeves, *Reality in Advertising*, Widener Classics, 2015.

Kunal Sinha and David Mayo, *Raw: Pervasive Creativity in Asia*, Clearview, 2014.

INDEX

(page numbers in italic type refer to illustrations and captions; the initials DO refer to David Ogilvy)

A

Aaker, David 54
A.C. Nelson 71
The Act of Creation (Koestler) 112
ad-blocking software 29
Addicks, Mark 114
Adidas 185, *187*
Ad.ly 29
advertising giants in digital age
 210–35
  Greenberg 210–16, *210*
  Kagami 216–20, *216*, *218*
  Nisenholtz 220–3, *220*
  Palm-Jensen 224–8, *224*
  Porter 228–35, *228*, *233*
Aegis. 227
Africa, and mobile phones 260
AGA Cooker *107*
Age of And 40, 150, 236, 264
Ainslie, George 246, *246*
Airbnb *16*, 17
Aldrich, Michael 27
Ali, Ben *193*
Alibaba 257, *258*, 260
Allianz 112
ALS Ice Bucket Challenge 168–9,
 168, *169*
AltaVista, search engine of 28
Always *67*
Amazon *161*, *183*
 and disintermediation 21
 and ecommerce growth 29
 making most of 184
 as one of digital "big three" 31
 and price comparison 182, *183*
 rising sales of 28
Amazon Echo 87
American Express *62*, 90, *91*, 222
Amin, Salman 188–9

amyotrophic lateral sclerosis (ALS)
 168–9
Anacin *102*
The Anatomy of Humbug (Feldwick)
 102, *102*
Andreessen, Marc 15, *15*, 211
Apple 174–6
 Macintosh launched by 27
Apple Safari, and ad-blocking software 29
Arab Spring 193, *193*
Arcade Fire 88, *89*
Under Armour 66, *67*
Armour bra *67*
ARPANET *12*, 26, 27 (*see also*
 internet)
  creation of and first message via 12
Arthur W. Page Society 57
AT&T 28, 48, *49*, 173, 222
Audi 165, *165*

B

Baidu 257
Baldwin, Jerry *25*
Bangladesh:
  disproportionate growth in 251
  middle-class consumers in *252–3*
  and velocity 254
Banksy 108, *108*
Baran, Paul 14, *14*
Barneys *90*
Barnum, P.T. 82
Bass, Saul 211
BAT 257, *258*
Bates, Ted 13, 266
Battelle, John 137
Battersea Dogs and Cats Home *206*
battlegrounds 164–91, *171*
  and continuous commerce 180–

 91, *181*, *187*
  mobile phones 174–80, *175*, *177*,
   178, *180*
  mobility 174–80
  social media 164–73, *164*, *165*,
   166, *167*, *170*, *171*, *172*
"The Beauty Inside" *116*, 117
Beckham, David 169
Being Digital (Negroponte) 34
Benjamin, Jeff 234
Beowulf 80, 115, *115*, 116, 117
Berger, Barndon 232
Berger, Jonah 78–9
Bernbach, Bill 13, 102, 213, 266
Berners-Lee, Tim 15, *15*, 27
Bernhardt, Sarah 268
Bezos, Jeff 180
BFME 267, 268
Bhalla, Surjit 251
Bieber, Justin 162, 169
Big IdeaLs 44, 60–1, *60*
Bildt, Carl 224–5
Blackshaw, Pete 35
Bland, Christopher 34
BMW 28, 72, *73*, 143, 213, 231
Bo, Armando *146*
Bogusky, Alex 230–4, *233*
Bogusky, Bill 230
Bottle Rocket *159*, 174, 176
Bowker, Gordon *25*
Bowman, Jeff 71
brain and behaviour 236–47, *238*,
 239, *241*, *243*, *244–6*, *247*
  and nudging, *see main entry*
"Brand X believes . . ." 60
branded content 72–5
brands (*see also individual* brands):
  and Big IdeaLs 44, 60–1, *60*
  and China 263–5, *264*

and content, *see main entry*

crisis of 54

death of, as we know them 34

errors of, concerning mobile users 181

four locations of 114

inclusive 66

and most-viewed videos 38

and one message at a time 20

origins of 54, *54*

performance 149

post-modern 54–71

as promise 113

and Starbucks, *see main entry*

360-degree stewardship of 137

and transparency 57

and videos 38

waves of *55*

well-behaved 64

BrandZ 45, 62

Branson, Richard 211

Brazil:

    disproportionate growth in 251

    middle-class consumers in 251, *252–3*

    and social networking 186

BRIC 251

Brien, Nick 228

Brinker, Scott *155*

Broadbent, Tim 106, *106*, 126

Built to Last (Collins) 40

Burger King *68, 69, 175*, 234

Burnett, Leo 210, 213, 266

Bush, George W. 28

C

Cabral, Juan 97

Cadbury 96–7, *96, 97*

Caesar's Palace *124*

Cailliau, Robert 15, *15*

Cameron, David 168, 241

Campaign for Real Beauty 44–5

Campbell, Joseph 116

Cannes 68, 98–101, *100, 101*, 106

    in author's predictions 272

Cannes Lions *228*, 230

Carter, Calvin 174–6, 178

Centennials 46, 47, 48, 51

Cerf, Vinton "Vint" 15, *15*

CERN 117

ChannelNet 27

The Chaos Scenario (Garfield) 34

Chapman, Phil 97

Chen, Joan *146*

Chick-fil-a *180*

Chicken McDo 261, *262*

China:

    and ad typo 217

    and brands 263–5, *264*

    companies' conference in 263

    disproportionate growth in 251

    first international email from 255

    and Huawei 264–5, *264, 265*

    and internet 255–60, *256, 258*

    internet *256*

    internet users in 20, *20*

    middle-class consumers in *252–3*

    and QI codes 257

    and rich symbolism 249

    and social as a mindset 258–9

    and velocity 254

    and Visit Britain 259, *259*

    and WPP revenue 248–9

Chipotl *61*, 85, *85*

Choose Beautiful 45

Chouinard, Yvon 188, *189*

Clark, Jim 211

Clark, Wendy 146

Clinton, Bill 224

Clinton, Hillary 196, *196*

cloud technology 120–1, *121, 124*

The Cluetrain Manifesto 61

COBOL 26

Coca-Cola *52, 59, 59*, 61, 62, 79, *80*, 103, *103*, 110, *110*

code 150–2, *151*

Coke Zero 92–3, *93*

Collins, Brian 113–14

Collins, Jim 40

Compact 27

Compuserve 27

Condé Nast 27

Confessions of an Advertising Man (Ogilvy) 8

Contagious (Berger) 78

content 72–92

    in author's predictions 272

    branded 72–5

    and Digital Revolution 72–3

    eight tips for 95

    immersive 82–5

    ". . . is King" 72

    magnetic 77–82

    matrix of 77–92, *77*

    as misused word 72

    organizing for 93–5

    practical 88–92

    smart 85–8

    thinking about 75–6

Content Studios 93–5, *94, 95*

continuous commerce:

    as battleground 180–91, *181, 187*

    and digitally enabled sales, growth in 182

    and emotion 186–7

    and experience 190

    omni-channel 185–6, *187*

    and relationship 186–9

Cook, Tim 216

Corporate Social Responsibility (CSR) 62

Cow & Gate 271

creative technology 150–64

    and back end 154–7

    and code 150–2, *151*

    and front end 153–4

    and marketing automation 156, *156*

    and virtual, automated and mixed reality 157–61, *158, 159, 160, 161*

creativity:

    and art-vs-science debate 101–2

    and Digital Revolution 98–119

    and ideas 110–14, *113*

    measuring 102

    pervasive 107–10

    and stories 115–16

    in technology, *see* creative technology

    word hated by DO 101

Crispin Porter 230, 232, *233*, 234

Crispin, Sam 230

Crockett, Molly 238
customer relationship management
   (CRM) 7, *31*, 147, 172–3

D

Dabur *263*
Damasio, Antonio 236, 237–8
Damasio, Hannah 236
"dark markets" 263
data:
   big, cautions concerning 122–3
   big, and emotion 186–7
   big, first reference to 120
   and cloud technology 120–1, *121*,
      124
   as currency of digital age 120–31
   and econometric modelling 127–8
   and insights 129–31
   and measurement vs effectiveness
      126–7, *127*
   and metrics, underdosing with
      128, *128*
   as "new oil" 122
   and optimal optimization 131
   pervasive nature of 122
   and platform impediments 125–6
   really useful, prerequisites of 125–
      31, *125*, *127*, *128*
   and single-enterprise point of view
      124, 125
   structured and unstructured 120
   value spectrum of *123*
DAVE 148–9, *148*, *149*
Davies, Donald 14, *14*
Davies, Russell 197, 199, *199*
Davis, Rob 41
Dawkins, Richard 79–80
de Luca, Peter 155, *156*
Dean, Howard 194
DEC 27
Dentsu 217, 218, 220
Descartes' Error (Damasio) 237, *238*
Descartes, René 237–8, *238*
Dhingra, Rishi 105
digital ecosystem *32–3*
   evolving nature of 31
   and traditional media 34

Digital Revolution:
   advertising giants in, *see* advertising
      giants in digital age
   and analogue vs digital *13*
   and aroma 109
   and brands, *see main entry*
   bright secrets from 244–5
   and changes in advertising 39–40
   connectivity as great gift of 48
   and content 72–3
   and creativity, *see main entry*
   data as currency of 120–31
   and ghettoization 35, 37
   and lessons for leaders 43
   primary motivation of 12
   and social contract *39*
   and storytelling 115
   timeline of 26–9
   transformations brought about by,
      see transformations in digital age
   and two-way communication 82
digital video 145–7
disintermediation 21
Domestos *205*
Domino's Pizza 234, *235*
DoubleClick 28, 29
Dove 35, 44–5, *44*, *58*, 59, *59*, 82,
   101
Dove Men +Care 105
Drax 226
Dunkin' Donuts 25

E

Eames, Charles 211, 268
Eames, Ray 268
Egypt:
   disproportionate growth in 251
   middle-class consumers in *252–3*
   revolution in *193*
Eisenhower, Dwight D. 12
Ellsberg, Daniel 245, *245*
eMarketer 29
Engel, Joel S. 27
Engelbart, Douglas 14, *14*
Enigma machine 26, *26*
The Epic Split 113, *114*
Equitable 222

ethnicity 70–1
Europcar 81, *81*
everyday.com 224
Evolution 44, *44*
EyeViewDigital.com *190*

F

Facebook 29, 82–3, *83*, *164*, *166*
   and ALS Ice Bucket Challenge 168
   in author's predictions 272
   and "The Beauty Inside" 117
   and Centennials 51
   change in nature of 31
   and CRM *31*
   and digital-media spend 31
   and disintermediation 21
   as ephemeral network 41
   growing use of 29
   and IFLScience 118
   launch of 28
   and Nestlé 209
   and nudging *247*
   and Old Spice 105
   as one of digital "big three" 31
   and politics *193*, 195, *195*
   revenue of 29
   and tourism *202*
   and Toyota 57
   and underserved communities 180
   and video 40–1, 42
Facebook Live 42
Facebook Messenger 166
Fairnington, Alan 132
Fallon, Jim 229
Fanta *86*
Farfar 226–8
FatCat 260
Feldwick, Paul 101–2, 107
feminism 66–8
Fetherstonhaugh, Brian *148*
Financial Times (*FT*) 223
Firefox, and ad-blocking software 29
5G 179
Ford *92*
Ford, Paul 150, *151*
Forgotify 73
Forster, E.M. 143, 149

Foster, Norman 213
French, Neil 119
Freud, Sigmund 268
Friendster *30*, 31
Frisch, Ragnar 127

G

Gage, Phineas 236, *237*
Gallop, Cindy 66
Galloway, Scott 34
Gambino, Melody 23
Garfield, Bob 34
Gates, Bill 72
GE 90
Gehry, Frank 213
Geico 147
General Foods 222
Generation C 46
Generation S 46, 51
Generation X 46, 47
generations:
    labelling 46–7, *46, 47*
    Millennials 46–53, *48, 50, 52–3*
Gensemer, Thomas 195
Gerber 138, *138*
Gilbert, Dan 53
Gillette 105
Goldman Sachs 251
Google 28
    AdWords of 28, 141
    as archival network 41–2
    and content consumption 178
    cost of, per person 17
    as database of intent 137
    and digital-media spend 31
    and disintermediation 21
    DoubleClick acquired by 29
    and Millennials' search behaviour
        138, *138*
    and non-internet channels 18, *18*
    as one of digital "big three" 31
    and page ranking 28
    PC Magazine's verdict on 28
    personalized search offered by 29
    revenue of 29
    and same-sex marriage 205, *206*
    and underserved communities 180

and video 40–1, 73
Google Chrome:
    and ad-blocking software 29
    and Arcade Fire video 88, *89*
Google Instant 29
Google Now 176, 179
Google Quality Score 145
GoTo.com 28
government, as transformation in
    digital age 197–9, *198, 199*
GOV.UK 199, *199*
Grace, Topher 117
Grapeshot 23
Graves, Chris 238
Green, Rick 230
Greenberg, Bob 210–16, *210*
Greenberg, Richard 211
Grindr, and disintermediation 21
Gropius, Walter 212
Guinness 10, 68

H

Haier 265
haptics 158, 160, *160*
Haring, Keith 221, *222*
Harrison, Steve 118–19
hashtags *166*
Heath, Robert 103, 106
Hegarty, John 18
The Hero with a Thousand Faces
    (Campbell) 116
Hershey 114
Hicks, Jeff 232
Higa, Ryan 146
Higgs boson 117
Holt, Douglas 55–6
Honey Maid *68*
Hopkins, Claude 101, 102, 210
HotWired, launch of 28
Howards End (Forster) 143
Huawei 264–5, *264, 265*
Huggies *91*, 186
Humby, Clive 122

I

IBM 10, *58*, 59, *59*, 112, 117, *117*,
    118

and CICS 26
and cloud technology *121*
and "PC" 27
and SCAMP 27
IBM Newsroom 89
IBM Watson 130, *130*
immersive content 82–5 (*see also*
    content)
Incredible India *200*, 201
India:
    and Ayurveda *263*
    disproportionate growth in 251
    general election in 192
    and Indianness 250, *250*
    less digital advertising stimulus in
        249
    middle-class consumers in *252–3*
    and non-internet channels 18
    and tourism 201
    and velocity 254
Indonesia:
    disproportionate growth in 251
    middle-class consumers in *252–3*
    and velocity 254
Instagram 73, 165, *165*, 260
    as ephemeral network 41
    in Philippines 262
integration:
    deep 135–6, 137
    evolution of *136*
Intel *116*, 117
internet (*see also* ARPANET; World
    Wide Web):
    advertising pays for 17
    advertising transformed by 13
    back-of-an-envelope beginnings
        of *12*
    birth of 12
    bubble, bursting of *28*
    and China 255–60, *256, 258*
    Chinese users of 20, *20*
    founders of 14–15, *14–15*
    looking for a commercial model 12
    march in progress of 26–9
    and media interests 17
    and memes 79–80
    and post-modern brands 64
    riven by conflict 13

and targeting 68
and "viral" 79
what to give up instead of 48–9,
    49
Internet Explorer, and ad-blocking
    software 29
Internet of Things 19, 161
intimacy in depth 147–8
Iran, disproportionate growth in 251
Islam 70–1
Isobar 227
Iwata, Jon 59

J

Jägermeister 157
Janmohamed, Shelina 71
Jim Beam 159
Jobs, Steve 174, 211
John Street 37
Johnnie Walker 56–7, 56
Jollibee 261
Jope, Alan 262
Journal of Advertising Research 34

K

Kagami, Akira 216–20, 216, 218
Kahn, Robert 14, 14
Kahneman, Daniel 238–9, 239, 245,
    245, 246, 246
Kaisi, Katsura 220
Kestin, Janet 44
KFC 261
Kimberly-Clark 242–3, 243
Kind Collective 228
Kindle 190
Kirkland, Mike 44
Klapp, Orrin 22, 22
Koestler, Arthur 112, 112
Kotler, Philip 54
Krazy Glue 113
Kuntz, Tom 105

L

Lange, Martin 174
Late Night with David Letterman 10
Lego 181

Lenovo 146, 265
Lever Brothers 44
LGBTQ 68–70, 68, 69, 70
Li Peng 255
Li, Robin 257, 257
libertarian paternalism 241
Licklider, Joseph Carl Robnett 14, 14
Lifeline 146
Lincoln, Abraham 59
LinkedIn, launch of 28
Lorinc, John 22–3
Luma Partners, chart developed by 21

M

Ma, Jack 257, 257
Ma, Pony 257, 257
McCann 230
McCarthy, John 15, 15
McDonald's 25, 261
MCI 28
Macintosh, launch of 27
McLuhan, Marshall 40
Madigan, Jamie 84
Maex, Dimitri 120, 122, 127
Magazine Luiza 190
Magids, Scott 186
magnetic content 77–82 (see also
    content)
Magnetic Resonance Imaging (MRI)
    236
marketing automation 156, 156
Marlowe, Christopher 268
Marsden, Paul 186
Marti, Bernard 15, 15
Mashable 90
Mather & Crowther 110, 111
mattering 63, 64
media (see also social media):
    "dead" claim concerning 132
    and Great Fragmentation 133
    new, fragmented nature of 30, 34
    old, and diminishing revenue 34
    old, DO's view of 132
    planning, and "connections
        planning" 134
    shifting landscapes of 132
    from traditional to digital 17

Meipai 260
memes 79–80
MetLife 125
Mexico:
    disproportionate growth in 251
    middle-class consumers in 252–3
Microsoft 72
    and ad-blocking software 29
middle-class consumers 251, 252–3
Miles, Steve 35, 44
Milk, Chris 88
Milko 226–7, 227
Millennials 46–53, 48, 50, 52–3
    and Coke 93
    and ethnicity 71
    search behaviour among 138
Miller, George A. 244, 244
MindShare 132, 133
MINDSPACE 241, 242
MINI 229
Minitel 27
M-Kopa 261
MMG 28
mobile phones:
    in Africa 260
    as battleground 174–80, 175, 177,
        178, 180
    and brands' errors 181
    enabling nature of 174
    first words on 27
    as new ad medium 174
    retail landscape 177
Mockapetris, Paul 15, 15
Modi, Narendra 192–3, 192
Motista 186–7
Motorola 27, 249, 249
Mozilla, and ad-blocking software 29
M-Pesa 261
Munn, Olivia 146
Museum of American History 168–9,
    168, 169
Museum of Feelings 78, 78
Mustafa, Isaiah Amir 105
Myanmar:
    disproportionate growth in 251
    middle-class consumers in 252–3
Myspace 30
    launch of 28

N

Nadal, Miles 232, 233
Nakamira, Hiroshi 220
Naked 136
NASA 117
NASDAQ, increase in 28
National Public Radio 176, *178*
Negroponte, Nicholas 34
Nescafé 208–9, *208–9*
Nest *19*
Nestlé 35, *175*, 208–9
Nestlé Milo *87*, 88
Netflix 120
neuroscience, *see* brain and behaviour
New York Times (*NYT*) 118, 221, 222
Newcombe, Zach 31
Nice 260
Nielson 178
Nigeria:
    disproportionate growth in 251
    middle-class consumers in *252–3*
Nike 54–5, 56, 212, 214–15, *214–15*
The 9-Inch Diet (Porter, Bogusky) 233
Nisenholtz, Martin 220–3, *220*
No Likes Yet 73
Nokia, first smartphone of 28
Norman, Don *153*
NSFNET 28
NTT DOCOMO 28
nudging 197, 240–7 (*see also* brain and behaviour)
NYPD 166, *166*

O

Obama, Barack 194, *194*, 195, 197, *199*, 241
Odagiri, Akira 216, 219
Ogilvy on Advertising (Ogilvy) 101, 132, 192, 202, 267, 272
    advertising giants chosen by, *see* advertising giants in digital age
    and brands 54–5
    cover of *10*
    favourite words in 40
    first chapter of ("Overture") 8, 11
    and foreign travel 200

    storming success of 8
    and US's top-nation status 248
    writing of 8
Ogilvy Change 238, 242, 244, 246
Ogilvy, David *7*, *99*, *100*, 272
    advertising giants chosen by, *see* advertising giants in digital age
    and art-vs-science debate 102
    book of quotations of *266*
    branding speech of 240
    centenary of 100, *100*
    "creativity" hated by 101
    culture created by 266
    death of 7
    and direct marketing 10
    and direct-response advertising 107, 122
    and disintegration 136
    film clip of 74
    first advertising work of 106, *107*
    on foreign travel 200
    4A speech of 23
    on good causes 202, *205*, 206
    Greenberg favourite 213
    "kingly" 228
    on Letterman show *10*
    on life-assurance firms 185
    on market research 247
    on media 132
    and Nisenholtz 223
    and partnership syndrome 270
    and political advertising 192
    on skills 268
Ogilvy, Francis 110–11
Ogilvy, Herta *7*, 263
    as Ogilvy & Mather's materfamilias 7
Ogilvy & Mather:
    and belief 62
    and Big IdeaLs 60–1, *60*
    and Cadre system 98
    and Cannes 98–101, *100*, *101*
    Content Studios of 93–5, *94*, *95*
    digital transformation of 7
    and Guinness 68
    Japan success of 217
    and political advertising 192
    Shanghai office of 248
    Social Lab acquired by 172

    social-media practice of 80
    and 360-degree stewardship 137
    and velocity 251
Ogilvy Noor 70–1
Ogilvy Pride 70, *70* (*see also* LGBTQ)
Old Spice 103, 104–5, *104*, *105*
Oliver, Richard 34
Oreo 36–7, *36*
Orkut *30*
Ortega y Gasset, José 267
Oscar Mayer 109, *109*
Owen, Clive *73*

P

page ranking 28
paid, owned, earned (POE) 74, 134, *134*, 167
Paivio, Allan 245, *245*
Pakistan:
    disproportionate growth in 251
    middle-class consumers in *252–3*
    Millennials in 46
    and non-internet channels 18
    and velocity 254
Palm-Jensen, Matias 224–8, *224*
Palmer, Tony *21*
Pandey, Piyush 192, 193, 201, 249–50
Pantene 66
Parker, Alan 112
Parker, George 220
Patagonia 188–9, *188*, *189*
Patches 45
Pepsi 25, 62
Periscope 42
    as ephemeral network 41
Perrier *86*
Petit Tube 73
PewDiePie *38*, 42
Philippines:
    and chicken fights *262*
    disproportionate growth in 251
    middle-class consumers in *252–3*
    and Wardah 262
Philips *31*, 64–5, *65*
Pickholz, Jerry 223
Pidilite 250

Piper, Tim 44, 45
Plouffe, David 195
Pokémon 162–3, *162*, *163*
politics:
    in author's predictions 272
    as transformation in digital age
        192–5, *192*, *193*, *194*, *195*, *196*
Polman, Paul 204, *205*
Porter, Chuck 228–35, *228*, *233*
"post-truth" 17
Postel, Jon 15, *15*
Practical Advertising 110–11, *111*
practical content 88–92 (*see also*
  content)
and predicted death of television 34
Procter & Gamble (P&G) 99, 105
programmatic advertising 143–5, *144*
Puri, Bharat 97

Q

QI codes 257
Qualcomm 89–90, *89*, *146*

R

Raphaelson, Joel:
    DO's letter to *9*
    and *Ogilvy on Advertising* 8
Raw 110
Ray-Ban 260
Red Bull 75
Red Label *68*, *69*
Reeves, Rosser 13, 102, 106, 266
Ren Zhengfei 264, *265*
Resor, Stanley 210
R/GA 212
Rhett and Link 147
Richards, Ben 134–5, *136*, 143
Ritson, Mark 36
Rizzolatti, Giacomo 246, *246*
Roberts, Kevin 102
Roberts, Lawrence 14, *14*
Robertson, Andrew 100
Roosevelt, Theodore 31
Rospars, Joe 195
Royal National Lifeboat Institution
  206, *207*

Rubicam, Raymond 210
Rumbol, Phil 96–7
Rust, Ronald 34

S

Saatchi, Charles 102
Sagmeister, Stefan 116
same-sex marriage 70, 205, *206* (*see
  also* LGBTQ)
Sammartino, Steve 133
Sanchez Lamelas, Javier 115
Saunders, Ernest 10
Schelling, Thomas 245, *245*
Schultz, Howard 24, 25, *25*
Schwab, Charles 211
Schwartz, Barry 240
Scientific Advertising (Hopkins) 101
search 137–8
    glossary of common terms for 139
    and keywords 137–8, *138*
    and Millennials' behaviour 138
Search Engine Marketing (SEM) 137,
  139
Search Engine Optimization (SEO)
  28, 137, 139
Searls, Doc 223
Selective 234
The Selfish Gene (Dawkins) 79
Senerchia, Jeanette 168–9
sexism 66
Sexy Little Numbers (Maex) 127
sharing economy 17
Sharp, Byron 102
Shazam *157*
Sherif, Muzafer 244, *244*
Shimizu, Ryo 220
Shiseido. 218
shopping online, first systems for 27
showrooming 182, *184*
Shy, Jean 44
Siegl, Zev 25
Simon, Herbert A. 240
Sina Weibo 257
Sinclair, Upton 227
Six Degrees *30*
Sketches 45
skipping ads 28, 29

Sloan, Robin 94
smart content 85–8 (*see also* content)
smartphones, first 28
Smith, Adam 34
Smosh *38*
SMS, arrival of 27
SnapChat:
    and Centennials 51
    as ephemeral network 41
social media (*see also individual
  outlets*):
    ad spending on 29
    and Arab Spring 193, *193*
    as archival networks 41
    as battleground 164–73, *164*, *165*,
        166, *167*, *170*, *171*, *172*
    as database of intent 137
    as ephemeral networks 41
    overclaims for 39
    search capabilities of 138
    and tourism *201*, *202*
social responsibility, as transformation
  in digital age 204–7, *205*, *206*, *207*
Social@Ogilvy 80
Song, TB *21*, 248
Sorrell, Martin 248
spam, first incidence of 27
Spark 90
SPG Keyless *182*
Spiff 225, 226
Spotify 73
Sprint 255
Staav, Yael *44*
Standard Oil 31
Starbucks 24–5, *24–5*
Starwood Hotels *182*
Stenbeck, Jan 224
Stitzer, Tod 96, 97
Stonewall 70
Stumbleupon 90
Sulzberger, Arthur 222
Sunstein, Cass R. 240–1
Super Bowl 27, *27*, 36, *36*
Surminski, Brenda *44*
Sutherland, Rory 143, 185, 238–40

T

Taylor, Robert William "Bob" 14, *14*
Ted Bates agency 266
teletext 221–2, *222*
television:
 and changing digital ecosystem
  34–5
 and DVR 28, 29
 linear viewership of 34
 predicted disappearance of 34
Tencent 257, 258, *258*
Thaler, Richard H. 197, 240–1
Tham Khai Meng 98, *99*, 108
Thomas, Gareth 68
Thompson Holidays 27
Thompson, J. Walter 51
Thorndyke, Edward 244, *244*
3G:
 debut of 28
 growing use of 29
Tiffany & Co. 70
Timberlake, Justin 169
Time Inc. 27
Tin Shed 188–9
Tone 178
Toothbrush Games *158*
Toshiba *116*, 117
tourism:
 as transformation in digital age
  200–3, *200, 201, 202, 203*
 and Visit Britain 259, *259*
Toyota 57
traditional media, and changing
 digital ecosystem 34
transformations in digital age 192–209
 and government 197–9, *198, 199*
 and politics 192–5, *192, 193, 194,*
  195, 196
 and social responsibility 204–7,
  205, 206, 207
 and tourism 200–3, *200, 201,*
  202, 203
Trump, Donald 195–6, *195, 196*
"The Truth" 231
Tumblr 209
Turing, Alan 26, *26*
TV, rising revenue from 28

Tversky, Amos 238, 245, *245*, 246,
 246
Twitter 105
 and ALS Ice Bucket Challenge 169
 and Cadbury 97
 launch of 28
 and Oreo 36–7, *36*
 in Philippines 262
 and politics *194*, 195, *195*
 and promoted trends and tweets
  29
 revenue of 29
2G mobile network 27

U

Uber 17, 120
 and disintermediation 21
Unilever 66, 105, 204–5, *205*
Uniqlock 219, *219*
UPS *75, 76, 77*, 83, *84*
UX (user experience) 153–4, *153*

V

Van Damme, Jean-Claude 113, *114*
van Nispen, Jost 266
velocity 251, 254
Vibe 28
Vietnam:
 disproportionate growth in 251
 middle-class consumers in *252–3*
 and velocity 254
"View from Touffou", still played 7, *7*
Vine 42, 260
virtual, automated and mixed reality
 157–61, *158, 159, 160, 161*
 in author's predictions 272
Visit Britain 259, *259*
Vittel *92, 93*
Volvo 113, *114*
Vonk, Nancy *44*

W

Walrus 22
Wang, Leehom *146*
Wardah 262

Wason, Peter 244, *244*
Watkins, Pearline 44
web advertising:
 and "banner" ads 28, *28*
 clickable, first 27, *28*
website, judging 138, 140–5
WeChat 166, 174, 257–8, *258*
 in author's predictions 272
Weed, Keith 204, *205*
Weinberger, David 223
Westheimer, Ruth 78
"What Is Code?" (Ford) 150–1, *151*
WhatsApp 166, 258
Wikipedia 169
World Wide Web (*see also* internet),
 and founders' idealism 17
World Wildlife Fund *205*
WPP 45, 62, 132, 248–9, 266

X

Xanga *30*
Xerox Alto 26
Xiaomi 260

Y

Yahoo!, search engine of 28
Ying Zhang 246, *246*
Yoshida, Hideo 220
Young Turks *41, 42*, 146
YouTube 105
 and ALS Ice Bucket Challenge 169
 as archival network 41–2
 and Cadbury 97
 and *Evolution* 44
 and live capabilities 42
 and Millennials 52, *52*
 and Millennials' search behaviour
  138
YouTube Red 42

Z

Zalis, Shirley 68
Zhang, Ying 246, *246*
Zucker, Jeff 222
Zuckerberg, Mark 169, *169*

ACKNOWLEDGEMENTS

Thanks are due first to Lammy, who put up with the fractured holidays and weekends when I mostly wrote this book, and who provided sanity throughout.

Then I must thank my predecessors at Ogilvy and Mather: Bill Philips, Graham Philips, Ken Roman, Charlotte Beers: without each of their contributions the brand would not be what it is. And special thanks go to Shelly Lazarus, my immediate predecessor, who guided and supported me in Asia and New York. My successor, John Seifert, has been an ardent supporter of the project. Herta Ogilvy provided encouragement, hospitality and friendship throughout my tenure: she is the direct line to David which all of us who have worked for the firm have felt and cherished. Joel Raphaelson generously gave his wisdom from "the first time round", and I crave his forgiveness for my latter day solecisms.

Any wisdom in the book is collective much more than personal. How can I properly thank my colleagues at Ogilvy and Mathew over the years? My creative partner Tham Khai Meng is the "best of the best": without him there would have been nothing. I was blessed to work with two inimitable strategists, each very different, Ben Richards and Colin Mitchell, as well as my Vice Chairman and Consulting Head, Carla Hendra. My brilliant colleagues throughout the organisation have been indispensable collaborators. Thanks in particular to:

Brian Fetherstonhaugh, Christopher Graves, Rory Sutherland, Calvin Carter, Piyush Pandey, the late Tim Broadbent, Kent Wertime, Thomas Crampton, Martin Lange, Pete Dyson, Mark Lainas, Madeleine Croucher, Julia Stainforth, Shelina Janmohamed, Andrew Barratt, Carlos Nunez, Paul Matheson, Dimitri Maex, Bjorn Stahl, Magnus Ivansson, Minoru Fujita, Maki Suzuki, Akira Odagiri, Mike McFadden, Jeremy Webb, Madeline Di Nonno, Jamie Prieto, Sean Muzzy, Mark Himmelsbach, Rajiv Rao, Maeve Countey, Mi hui Park, Beth Ann Ingrassia, Sabrina Allen, Robert Lear, Peter DeLuca and Liam Parker.

A thank you to all the Ogilvy Discipline Heads, GBM leaders, Account and Creative teams that helped us gather all the material needed to put this publication together.

I must also thank Steve Goldstein, Stacey Ryan-Cornelius and Lauren Crampsie for all their practical support; and the "home team" of Nikolaj Birjukow, Alexander Banon, Harley Safter and John Vetrano. Joan Huber, Mariah MacCarthy, Laird Stiefvater and Ellen Pierce, Eleanor Tsang, Erin Clutcher, Lynn Whiston and Arlene Richardson all went beyond the call of duty.

Jeremy Katz, and Samar Taher Khan helped produce the book at Ogilvy, and Samar assisted in a myriad of essential ways alongside me from beginning to end. Mark Dewings gave me completely invaluable help. Tuan Ching, Joohee Park and Jess Xuan contributed many design elements.

My deepest thanks go to them all.

Outside of Ogilvy, I am indebted to my clients first and foremost. I have been blessed to know and work with them, and these are just a few who have helped push their "partners" into better and better work:

John Hayes, Alison Bain, Tony Palmer, Clive Sirkin, Rishi Dhingra, Keith Weed, Marc Mathieu, Walter Susini, Steve Miles, Fernando Machado, John Iwata, Bharat Puri, Phil Chapman, Nikhil Rao, Dana Anderson, Salman Amin, Ann Mukhurjee, Patrice Bula, Tom Buday, Quique Pendavis, Sean Murphy, Christine Owens, Maureen Healy, Peter Nota, Jeanette Senerchia, Javier Sanchez Lamelas and Rodolfo Echeverria.

It was Jonathan Goodman of Carlton Publishing who had the idea for this book, and then pushed and prodded until I finally wrote to him. I thank him, editors Alison Moss and Gemma Maclagan Ram, Art Director Russell Knowles and the whole team at Carlton for turning my untidy pile of pages and images into reality.

Finally, there are others who have given freely of their time and knowledge: the "famous five" – Bob Greenberg, Akira Kagami, Martin Niesenholtz, Matias Palm-Jensen, Chuck Porter – and also Thomas Gensemer, Russell Davies, Surjit Bhalla, Phil Rumbold, Tim Piper, Adam Smith, Jeff Bowman, and Rob Norman.

PICTURE CREDITS